From Bristol to the Sea

From Bristol to the Sea

Artists, the Avon Gorge and Bristol Harbour

FRANCIS GREENACRE

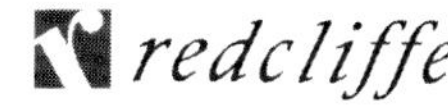

Redcliffe Press
in association with
Bristol Museums and
Art Gallery

First published in 2005 by Redcliffe Press Ltd., 81g Pembroke Road, Bristol BS8 3EA

ISBN   10 1 904537 39 1
ISBN   13 978 1 904537 39 7

British Library Cataloguing-in-Publication Data
A catalogue record for this book is available from the British Library.

Design and typesetting by Stephen Morris Communications, smc@freeuk.com Bristol and Liverpool.
Printed in Malta by Gutenberg Press Ltd.

Contents

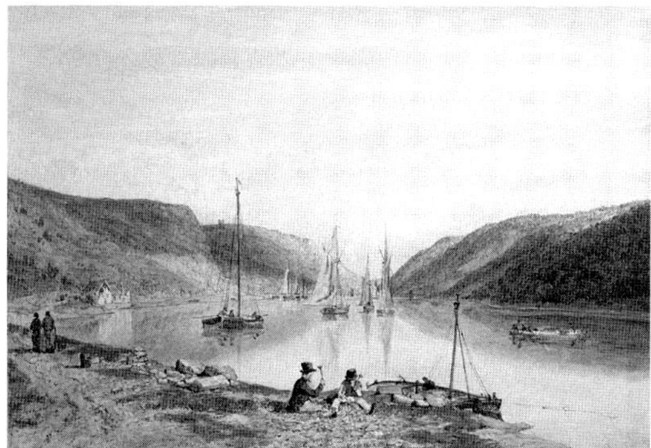

Francis Danby ARA 1793-1861
The Avon Gorge from beneath Sea Walls, 1820

Introduction

Bristol's inland port has the most various and spectacular approach in the world. This book celebrates the response of artists to this dramatic landscape and to the changing appearance of the city's historic harbour over three hundred years.

No other city has such a complete record of its past appearance. The collections of Bristol Art Gallery, which celebrates its centenary this year, are especially strong in paintings and drawings of Bristol from the early nineteenth century. This is the period of the Bristol School of Artists, when Bristol painters were making an important contribution to the history of British art.

There is a third superlative. At Bristol the 'water floweth at an high spring tide neere 40 foot in height.' The mouth of the Avon has the second highest tidal range in the world and there is no port that has a larger rise and fall. This visual anthology emphasises the 'wonderfull passage through a mighty hill…& stupendious Rocks', but it also draws attention to the difficulties that the tortuous Avon and its tides created. The images may help to contradict the tendency of historians of the port to tell its story as a succession of missed or delayed opportunities; instead, it can be argued that the port's history is a continuing tale of triumphs against the odds.

Thirty-six years ago Bristol's Floating Harbour was threatened with flyovers and large-scale infilling. Now, once again, the river is a determining factor in the pleasure that both residents and visitors take in the city. The landscape between the harbour and the Bristol Channel has retrieved much of its distinctive character. The peregrine falcon and the raven have returned to nest in the Avon Gorge, where some of the world's rarest plants now thrive under conservation management.

The pictures are in approximate chronological order, but with certain of the artists – Nicholas Pocock, S.H. Grimm, Samuel Jackson, T.L. Rowbotham and Joseph Walter – it has, in effect, been possible to travel down the river in their company. These topographical sequences from the centre of Bristol to the Avon Gorge and beyond may encourage the reader to walk around the Floating Harbour on a fascinating route deliberately engineered by the City Council's planners in recent years. Alternatively, one can take advantage of Bristol as the birthplace of Sustrans and walk or ride the cycle path to Pill (River Avon Trail), much of which follows the hobblers' towpath. There is also the route that many eighteenth-century Hotwell visitors took on horseback, up through Clifton, across the Downs to Shirehampton and Kingsweston (Forest of Avon's Community Forest path) and on to Penpole Point. Or take a boat: hire Bristol Packet's *Tower Belle*, circle the Floating Harbour, descend by the lock at Cumberland Basin and go down river on a summer's evening to a sunset at Avonmouth, returning at speed on the flood tide.

Our pleasure in contemporary Bristol can surely be much enhanced by familiarity with the city's past appearance and history. Artists have supplied many original and inspiring images and these images can often be illuminated by local history. The following combination of illustration and text, of art and history, is intended to increase the enjoyment of resident and visitor alike in this remarkable city.

In the words of one great Bristol artist about another: 'Paintings form part of the quality of life. Francis Danby's paintings are a celebration of nature. I hope they serve to remind us that nature… is still the foundation stone and that an awareness of our environment and its resources is a pre-condition to the quality of our lives.' – Richard Long.

The Cittie of Bristoll standeth upon ye borders of Somersett &
Gloucester sheirs, yet belongeth to neither, but is a Cittie & Countie
of it self: It's Scituation is in a pleasant Vale upon ye two Rivers of
Avon & Froome. The river Froome is much the Lesser river yet on it
standeth the Cheif Key of this Cittie: The water there floweth at an
high-spring tide neere 40 foot in height bringing up thither shipps
of great burthens, but theire greatest ships ride about three miles
downe the river and are for the most part discharged by lighters.
Just below this Cittie the river Froome falleth into the river Avon
which about Six miles lower falleth into the great River Seaverne
but by the way hath a wonderfull passage through a mighty hill
leaveing on each side very high & stupendious Rocks, that on the
North side is called St Vincents rock, where are found those
adamantine like stones or Bristoll-Diamonds which are famous in
most parts of Europe & elswhere & which (as Cambden affirmeth)
only in point of hardness come short of ye Diamonds of India. On
ye top of this rock are seene ye footsteps of some larg, but very
antient fortification And out of ye bottom thereof issueth a famous
medicinall warme Bath water, comonly called ye Hotwell, much fre-
quented at all convenient seasons of ye yeare both by ye neigbour-
ing Cittizens & also by Others, who liveing farr remote resort thith-
er for health sake.

James Millerd 1673

A short history of the port of Bristol

On Durdham Down, just to the south of Stoke Hill Road, a broad but slight ridge runs for about a hundred yards. It is the remains of the Roman road that ran directly between the Roman settlement at Sea Mills, *Portus Abonae*, and Bath, *Aquae Sulis*. Bristol did not yet exist; indeed we do not hear of Bristol for another thousand years, when it is first mentioned in the Anglo-Saxon Chronicle in 1051. Its growth thereafter is impressive. By the time of the Norman Conquest, Bristol was one of the chief trading ports of the country and from the Domesday Book, completed in 1086, we learn that only London, York, Lincoln and Norwich were taxed at a higher sum than Bristol.

In 1240 one of the most ambitious feats of medieval engineering was begun. At this time the River Frome ran below the town wall to the east of St Stephen's Church and along the approximate line of today's Baldwin Street, entering the Avon just below Bristol Bridge. Over the following seven years a great trench was dug from Lewin's Mead through St Augustine's Marsh to the Avon below the bend at Redcliffe. It was nearly half a mile in length and about 5 1/2 metres deep and 36 metres wide. In 1247 this became the new course of the Frome, providing a much extended harbour with a long quay and a ground of soft mud, free of rocks, to lie on at low tide.

The earliest visual record, albeit symbolic, of the port of Bristol comes just a few decades later. On one side of the late thirteenth-century common seal of the burgesses of Bristol a trumpet is being sounded from a tower of the great stone keep of Bristol Castle. On the other side, a merchant ship approaches the castle watergate along the Avon (Fig. I). The river teems with fish, including a particularly large eel. A man on the watergate appears to point heavenwards, but his gesture is explained by the surrounding Latin inscription, which has been translated: 'I am the key of the hidden port. The sailor watches the port side of the ship. The watchman points out the port with his finger.'

It is a symbolic image that admirably describes the arrival of a ship in the safety of Bristol's harbour protected by the castle after the tortuous journey up the river.

Mariners would have passed below two other symbols of Bristol's status in the thirteenth century. Both still dominate the harbour. The great choir of the Augustinian abbey, now Bristol Cathedral, is the work of an architectural genius and it was still bolder and more revolutionary in design than the new harbour itself. The noble tower of St Mary Redcliffe was built later in the same century and proudly proclaimed both the wealth of Redcliffe and its separation from Bristol by jurisdiction as well as by the river.

The men of Redcliffe had been reluctant to assist in the building of Bristol's new harbour on the Frome until specifically commanded to co-operate by King Henry III. No encouragement was apparently required over the replacement of the old wooden

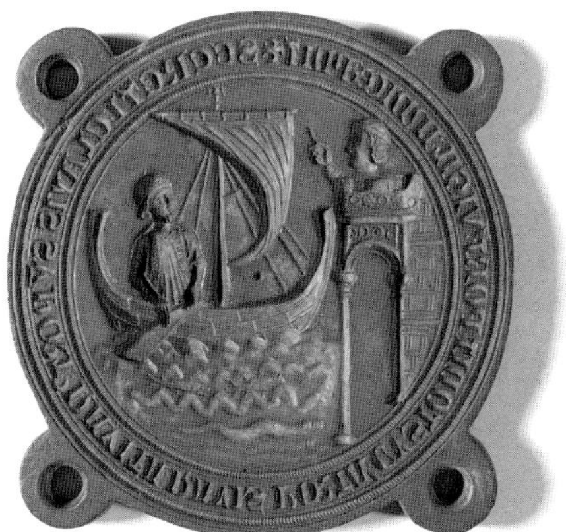

fig.I Cast of the thirteenth-century matrix of the common seal of Bristol. (Bristol Record Office)

bridge across the Avon. The building of a stone bridge of four arches followed immediately upon the completion of the harbour. For the next four centuries Bristol Bridge (Fig. II) was the only bridge across the Avon until shortly before Bath. Narrow and congested, with some thirty many-storied houses along its sides, it was finally replaced in the 1760s by the elegant bridge that survives today (59), hidden beneath Victorian cantilevered extensions. It still rests on the thirteenth-century foundations.

The unification of Bristol and Redcliffe came in 1373 when Bristol and its castle in the county of Gloucester and the prosperous suburbs of Redcliffe and Temple, which were part of Somerset, became a new and independent county. The boundaries took due account of Bristol's desire to protect its trade and they extended down the Avon and into the Bristol Channel as far as the islands of Steep Holm and Flat Holm. Bristol was now the wealthiest provincial town in England.

The earliest actual depiction of Bristol may be the illustration in Ricart's Calendar (Fig. III), a chronicle of the town, written in 1479. It is a very stylised view of a symmetrical town with four roads leading out from the High Cross to the four gates of the fortified city. Robert Ricart was the Town Clerk and this is very much a civic image of his town. Surprisingly, there is no water to be seen and the city's dependence upon its maritime trade is ignored. Towards the end of the fifteenth century Bristol's export of cloth was at its peak.

At much the same time a growing number of important voyages of exploration were being made from Bristol, of which the best known is that of the Venetian citizen, John Cabot, who

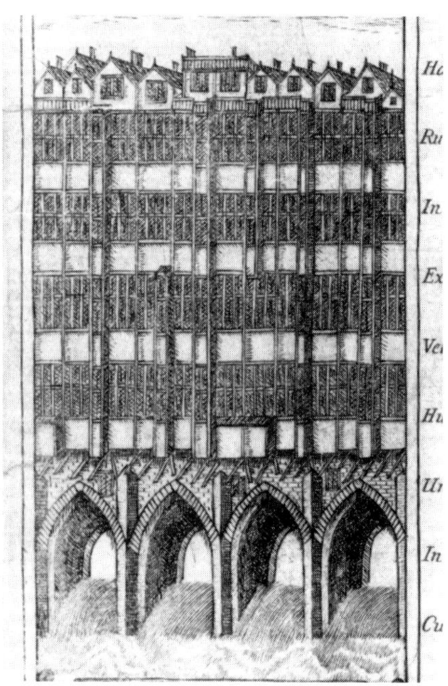

James Millerd: *Bristol Bridge*, a detail from the map of Bristol (see 1 on page 20), 1673 engraving (Bristol Museums and Art Gallery)

fig. II

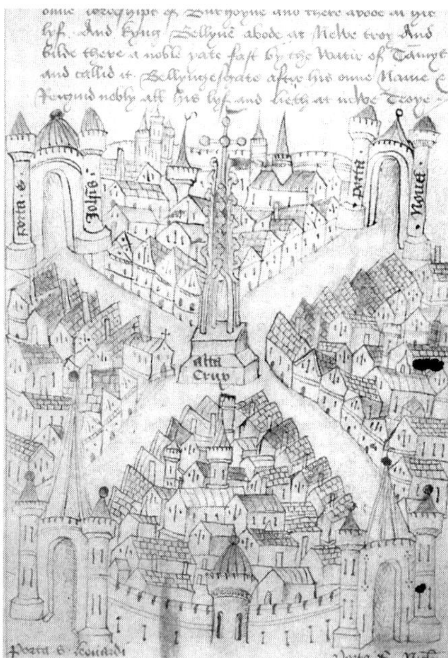

Robert Ricart: *Plan of Bristol from the Mayor's Calendar*, late fifteenth-century watercolour (Bristol Records Office)

fig. III

sighted Newfoundland on 14 June 1497. It was the first definite landing of an English crew on the north American continent. Today, the studied but very approximate replica of Cabot's small ship, the *Matthew*, is usually moored near the *Great Britain*. Launched in 1996, it is more accurate than that in Ernest Board's crowded costume drama depicting the departure of John and Sebastian Cabot, which was painted in 1906 (Fig. IV).

Bristol's fame for its role in the exploration of the New World was acknowledged in the seventeenth century. The Anglican divine and scholar, Thomas Fuller, wrote in *The Worthies of England* published in 1663:

> No city in England (London alone excepted) hath, in so short a time, bred more brave and bold seamen, advantaged for western voyages by its situation. They have not only been merchants, but adventurers, possessed of a public spirit for the general good; aiming not so much to return wealthier, as wiser; not always to enrich themselves, as inform posterity by their discoveries.

It is unlikely that Thomas Fuller was making a veiled reference to the Society of Merchant Venturers of Bristol. As a corporate body, the Society's attitude to exploration and colonisation was cautious. Initially it was essentially a trading cartel for the betterment not only of the merchants, but also of the mariners of Bristol and the customs officials of the state. Its formal incorporation with letters patent from Edward VI came in 1552. From the beginning of the seventeenth century the Merchant Venturers collected the wharfage dues on behalf of the City Corporation. In return the Society took on increasing responsibility for the management, maintenance and improvement of the harbour, together with its quays and cranes. The licensing and discipline of the pilots, so vital to the safe navigation of the Bristol Channel and the Avon, was managed by the Society. This responsibility continued until 25 June 1861, long after the Society's other port duties had ceased. On that day the

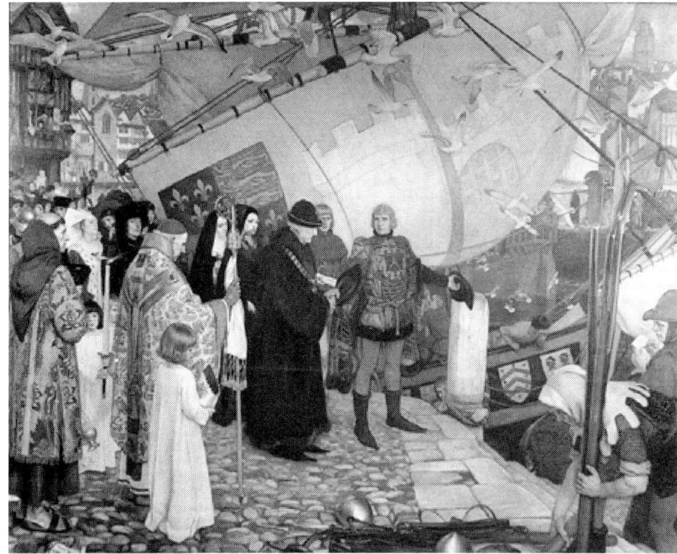

Ernest Board: *The Departure of John and Sebastian Cabot from Bristol... 1497*, 1906, oil (Bristol Museums and Art Gallery K102)   fig. IV

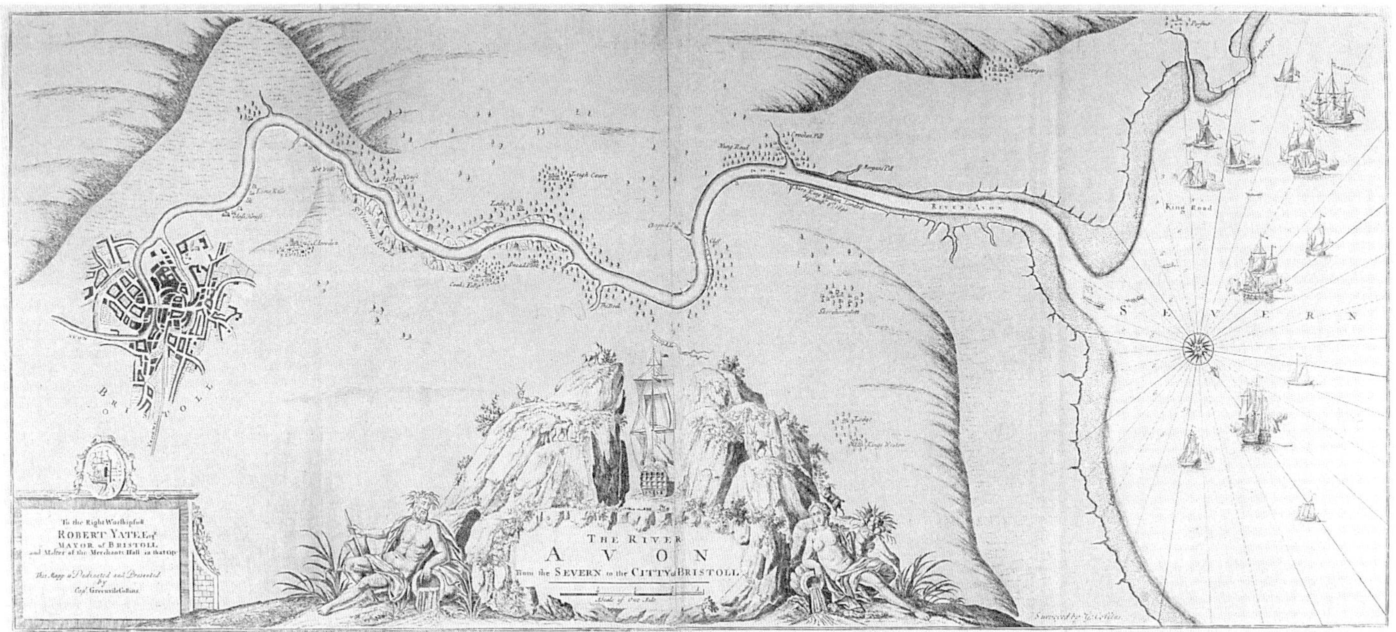

fig. V   Capt. Greenville Collins: '*The River Avon from the Severn to the Citty of Bristoll*' c.1694 engraving with watercolour
(Bristol Museums and Art Gallery J1124)

Treasurer recorded in his journal: 'The Town Council… repaid the Society for all their good deeds by a Kick in the Bum. They appointed their Docks Committee as Managers of the Pilots, the Society having by delegation from the Corporation conducted the same since the year 1612 – 249 years, and they never said Thankee even!'

In the 1670s and '80s the Merchant Venturers acquired the Manor of Clifton in two parts. They became owners of one side of the Avon Gorge, half of the common land of the Downs, much of the then barren slopes of Clifton and of the Hotwell. Robert Yate, twice Master of the Society, was soon to be one of the key developers of the Hotwell spa in the 1690s. It is also to Robert Yate, as both Mayor of Bristol and Master of the Merchant Venturers, that Captain Greenville Collins dedicated his upside-down map of the River Avon from Bristol to King Road (Fig. V). The dedication admirably illustrates the very close links between the Merchant Venturers and Bristol Corporation that were to last well into the nineteenth century.

A map of similar date of 'The Severn or Channel of Bristol' has a vignette that graphically illustrates the prime solution to the difficulties associated with Bristol's inland port (Fig. VI). Many vessels simply transferred their cargoes at King Road at

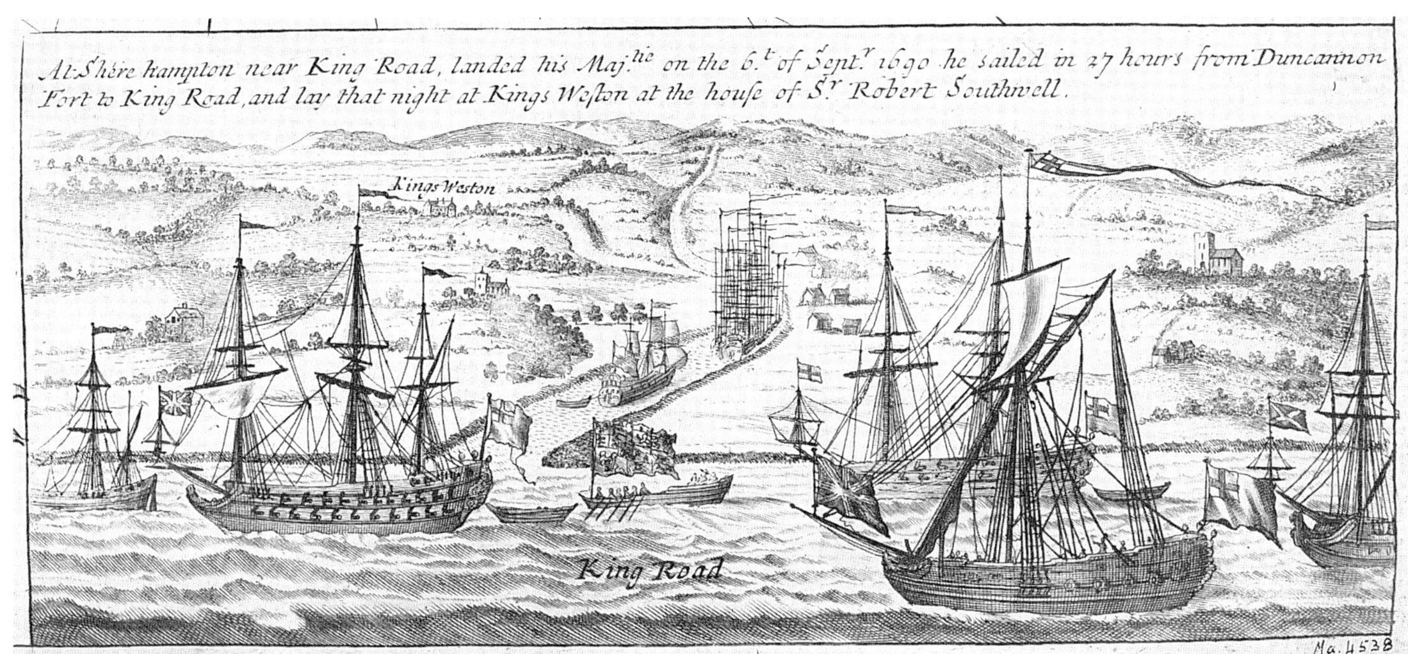

fig. VI William III and the fleet anchored in King Road 6th September 1690; detail from a map of 'The SEVERN or Channell of BRISTOLL' c.1700
engraving (Bristol Museums and Art Gallery Ma4538)

the mouth of the Avon or, more often, at Hung Road two miles up the river. With a certain triumphalism, the vignette shows the fleet of William III anchored in King Road on 6 September 1690 after an unusually fast voyage from Duncannon in 27 hours following the defeat of James II at the Battle of the Boyne. The royal barge is about to transport the King to Shirehampton, whence he continued to King's Weston to stay overnight with the new owner of the house, Sir Robert Southwell, his Secretary of State for Ireland.

The Bristol Channel was treacherous with shifting banks, complex currents and persistent contrary winds. King Road at the entrance to the Avon provided a relatively sheltered and deep anchorage on good holding ground. The concentration of masts in the centre of the vignette also shows that several vessels have entered the Avon. They may be anchored at Broad Pill, downstream from Pill, but it is very much more likely that the artist's perspective is poor and that they were anchored at Hung Road, just upstream from Pill. Here, as S.H. Grimm's drawings will show (29-31), was a low cliff, where the vessels' masts could be secured to the bank and remain upright at low tide. Cargoes were then unloaded into Severn trows or lighters for transfer to Bristol and elsewhere.

A period of peace and stability followed the death of William III in 1702 and the colonial trade, especially the slave trade, brought great wealth to Bristol. The inscription on Samuel and Nathaniel Buck's engraving of 'The South East prospect of the City of Bristol' published in 1734 reads: 'This City is most valuable for its extensive Trade, to all Parts of the World; in which it exceeds, all other Cities and Towns in Great Britain, except London…' The Bucks were brilliant and prolific engravers of panoramic views of British cities. It is the pair to that engraving, Bucks' 'North West Prospect' (Fig. VII) published in the same year, which best illustrates the two prongs of the Avon and the Frome entering into the heart of the city, which is densely packed with ships' masts.

The Bucks' panorama also shows Queen Square between the towers of the Cathedral and St Mary Redcliffe. This square, very much a demonstration of Bristol's second-city status, was completed in the 1720s and Michael Rysbrack's statue of William III, the finest equestrian monument in northern Europe, was erected in its centre in 1736. This statue is a relatively lonely masterpiece of the fine arts in eighteenth-century Bristol, architecture excepted. It was in the decorative arts – the industries of glass, pottery and porcelain especially – that Bristol excelled. Joseph Flower's blue-and-white delftware plate can be dated to early 1742, and was almost certainly painted to celebrate his marriage (Fig. VIII). He chose to decorate it with an image of the Hotwell, then at its most fashionable, and of the Avon Gorge. It is based

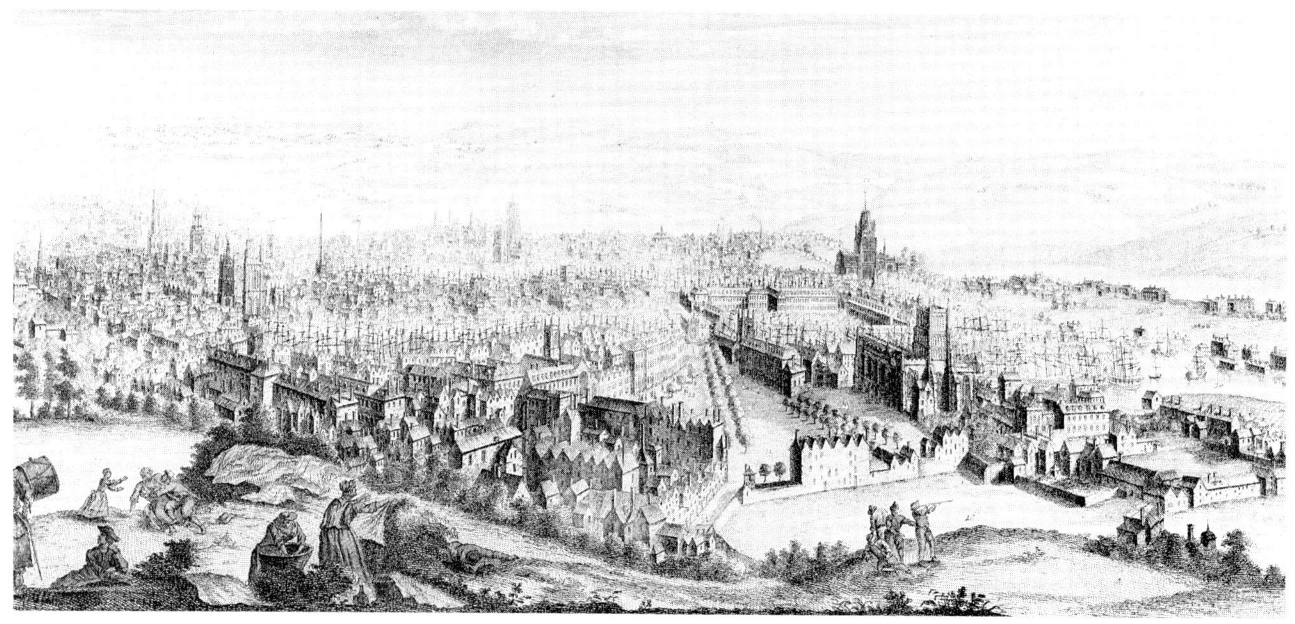

fig. VII   S. and N. Buck: *The north west prospect of the City of Bristol*, 1734 engraving (Society of Merchant Venturers)

on two engravings, which he confidently adapted to the circular format. The landscape is taken from one of the earliest engravings of the Hotwell by the architect William Halfpenny, published in 1731. Several of the vessels and the figures derive from an engraving of Admiral Vernon's victory at Chagres in the West Indies in 1740, an event of particular importance to Bristol's trade.

The Hotwell's fame was to decline sharply towards the end of the eighteenth century. Robert Southey noted tartly in 1807 that doctors 'still send the paralytic to find relief at Bath, or to look for it, and the consumptive to die at the Hot-wells.' Clifton now became a resort in its own right, with its new Assembly Rooms opening in 1811. With a cynicism that has completely lost its bite, Southey described Clifton as 'once the most beautiful village in England, and… now… the finest suburb.'

James Blackamore's pen and ink drawing of Clifton (21), published here for the first time, reveals that the developments planned for Clifton in the late 1780s were still more ambitious than has previously been recognised. Several of the projects were to take up to thirty years to complete, even in a truncated form. Innumerable builders were to go bust. And yet it is within this period – 1804-09 – that the Floating Harbour was constructed.

Fifty years earlier in 1765, the distinguished engineer, John Smeaton, at the behest of both the Corporation and the Merchant Venturers, produced the first detailed proposals for floating the harbour. At the height of Bristol's prosperity, it was an ominous admission of the increasing problems and competition with which the port had to contend. Although the annual traffic of the port was growing steadily at this time, there was already an understanding that Bristol's relative prosperity was in decline and, indeed, by the end of the century the city had slipped from second to ninth place. More important, however, is the statistic revealing that in the year ending March 1793, the

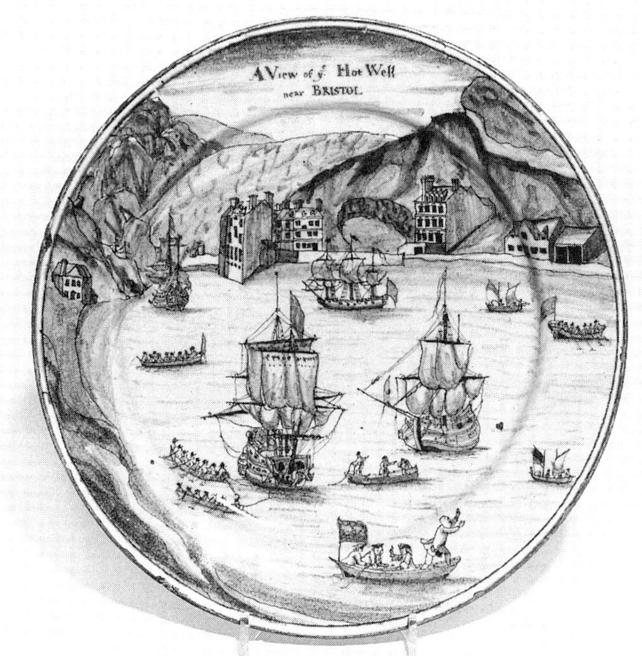

Joseph Flower: The Hotwell plate, 1742 tin-glazed earthenware   fig. VIII
(Bristol Museums and Art Gallery N7461)

more extreme tides had made navigation on the river impossible on 150 days, and 'improper' for outgoing ships on a further 89 days. This was a crippling handicap and an undoubted impetus for change.

Among many various proposals, separate and detailed plans for the floating of the harbour were put forward by William Champion and Richard Tombs, both dock owners and by Richard Bright, the merchant, and by William Acraman, the iron founder. It was the plans of the professional engineer, William

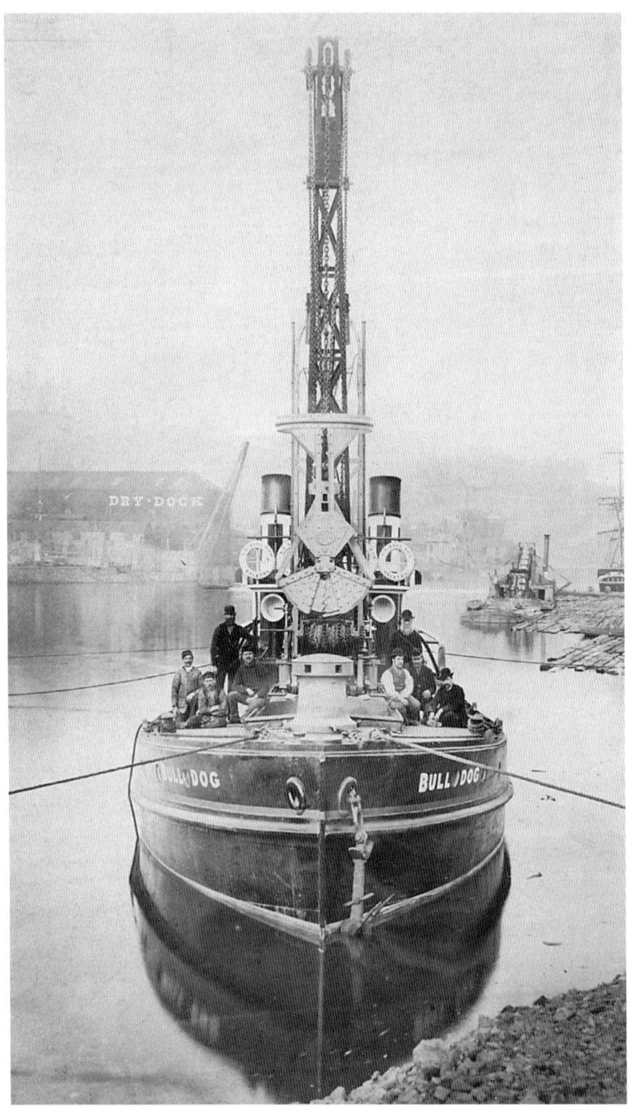

fig. IX *Bulldog* at Underfall Yard, c.1884, photograph
(Bristol Museums and Art Gallery J597)

Jessop, that finally gained parliamentary approval in 1803.

Jessop's plan involved the damming of the Avon at Rownham, near Hotwells, and above Temple Meads. The basins and locks at both Cumberland Basin and Bathurst Basin provided access into the vast non-tidal area thus created. The tidal flow of the river was diverted into a man-made trench called the New Cut, which ran from Rownham to the river above the dam at Temple Meads. A mile-long Feeder Canal was dug from near this point to above Netham Weir where it rejoined the Avon. A lock into the Feeder Canal gave access to the Floating Harbour and kept open navigation from Bristol to Bath. The Feeder also maintained water levels in the Floating Harbour but failed in its intended role of helping to flush out the stagnant harbour.

By completion in 1809, costs had increased nearly threefold from over £200,000 to nearly £600,000. The Floating Harbour was now owned and managed by the Bristol Dock Company. Equal numbers of members of Bristol Corporation and the Merchant Venturers made up two-thirds of its board members. On top of the port dues payable to the Corporation and the Society there were substantial charges payable to the company. Soon Bristol's costs far exceeded those of its main rival, Liverpool, and the advantages of the Floating Harbour's eighty acres of deep water were nullified.

In 1846 an impressive public campaign was orchestrated by the Free Port Association with a rare unity between merchants, tradesmen and artisans. Following an Act of Parliament two years later, Bristol Council bought the Dock Company. The dues were very quickly reduced and much needed improvements to the harbour were begun.

Joseph Walter's moving image (96) of the *Great Britain* disappearing down the Avon Gorge in December 1844, never to return, illustrated the essential problems of Bristol's inland port. Substantial improvements to the harbour, some of which were designed by Brunel, could not resolve them.

Brunel had first proposed a deep-water dock at the mouth of the Avon in 1839 (100). Finally two were built; the first at Avonmouth was completed in 1877 with the second at Portishead opening two years later. These two privately owned docks battled it out until both were acquired by Bristol Corporation in 1884, when it was already becoming evident that there were ships being built which were too big for the locks of these river-mouth docks. In 1908 King Edward VII opened the Royal Edward Dock (116), a vast extension to Avonmouth Dock with an entrance lock that can still take middle-range bulk carriers. It was a triumph of civic initiative.

It might well be assumed that Bristol's inland harbour was now on the decline. Instead it had been expanding rapidly. A major factor was the development of a complex system of rail access to almost the entire Floating Harbour, first to the south side in the early 1870s involving a tunnel under St Mary Redcliffe's churchyard. Finally in 1906 an extension reached Canon's Marsh via Cumberland Basin. The Explore building, opened in 2000, incorporates the goods shed designed in 1904 and built using the new *Hennibique* system of reinforced concrete construction.

The works of Albert Goodwin (109, 110) C. B. Branwhite (113) and Wilde Parsons (116) admirably illustrate this period. So too, do many photographs, which have been necessarily excluded from this anthology. The anonymous photograph of about 1884 (Fig. IX) of the *Bulldog*, for example, encapsulates the revitalised Floating Harbour. The crew of this brand new and very powerful tug had cause for pride. The *Bulldog* could be employed in dredging, salvage work, heavy lifting and icebreaking and she had a variety of pumps for refloating vessels and for fire fighting. Fifty years on, the photograph of the paddle steamer *Britannia* gliding beneath the Clifton Suspension Bridge (Fig. X)

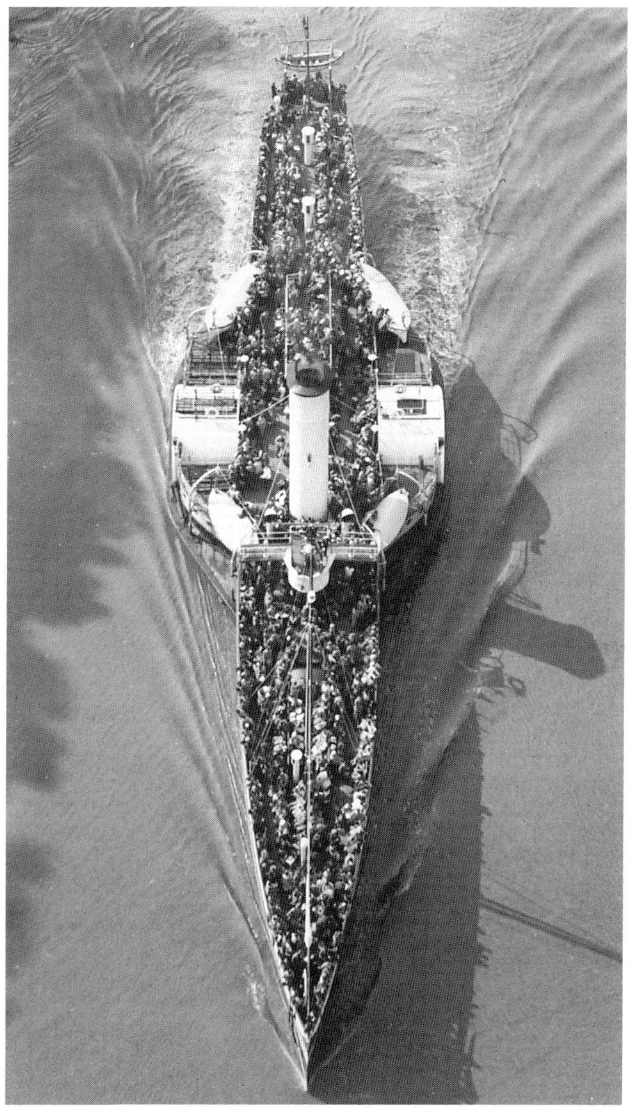

The *Britannia* photographed from the Clifton Suspension Bridge, fig. X 1938 (Bristol Museums and Art Gallery, Keen Coll. 2/62)

marvellously captures another aspect of the history of this inland port: the pleasure cruise. Two of the twentieth century's finest watercolourists, John Nash (122) and Eric Ravilious drew this vessel in 1938, but a more striking illustration of history is a poignant photograph recording the return of the same vessel to Bristol in 1945, now renamed H.M.S. *Skiddaw* and in zigzag camouflage as she enters Cumberland Basin after service as a minesweeper in World War II.

In the 1960s the City Council became determined to meet new demands by the building of Royal Portbury Dock opposite Avonmouth, despite the refusal of the British Government to provide any assistance. Begun in 1972, it was opened in 1978 by H.M. The Queen (Fig. XI). Following the example of the Royal Edward Dock, it had Britain's largest entrance lock of its day. However, it was soon hit hard by sharp fluctuations in the shipping markets. Designed specifically for containerised traffic that could take advantage of the nearby motorway and specialised off-loading equipment, the dock became, instead, a refuge for laid-up container ships. Bulk cargoes were now seen as the way ahead, but the Council, whose other services were being very seriously affected by debt repayments, was in no position to invest further, nor was it able to reduce the workforce to match the shrinking trade.

In 1991 First Corporate Shipping leased both Avonmouth and Royal Portbury Docks for 150 years, renaming themselves The Bristol Port Company. Cars, coal, animal feed and fertilisers, forest products and aviation fuel, as well as substantial investment helped to triple tonnage in the ensuing twelve years. It is a very impressive achievement.

In June 2005, The Bristol Port Company announced that it was applying for consent to build a new deep-water container terminal off Avonmouth that, once again, will anticipate the demands of ships that have yet to be launched. Vessels with a

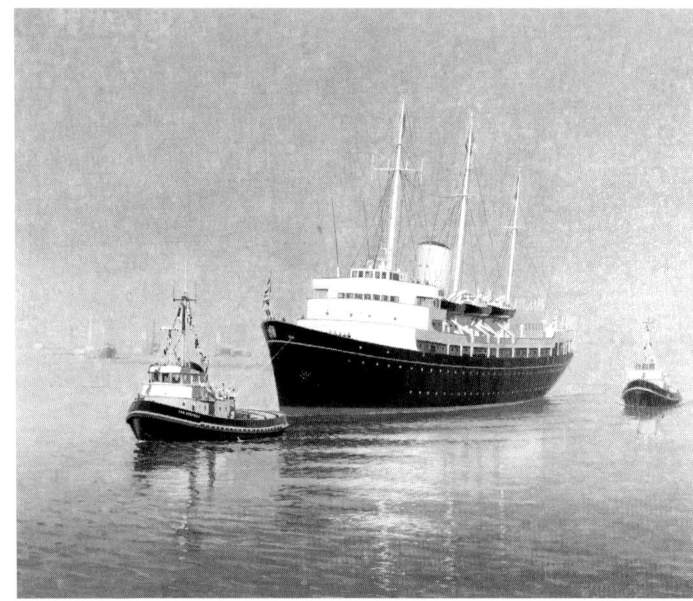

Frank Shipsides: *H.M. Queen Elizabeth II, aboard The Royal Yacht* Britannia *assisted by C.J. King & Sons' tugs* Sea Challenge *and* Sea Merrimac, *arrives to open the Royal Portbury Dock, August 1977* fig. XI
oil (Private collection)

draught of sixteen metres will be possible. It is a project that could involve the dredging of a 10-mile trench in the midst of the Bristol Channel. The long saga of the port of Bristol – from Bristol to the sea – continues.

From Bristol to the Sea

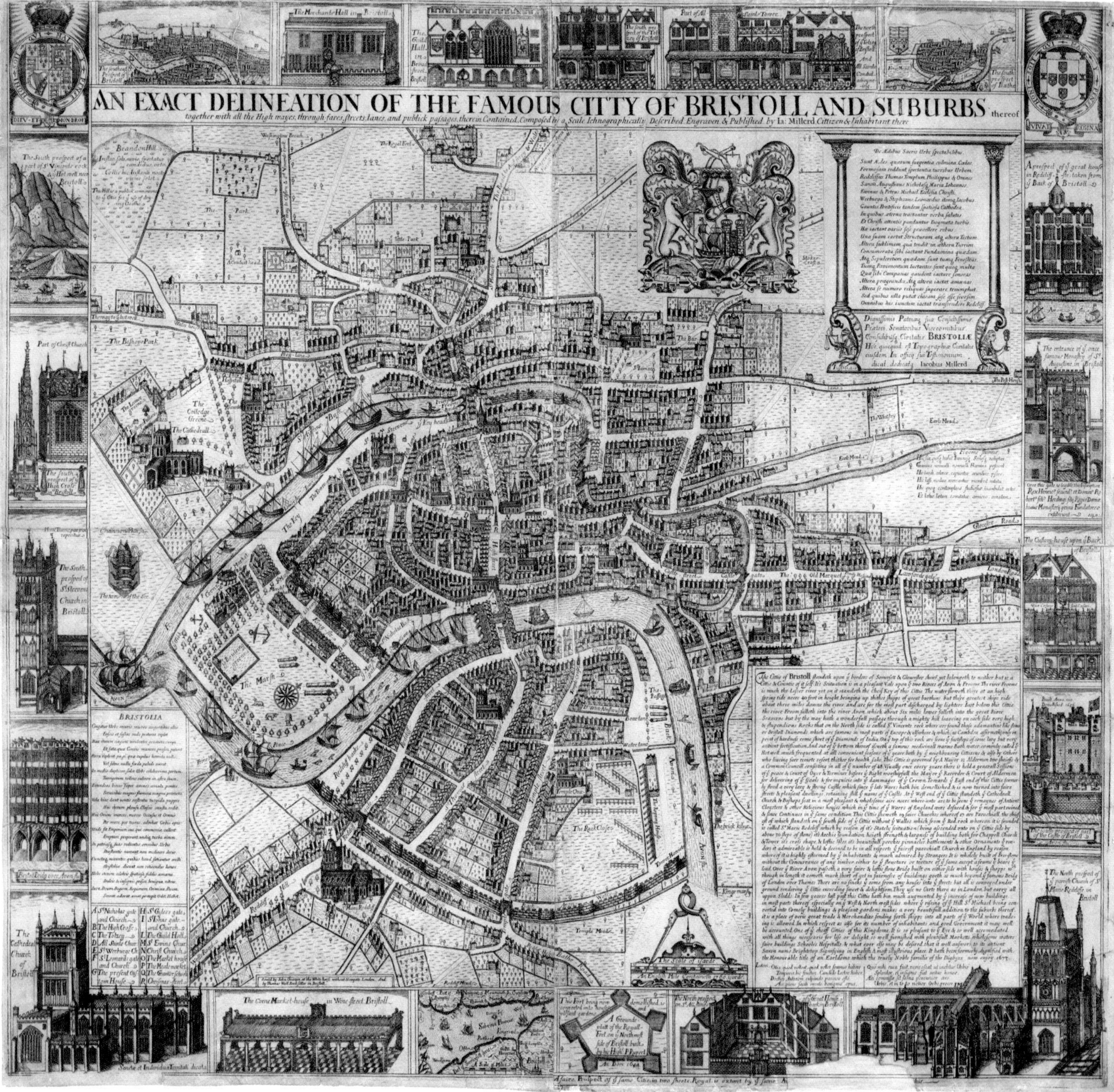

1 James Millerd c.1635–c.1715
'AN EXACT DELINEATION OF THE FAMOUS CITTY OF BRISTOLL…' 1673
Line engraving   770 x 840 mm   Bristol Museums and Art Gallery

JAMES MILLERD'S MAPS AND PERSPECTIVE VIEWS of Bristol in the 1670s are accurate, detailed and very recognisable images of Bristol and its immediate surroundings. They are early master-pieces of both cartography and view painting.

Unlike most of the mapmakers before him, Millerd knew the city intimately. He was a Bristol mercer and a guardian of the poor; he served as coroner and stood unsuccessfully for election as civic chamberlain. On this map he proudly describes himself as 'Cittizen and Inhabitant' of Bristol and that pride is evident in his work.

Despite the three-dimensional buildings that rise from his two-dimensional ground plan, archaeologists continue to be sur-prised by the accuracy of Millerd's maps. Vignettes of churches, public buildings and great houses and even of the natural fea-tures of the Avon Gorge and the Hotwell surround the map. The border picture of 'St Vincent Rock & ye Hotwell near Bristol' in this 1673 edition shows a simple pipe spewing water into the Avon beside a great rock that juts out into the river. It is the only image we have of the rock that was to form the foundations of the Hotwell House built in the 1690s.

The map was dedicated to both the city's elected Corpor-ation and the Society of Merchant Venturers. This was signifi-cant recognition of the role of the Society in the management of the port and the Society duly rewarded Millerd with a gift of plate, probably a silver salver engraved with their coat of arms.

Millerd emphasised Bristol's maritime character with a proces-sion of mottled seals in the heart of the city. Today, we have con-firmation that this was not a cartographer's fanciful elaboration. In August 2005 a seal was to be seen day after day in the Floating Harbour.

Bristol Museums and Art Gallery has recently purchased Millerd's original pen and ink drawing (2) for the earliest of his maps of 1671. It is a most remarkable survival and it is pub-lished here for the first time.

2 James Millerd c.1635–c.1715
'AN EXACT DELINEATION OF THE FAMOUS CITTIE OF BRISTOLL…' 1671
Pen and ink   235 x 211 mm
Bristol Museums and Art Gallery R364

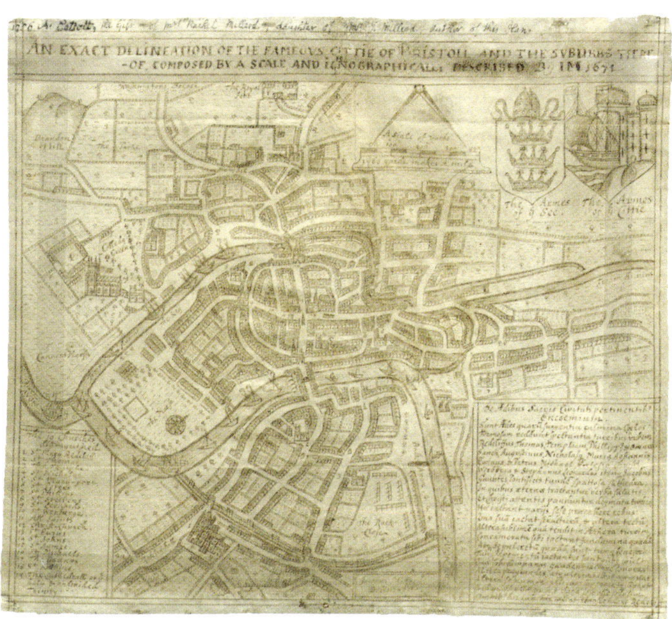

3 British School
Hotwells, with a view of the Avon Gorge   c.1730
Oil   979 x 1960 mm   Bristol Museums and Art Gallery   K4646

THE EARLIEST MENTION OF THE HOTWELL is in William Worcestre's careful account of Bristol in the late fifteenth century. He describes the Hotwell water as being as warm as milk and much like the waters of Bath. By the following century the water's efficacious effects had become widely known. It was celebrated in 1634, for example, for working inwardly upon the kidneys and outwardly on old sores, but by the end of the eighteenth century its medicinal properties were said to cure innumerable ailments.

In 1676 the Society of Merchant Venturers acquired the Hotwell as part of the purchase of the manor of Clifton. In the following year the Queen of England, Charles II's somewhat neglected Portuguese bride, Catherine of Braganza, visited the Hotwell. Then in 1695 the Society granted a 90-year lease to a group of developers including Robert Yate, who had been twice master of the Merchant Venturers, on condition that a Pump House was built together with lodgings and provisions for the visitors. The more serious exploitation of the Hotwell had begun.

At one extreme of this panoramic view is the Avon Gorge together with the Hotwell House; at the other are the few houses around Clifton's first parish church on the skyline. The central subject is the Hotwell spa, a conglomeration of lodging houses for the fashionable visitors to the Hotwell, which developed so rapidly in the early years of the eighteenth century.

This large oil painting may date from about 1730, much earlier than previous estimates. In the centre is the first of the public rooms, the upper Long Room, opened in 1722. To the right are some of the earliest houses in Dowry Square which was laid out for building in about 1720 but which was not to be completed until 1748. No 9, The Dove House, stands alone on the north side of the square. It was first offered to let as a lodging house in 1727.

4 British School
The Hotwells with Mr Warren's glass house   c.1745
Pen and ink with grey wash   280 x 455 mm   Private collection

IN THIS PEN AND INK DRAWING, The Dove House in Dowry Square is now surrounded by houses, but it is the growth of private houses on the hill, built for Bristol merchants rather than for visitors to the Hotwell, that suggests the drawing's approximate date. Well to the left of St Andrew's Church on the skyline is Clifton Court, now the Chesterfield Hospital, an elegant pedimented mansion built in about 1742 for Nehemiah Champion and Martha Goldney. Partly obscured by the glass kiln is Goldney House, but there is no hint of Thomas Goldney's bastion below it, which was to be completed by 1748.

In the foreground is Mr Warren's glass house. It stands on Red Cliff, a very small hill of red soil that had been worn by the tidal waters of the Avon into a meagre cliff. Its scale and perspective has defeated the artist.

When Daniel Defoe noted in 1724 that there were now fifteen glasshouses in Bristol, he acknowledged that many of them were engaged in making bottles for 'sending the water of the Hotwell not only over England but over all the world'.

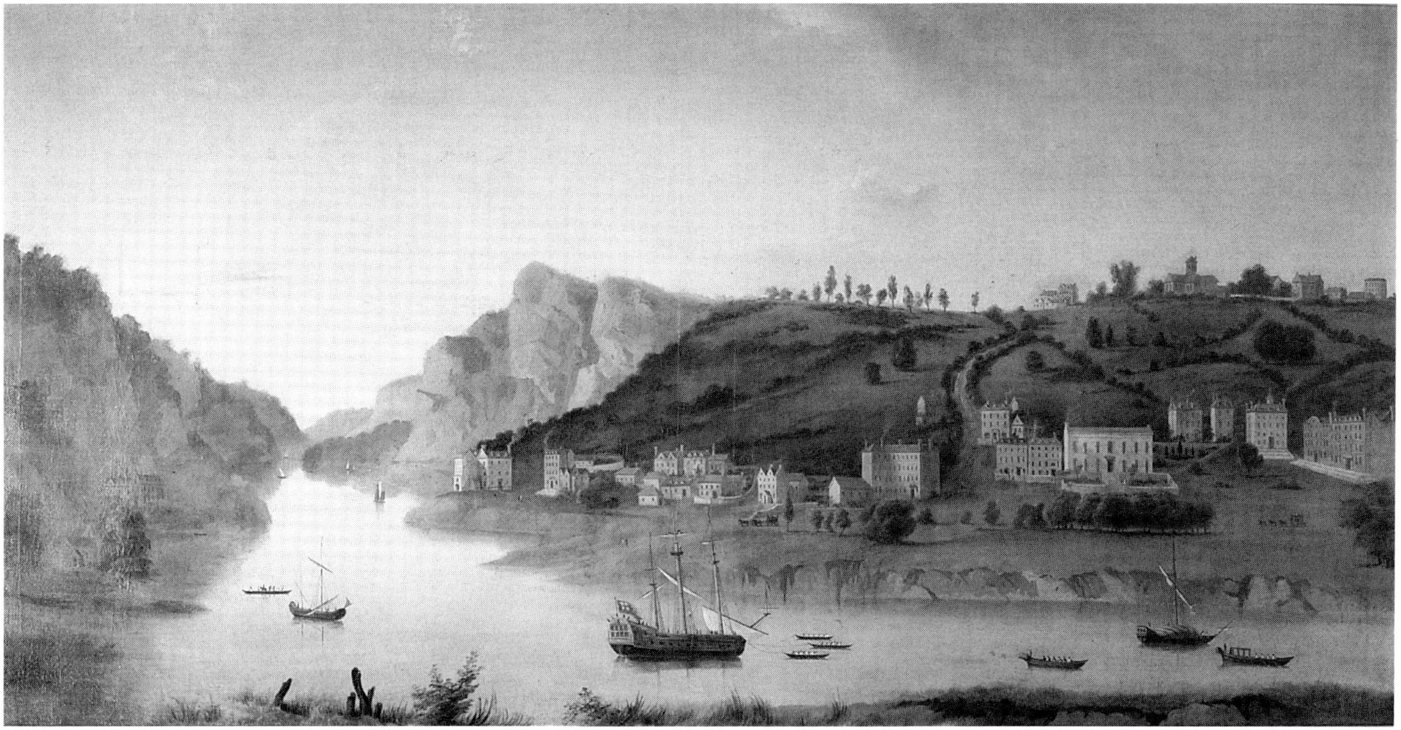

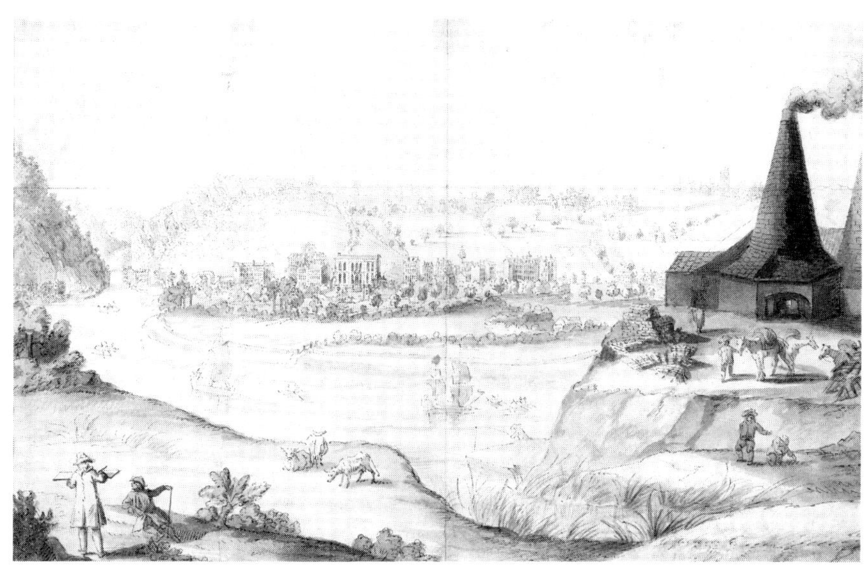

5 British School

Broad Quay c.1765
Oil 900 x 1150 mm Society of Merchant Venturers

WHEN THE POET, ALEXANDER POPE, visited Bristol in 1739, he first saw this view from the opposite end of the long quay. He had walked through the centre of the city from Bristol Bridge, down Broad Street and out under St John's Gate. With a delighted amazement, he described the scene in a letter to friend:

> From thence you come to a Key along the Old Wall with houses on both sides, and in the middle of the street, as far as you can see, hundreds of Ships, their Masts as thick as they can stand by one another, which is the oddest and most surprising sight imaginable. The street is fuller of them than the Thames from London Bridge to Deptford, and at certain times only, the water rises to carry them out; so that at other times, a Long Street full of ships in the Middle and Houses on both sides looks like a dream.

The tree on the left marks the entrance to College Green. It rises above the east end of St Augustine-the-Less, which was to be damaged in the Blitz and later demolished. Beyond the tree are Brandon Hill and the Mayor's Chapel. Above the centre of the view is St Michael's Hill and the tower of St Michael's, surrounded by many fine Tudor and early Georgian houses.

The artist concentrates on the unusual breadth of Broad Quay and the striking proximity of a commercial harbourside, with elegant figures window shopping. The viewpoint is from an upper window at the junction of Narrow Quay, behind us, and Thunderbolt Street, which led directly to the Merchants' Hall and King Street. As if he were celebrating Bristol's wealth and good governance at this time, the artist diligently records Bristol's early street lighting – the globe lamps along the quayside and by the shops.

The shop at the far right of the painting is almost certainly the shop of the Bristol pewterer, Richard Going. The enormous brewer's copper may be one of his products. It is carried on one of Bristol's notorious sledges. Daniel Defoe observed in the 1720s that 'They draw all their goods here on Sleds, or sledges without wheels, which Kills a Multitude of Horses…'

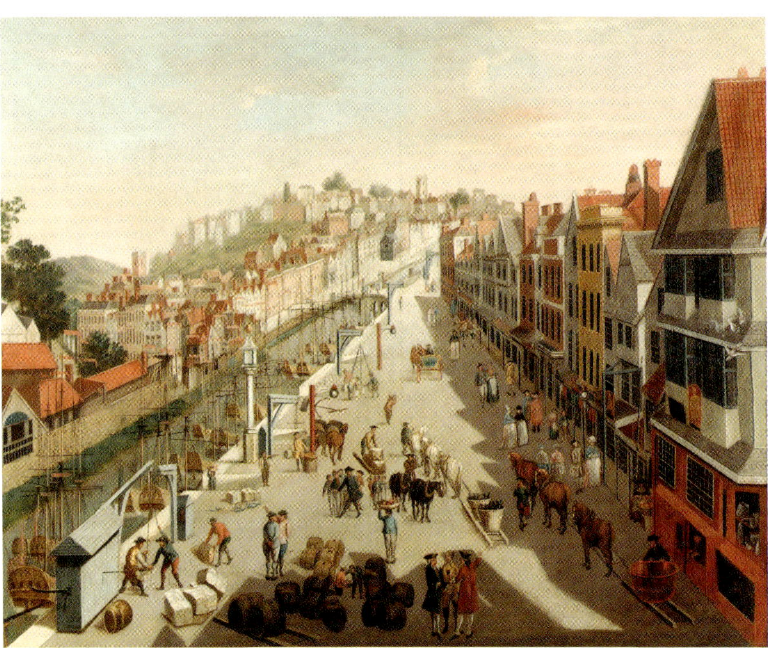

6 William Halfpenny died 1755
'The Great Crane…ERECTED by Mr John Padmore in the year 1735'
Pen, ink and grey wash   320 x 470 mm   Bristol Museums and Art Gallery Mb3450

THIS DETAILED, EXPLANATORY DRAWING is by William Halfpenny, architect of the Coopers' Hall in King Street, now the entrance hall of the Theatre Royal. He was also the author of several pattern books, including *Perspective made Easy* published in London in 1731.

The Great Crane had three jibs operated either by hand-windlasses or by two treadmills inside the long house, which was raised on fourteen columns clad in cast-iron. There was also an innovative braking system. It stood just to the north east of the future Prince Street Bridge and survived until the creation of the Floating Harbour.

John Padmore – 'the ingenious Mr Padmore', as Daniel Defoe called him – was one of the most influential engineers of the eighteenth century. In the late 1720s he was closely involved with the design and construction of the cranes and tramway system that transported stone from Ralph Allen's quarries above Bath to the wharves on the Avon. The river had been made navigable between Bristol and Bath by 1727. Padmore submitted a pioneering proposal for a dam and lock below the Hotwell House in the 1720s and he may also have been involved with the design of the docks at Sea Mills. Towards the end of the century when the Society of Merchant Venturers asked John Smeaton to improve the pumping machinery at the Hotwell House, Smeaton demurred, saying that it would be improper to interfere with machinery installed by so able an engineer as Mr Padmore.

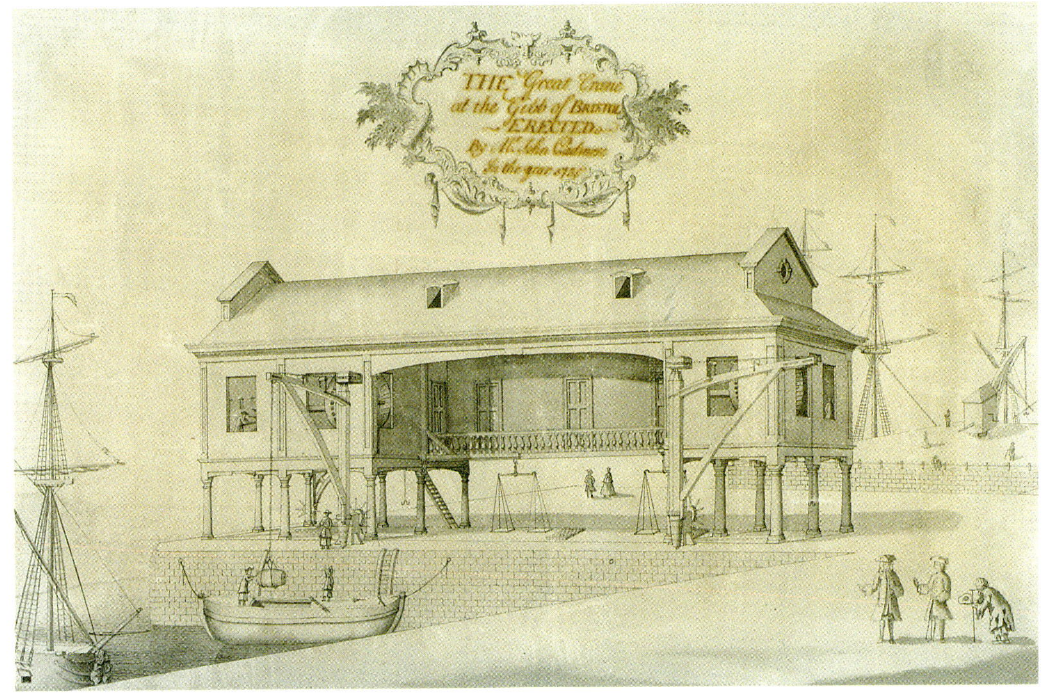

7 Nicholas Pocock 1740-1821
Wapping c.1760
Pen, ink and grey wash 435 x 572 mm Bristol Museums and Art Gallery M3022

THIS IS BOTH THE EARLIEST AND THE MOST DETAILED visual record of shipbuilding and repair in Bristol. It depicts the docks and yards of Sydenham Teast at East Wapping, the site from which Prince Street Bridge now springs. The lower right-hand vignette depicts the launch of a privateer from the Teasts' yard opposite the Great Crane with St Mary Redcliffe in the distance. Four successive Sydenham Teasts built and refitted vessels here from about 1750 to 1841.

In the centre of the drawing is a dry dock with its gates open at low tide. To the left, a new hull is ready for launching although the artist has omitted the supporting beams. Next to it a smaller vessel has been careened and is having its bottom cleaned of incrustations. To the right, passengers await the Gibb ferry, which can be seen in the foreground. The fine houses in the background attest to the Teasts' success.

At the feet of the right-hand figure supporting the blank cartouche are the tools of the shipbuilder's trade and it is possible that this drawing was intended as a tribute to Sydenham Teast, whose initials are on a log outside the saw pit above the Gibb ferry. The artist, Nicholas Pocock – still very much an amateur artist and not yet a ship's captain – may have been patiently awaiting his next voyage.

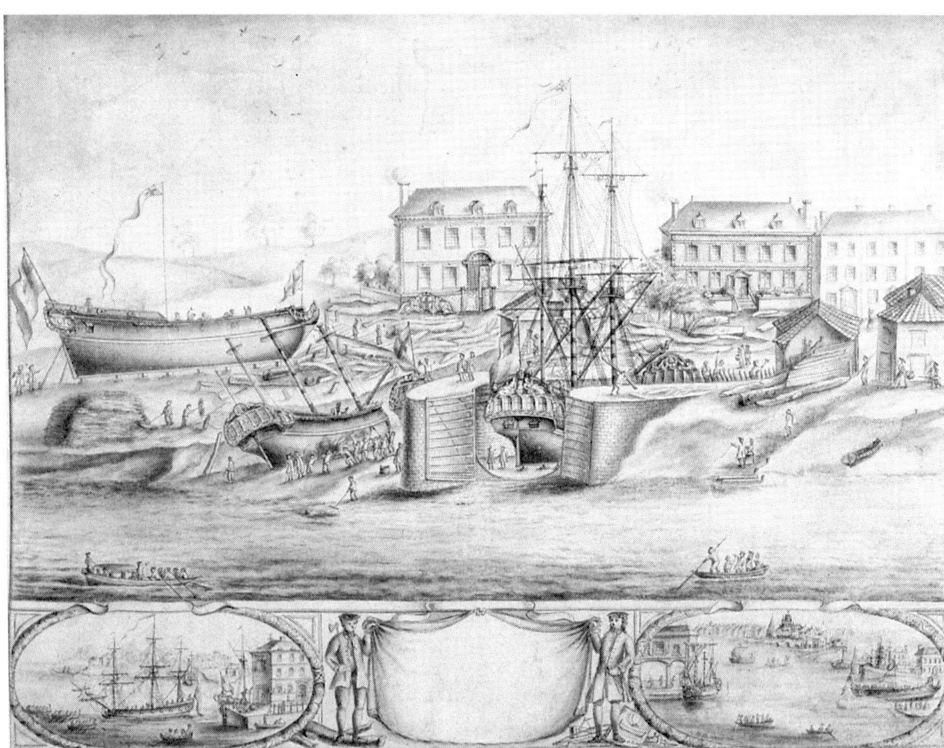

8 Nicholas Pocock 1740-1821
The ship Lloyd *in King Road at the entrance to the Avon with Blaise Castle and King's Weston* 1768
Pen, ink and grey wash   180 x 206 mm National Maritime Museum (LOG/M/54)

ON ALMOST EVERY DAY OF HIS VOYAGES as a ship's captain, Nicholas Pocock drew his ship in the logbook, depicting it from one viewpoint or another according to the weather conditions of the day. This view is the frontispiece to the logbook for Pocock's voyage to Charleston, South Carolina, in 1768/9.

The *Lloyd* is seen in King Road before setting off down the Bristol Channel. On the hill to the left are Blaise Castle, King's Weston House and the gateway or lodge near Penpole Point.

Beyond the *Lloyd* is the muddy expanse of Dumball (Dunball or Dungball) Island at the entrance to the Avon, which is today incorporated into Avonmouth Docks. This treacherous island was covered at high tide and is shown here complete with its gibbet. Pocock and his crew would have known the story of the sailors who were gibbeted here in 1741 after carrying out their Captain's orders – to murder the Captain's elder brother, the baronet Sir John Dinely Goodere.

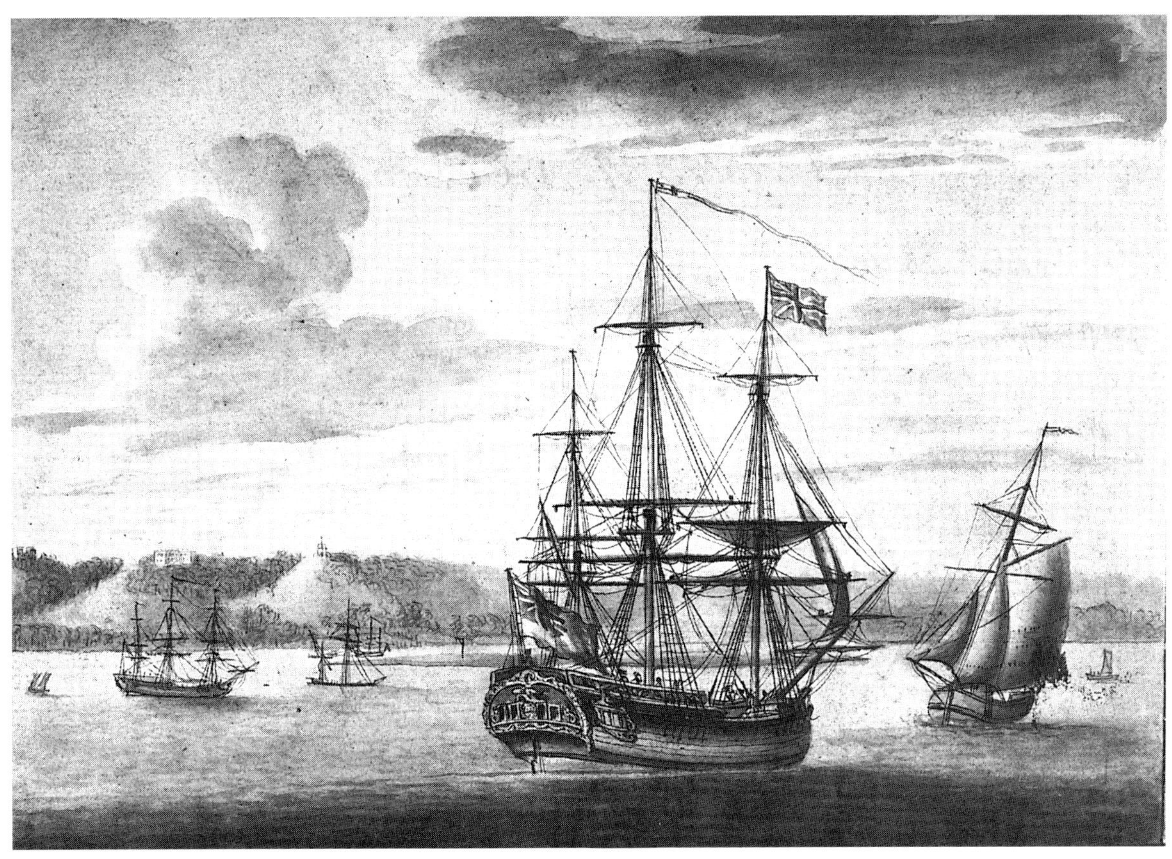

9 Thomas Smith of Derby c.1720-1767
View from Durdham Down c.1756
Oil 490 x 1170 mm Private collection

ONE OF THE ADVERTISED FEATURES of a visit to the Hotwell was the pleasure of riding on the broad unbroken stretches of turf on the Downs. Here, on the far right, an elegant carriage with postillions and outriders approaches Sea Walls. Mr E Owen in his guide to the Hotwell published in London in 1754 wrote: 'For those who love riding there is the finest country in the world; and, even for carriages, nothing can exceed it; the Downs are spacious and open, and we enjoy healthful exercise in a pure air…'

The artist, Thomas Smith of Derby, may have come to the Hotwell for his health, for we know that he was to die here on 5 September 1767. It is also possible that it was the growing reputation of the spectacular landscape of the Avon Gorge that first attracted him to Bristol.

He painted two opposing views of the Avon Gorge from the Downs, one looking back towards the Hotwell and the present view which is also known in two other versions. This particular elongated version was probably a commission for an overmantel or overdoor. Both views were engraved in 1756.

Smith was self-taught and much of his work, especially his many landscapes of his home county, is unencumbered with the self-conscious allusions to the work of earlier Continental painters such as Claude Lorrain, Gaspard Dughet or Salvator Rosa that are found in the work of many landscape painters at this time. He did, however, give the middle names of Correggio to one son and of Raphael to the other. In this painting the sparring goats in the foreground are probably derived from engravings after Claude.

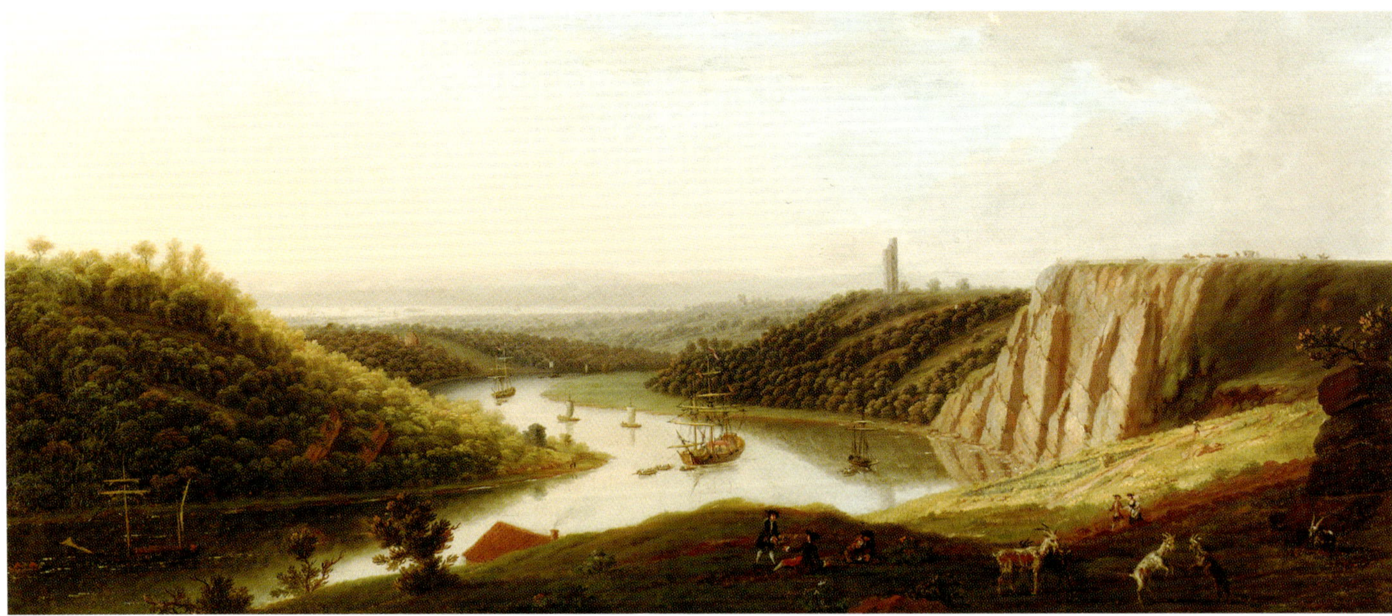

10 Edmund Garvey RA op. 1767 - d. 1813
Bristol with Clifton Wood and Merchants' Dock   c.1770
Oil   880 x 1230 mm   Society of Merchant Venturers

THIS IMPORTANT RECORD of Bristol's first major wet or floating dock is almost certainly by Edmund Garvey, an Irish-born artist of modest ability. He worked in Bath in the 1770s and was friends with Thomas Gainsborough. His one moment of renown came later when he was inexplicably elected a full member of the Royal Academy, defeating the far superior artist, Joseph Wright of Derby. That prompted the venomous critic, Anthony Pasquin, to refer to him as that 'insignificant mushroom…Edmund Garbage.'

On the hill to the left are Thomas Goldney's rotunda and the engine tower erected in 1767. In the centre is the Cathedral and to the right, past rows of ships' masts and glass kilns, is the truncated spire and tower of St Mary Redcliffe.

The large floating dock to the left was initially called the Great Dock. It was built 1762-1768 by William Champion. Merchant, manufacturer, privateer owner and ship builder, he even put forward his own proposals for the floating of the whole harbour by damming it at Rownham, the point at the very foreground of this painting. Over-stretched by his development of the brass and copper industries at Warmley and by difficulties with the Great Dock itself, he was declared bankrupt in 1769. The following year the Society of Merchant Venturers bought the dock and renamed it Merchants' Dock. The Society successfully obtained an Act of Parliament in 1776 that required all vessels with seriously combustible materials such as timber, tar and turpentine to off-load within the dock rather than in the heart of the city.

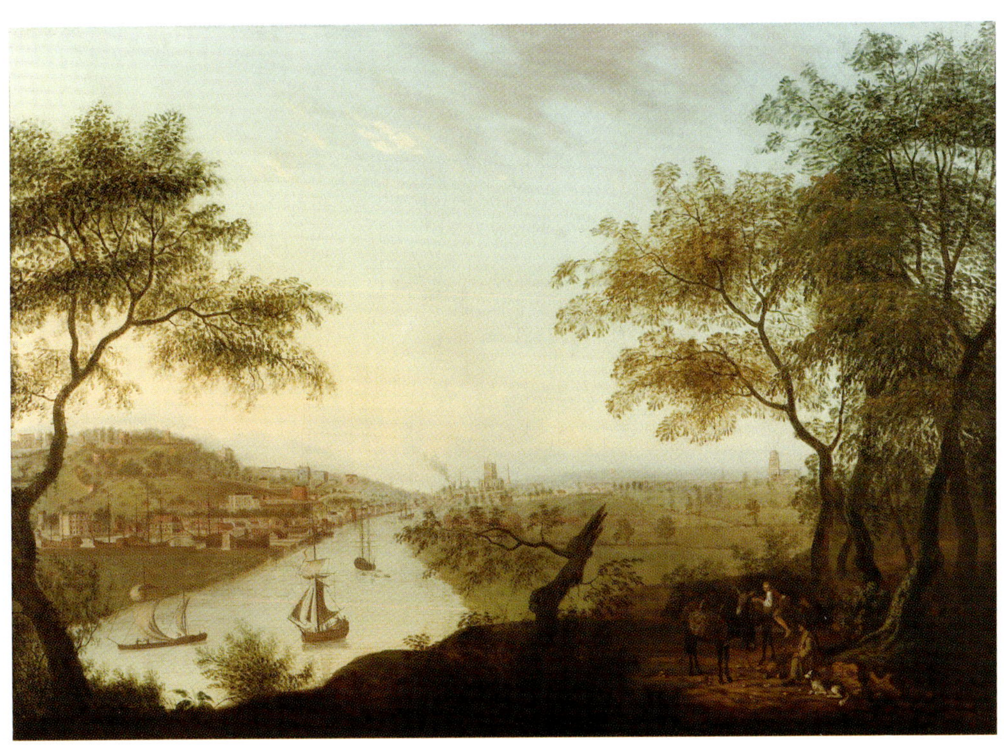

11 William Milton after S. Pye
'A North east Perspective View of Bristol Hot-well House, and St Vincent's Rock…' c.1747
Line engraving   248 x 408 mm   Bristol Museums and Art Gallery M712

FEW IMAGES BETTER SUGGEST THE CONTRAST between the Bristol and Bath spas. Bath was a predominantly winter spa, sophisticated and highly fashionable. Bristol was a summer spa, essentially May to September, and the fresh air and spectacular landscape were just as important as the medicinal waters. It was almost as fashionable as Bath with a respectable number of visiting nobility. One bookseller moved from one spa to the other according to the season.

This engraving presents the landscape setting of the Hotwell as a rural idyll. An appealing rococo maiden approaches a rather Falstaffian youth in the left-hand corner. The Hotwell House has no colonnade as yet, but an avenue of trees has recently been planted and extends to Rock House, a lodging house that survives today between the Colonnade and St Vincent's Parade. Beyond Rock House is a haystack – a necessary convenience for the horses.

An earlier state of this engraving is dated 1747 and it is one of the earliest prints of the Hotwell. This impression was printed and published in London. William Milton, the Bristol engraver of the plate for this print, is known for his superb rococo trade-cards made for local shopkeepers and craftsmen and for an album of original designs in Bristol Reference Library.

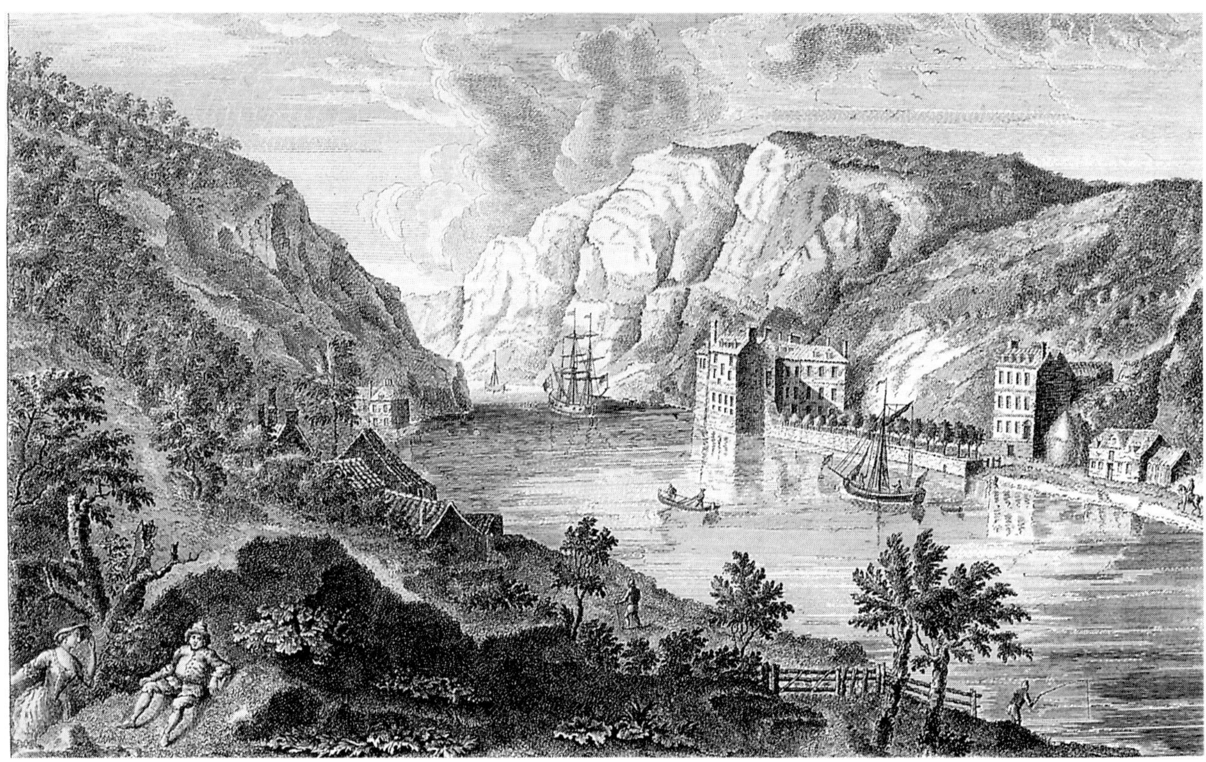

12 P. Angier after Jean Baptiste Claude Chatelain 1710-1771
'A South View of the Cliffs called St Vincents Rock…Taken from the Top of the Rock behind the Hotwell' 1753
Line engraving   235 x 350 mm   Bristol Museums and Art Gallery M711

ELEGANT AND FASHIONABLY DRESSED VISITORS to the Hotwell clamber on the rocks. Those at the summit look more like the robbers or *banditti* that so often bring an edge of terror to the dramatic landscape paintings of Salvator Rosa or to the etchings of Marco Ricci. Such Italian artists were very popular in England in the earlier eighteenth century, appealing both to artists and to sophisticated travellers, who were eager to recognise such exotic imagery in the English landscape.

Even the poet Alexander Pope, who delighted in satirising fashionable affectations, was carried away by this view from beyond the Hotwell House in 1739:

…you go in the [Hotwell] house, and looking out at the back-door a vast rock of an hundred feet of red, white, green, blue and yellowish marble, all blotched and variegated, strikes you quite in the face; and turning on the left there opens the river at a vast depth below, winding in and out, and accompanied on both sides with a continued range of rocks up into the clouds, of a hundred colours, one behind another…very much like the broken scenes in a play-house…

Chatelain was a London artist, engraver and drawing master of French Huguenot extraction.

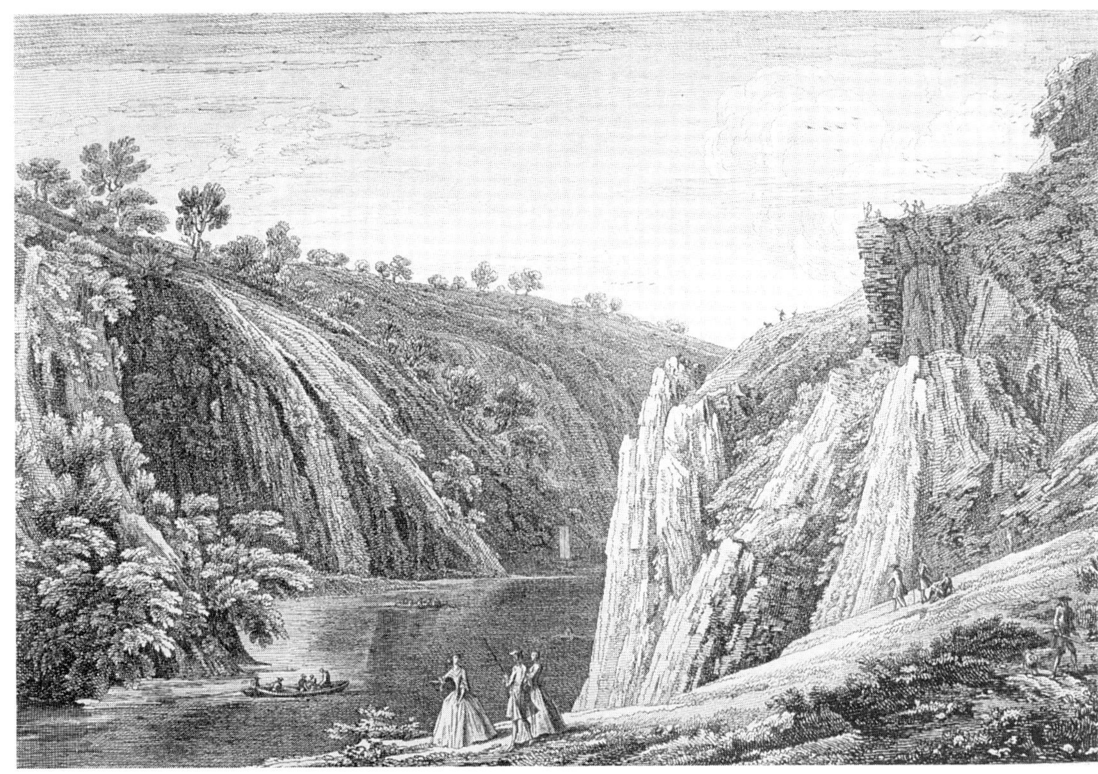

13 Nicholas Pocock 1740-1821
The Avon Gorge at Sunset   c.1785
Oil   915 x 1320 mm   Society of Merchant Venturers

A HEAVILY ARMED MERCHANTMAN carrying at least thirty-four guns is being towed downstream by some forty oarsmen in five boats. With a man at the tiller and another to bellow orders, there could be ten men to a boat. There are records of payment to as many as fifty-nine men in six boats. This was a journey that the artist, Nicholas Pocock, had undertaken many times when he was a ship's captain, albeit in a smaller vessel (8). Although there are other images that illustrate the difficulties of passage up or down the Avon, it is Pocock's views of the river, and this painting especially, that have unrivalled authenticity.

The view looks downstream with Sea Walls high on the right and Cook's Folly beyond. This building, so important to the compositions of innumerable artists and not always very accurately described by visiting painters (9), was built at the end of the seventeenth century by John Cook, the City Chamberlain, to embellish his estate of Sneyd Park. Today, part of the folly survives incorporated into a Victorian house.

Pocock had almost certainly become a professional artist by the time of the insolvency of his employer, Richard Champion, in 1778. In 1782 he first exhibited at the Royal Academy in London. A smaller variant of this view in a private collection is dated 1785.

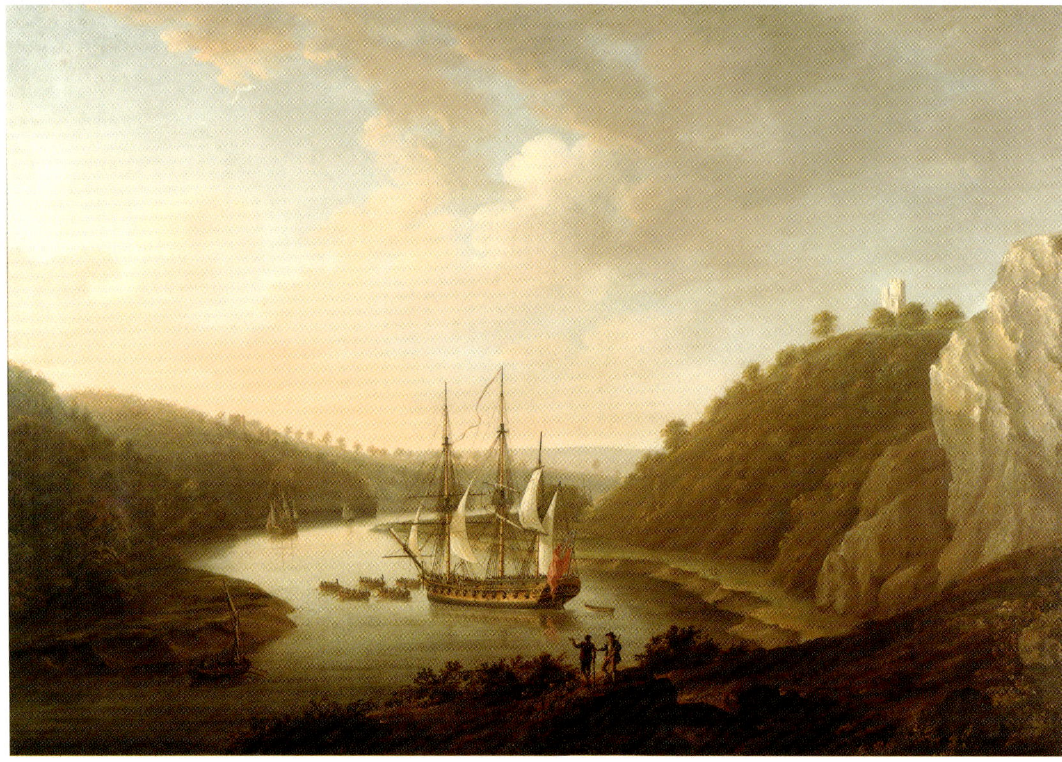

14 Nicholas Pocock 1740-1821
Bristol Harbour with the Cathedral and the Quay 1785
Oil 571 x 813 mm Bristol Museums and Art Gallery K742

THIS VIEW FROM WAPPING looking towards St Augustine's Reach with the densely packed quaysides of Narrow and Broad Quay running up to St Stephen's Church, is one of the most familiar images of Bristol's eighteenth-century prosperity, its so-called Golden Age. Statistics paint a very different picture – of a city failing to expand at the rate of its rivals in the Midlands and the North. But there was justification for Pocock's apparent confidence and pride in his native city. 1785, the date of this painting, was a year of relative peace. War had broken out with the American colonies a decade earlier and in 1778 France had joined forces against Great Britain, followed by both Spain and Holland in 1780. But now in 1785 catastrophe had been avoided, trade had returned and there were exciting plans for the port's expansion.

We know that this painting was later in the possession of descendants of Thomas Daniel, by whom it may have been commissioned. Mayor in 1797 and Master of the Society of Merchant Venturers in 1805, he had first been elected a common councillor in 1785. Merchant, ship-owner and West India planter, he was also one of the most powerful defenders of slavery.

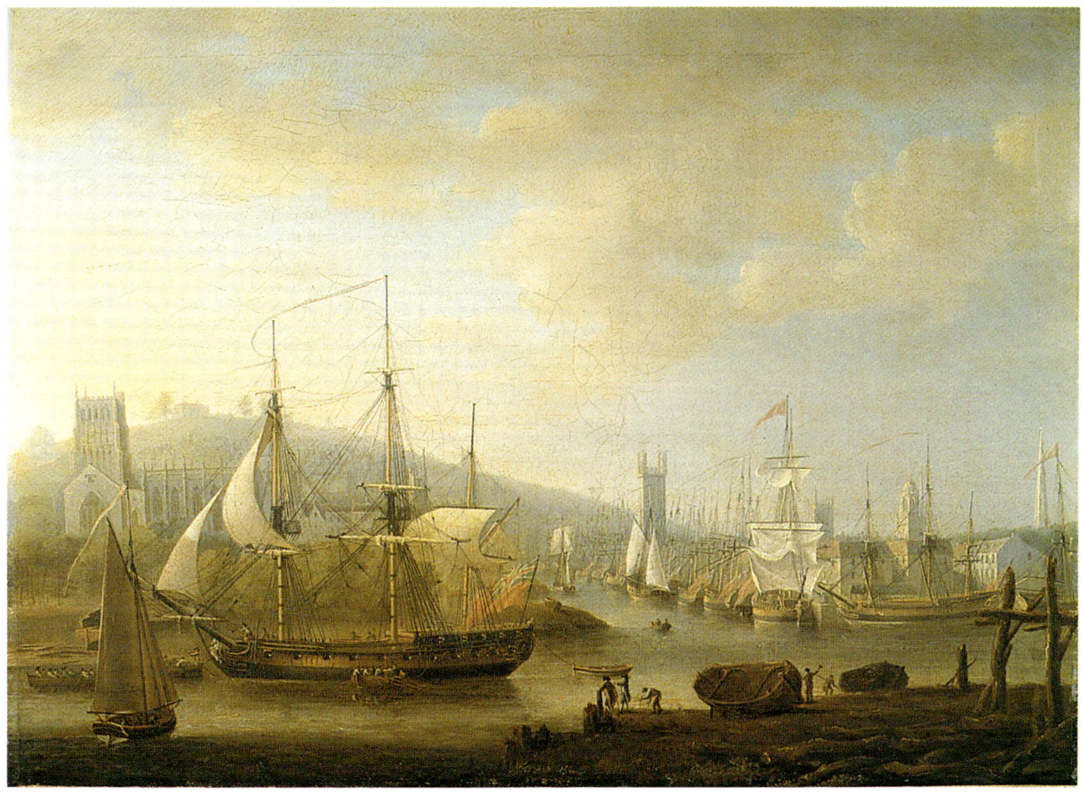

15 Nicholas Pocock   1740-1821
St Mary Redcliffe from Sea Banks c.1785
Etching, aquatint and watercolour   245 x 370 mm   Bristol Museums and Art Gallery M4358

FROM THE EARLY 1780S and for more than twenty years thereafter Pocock produced impressions of eight etched and sometimes also aquatinted views on the Avon from the harbour to the Channel — from Bristol to the sea. To each engraving Pocock added watercolour with exemplary care. The etched outline is sometimes so slight that, today, they are still innocently sold as original watercolours over pen and ink. They were not an indivisible set, but a series, sold in varying groups over a very long period.

This view, the second in the sequence, was based on a larger watercolour dated 1781. The date is of significance for it confirms that the ships being built in Sydenham Teast's dry docks, on the right, are likely to be King's ships, commissioned by the Admiralty. Orders for men-of-war were then at their height.

Above the yard, the west end of Teast's development of Redcliffe Parade is complete. It was the second of the four successive Sydenham Teasts who had first promoted the building of the Parade in 1768. St Mary Redcliffe is surrounded by glass kilns and the Great Crane can be seen on the quay by The Grove. The entrance to St Augustine's Reach is on the left and the viewpoint is from today's piazza by Lloyds Bank headquarters.

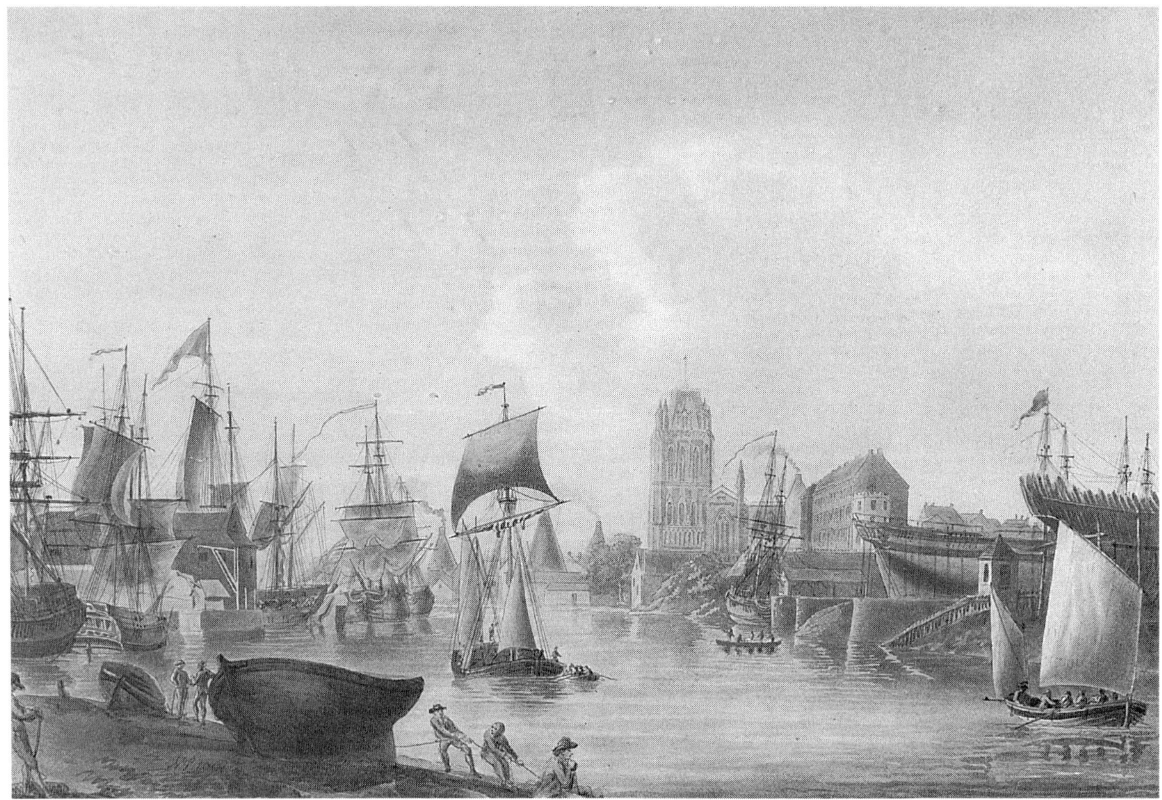

16 Nicholas Pocock 1740-1821
Clifton Hill from Sea Banks c.1786
Etching and aquatint   250 x 380 mm   Bristol Museums and Art Gallery M728

FROM ABOUT 1786 POCOCK added an aquatint ground to the etched outlines of his print series to help with modelling and shading. This impression was left uncoloured, probably because the aquatint tones were felt to be too dark for the successful addition of watercolour.

Sea Banks, the meadow bordering Canon's Marsh below the Cathedral, was soon to be developed as timber wharves. The Limekiln Lane glasshouse at the bottom of Jacob's Wells Road was a major supplier of bottles for the medicinal waters of the Hotwell and other nearby springs. Also puffing smoke above it is the tower built by Thomas Goldney to house the steam engine to pump water to his famous grotto and fountains.

On the far right is Clifton Hill House, the grand Palladian villa with its distinctive pedimented façade. It was built by the son of Paul Fisher, a very successful West India merchant, who had been much involved in the slave trade and in privateering. It bears the date of 1747 and was designed by the eminent London architect, Isaac Ware.

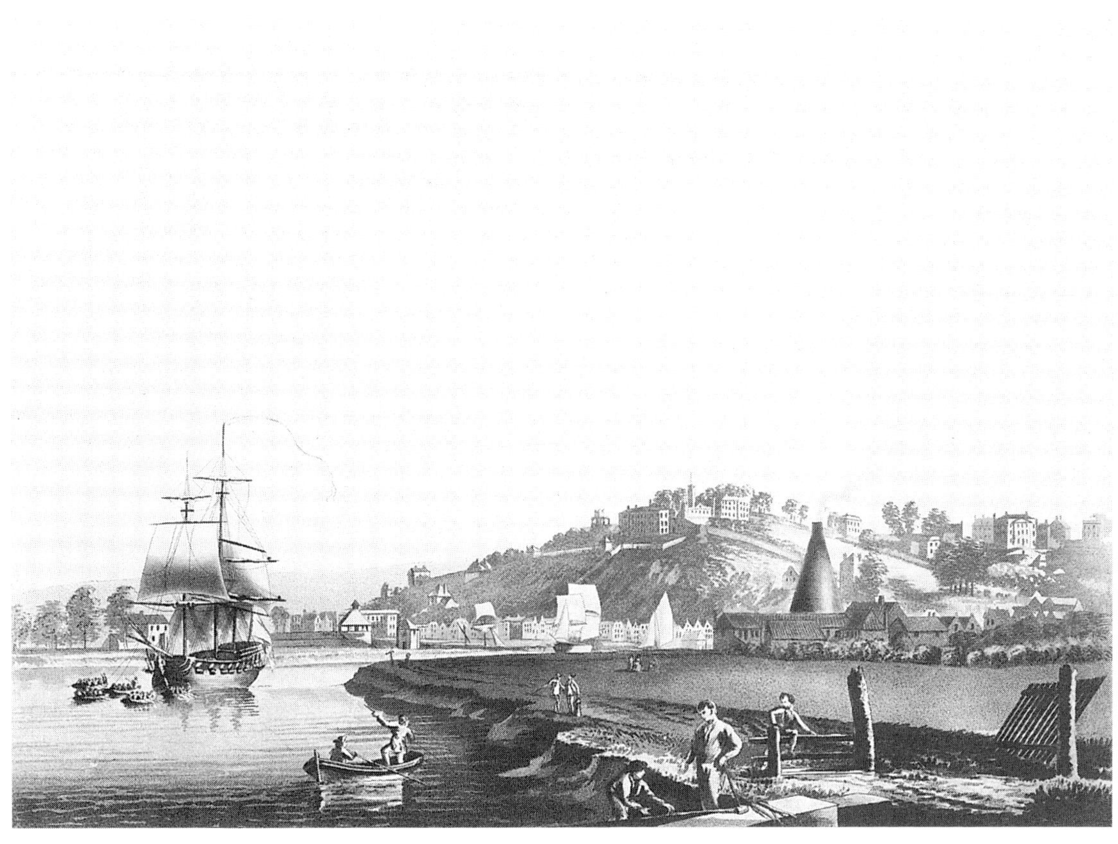

17 Nicholas Pocock 1740-1821
The Avon Gorge from below Cook's Folly 1786
Watercolour 400 x 520 mm Private collection

THIS RUSTIC LANDSCAPE WAS PROBABLY OF THE KIND to which
Pocock most aspired when he became a professional artist, but
from which he was to be diverted by demands for his ship portraits and naval battle scenes. He moved from Bristol to London
in 1789 and the extent and accuracy of his records of Nelson's
victories were to be unrivalled. He was even to be present at the
battle of the Glorious First of June in 1794.

The view is unusual and the watercolour itself is in superb
condition. Above the picturesque foreground are Sea Walls
with elegant travellers in a horse and carriage enjoying the view,
the gatehouse of the Clifton Turnpike, the ruined windmill and
the Hotwell House at the foot of St Vincent's Rocks.

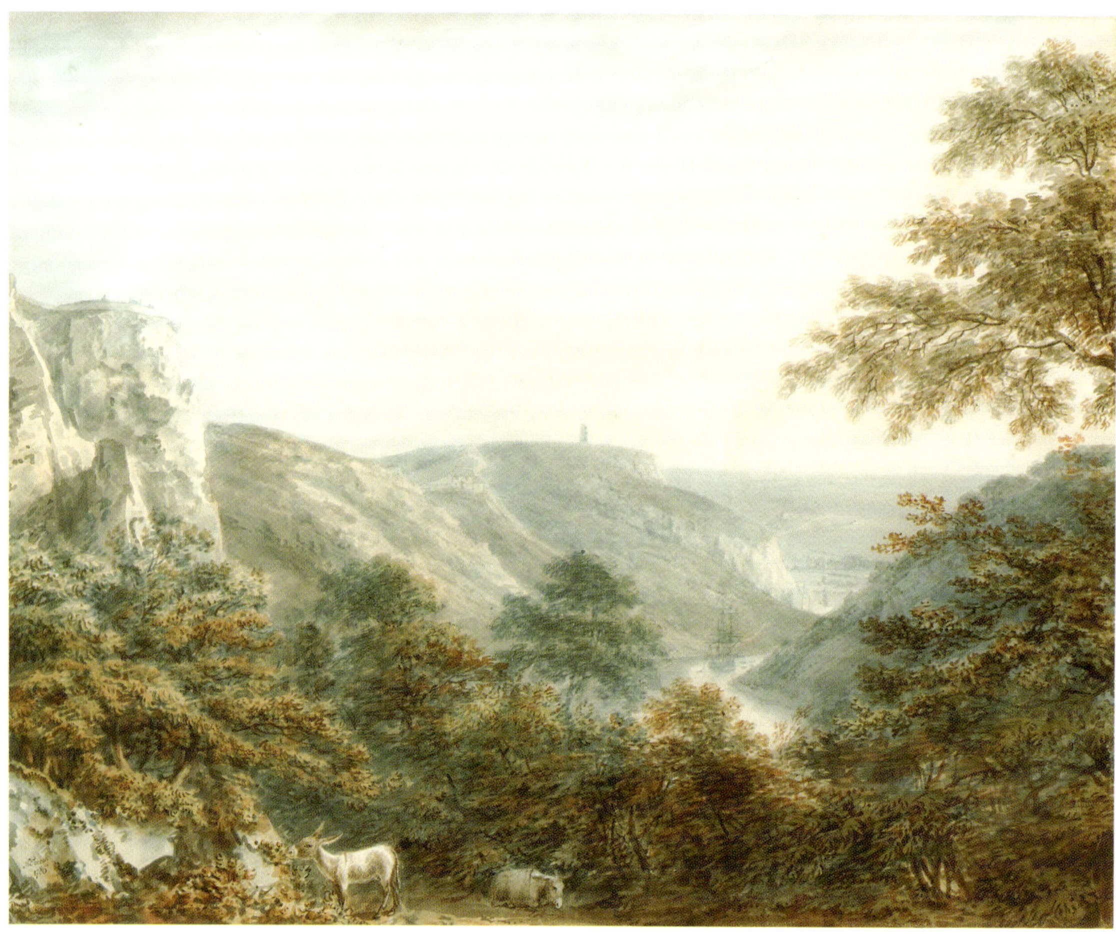

18 Nicholas Pocock 1740-1821
View over King's Weston to the Bristol Channel c.1785
Watercolour 440 x 600 mm Bristol Museums and Art Gallery K2392

THE SUBTLE COLOURING OF THIS WATERCOLOUR and the rhythmic entwining of the foreground trees demonstrate the great maturity of Pocock's art before he left Bristol for London in 1789. There he was to be one of the founder members of the Society of Painters in Watercolour in 1804, actually turning down the presidency of the society two years later.

In the centre are the stables to King's Weston House. These were designed by Robert Mylne in 1763, two years after his return from Rome. The great baroque mansion itself was designed by John Vanbrugh, 1709-19. Vanbrugh was also responsible for Penpole Lodge, above it. This was, in effect, an eye-catcher, but also a distant dining room and a spectacular vantage point. Despite its church-tower appearance, it was entirely classical in its detail. It was demolished in 1950. In the distance vessels await a favourable wind and tide in King Road and beyond is the bosom of Portishead Point.

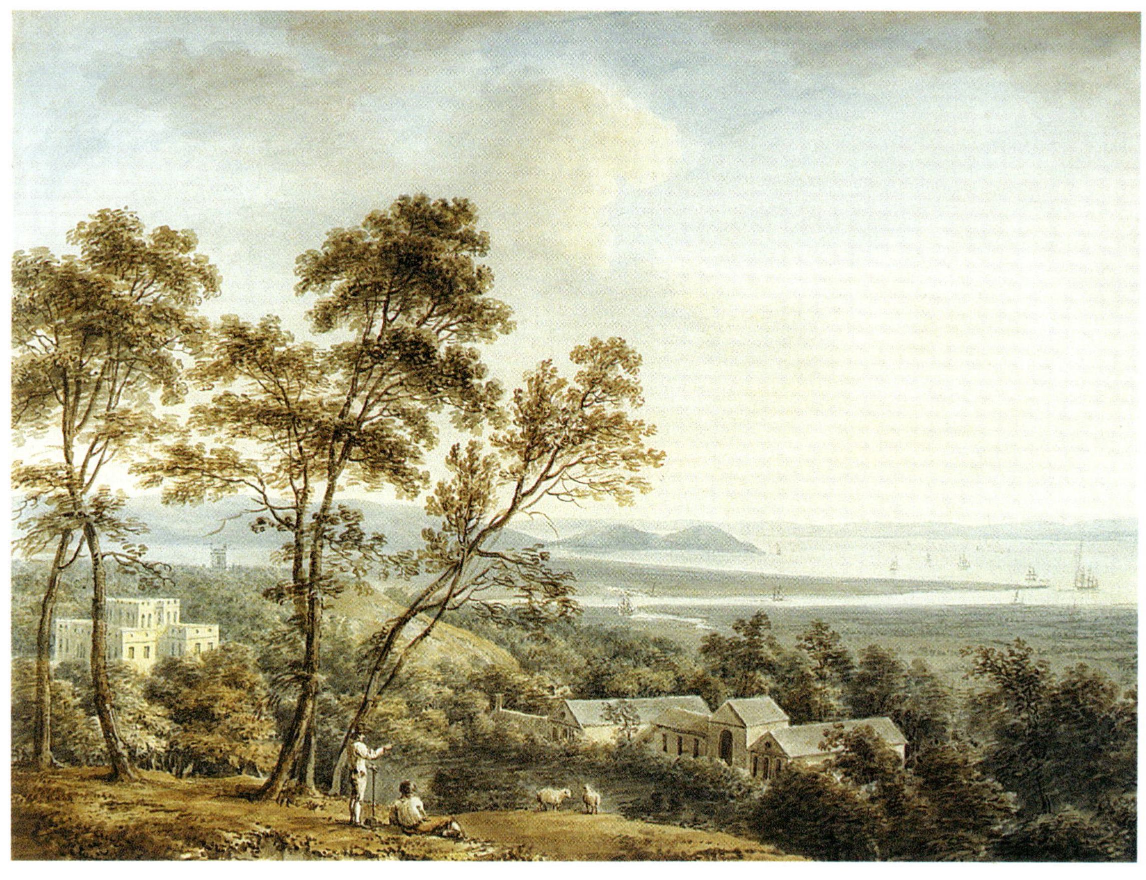

19 Nicholas Pocock 1740-1821
The Avon at Sea Mills from Kingsweston Down c.1785
Watercolour 185 x 240 mm Private collection

THIS UNUSUAL VIEW LOOKS UPSTREAM from above today's Shire-hampton golf course. Just to the left of the centre is a terrace of houses that marked the site of Sea Mills Dock. These houses were to be recorded in greater detail by Joseph Walter (97). The building of these docks, only the third floating dock to be built in England, had begun in 1712. They were always to be too inconveniently placed for continuous commercial success and when Pocock drew this view in about 1785, the dock buildings were probably already derelict.

Nicholas Pocock, when still a mariner, had drawn portraits of two ships which were refitted in these docks in the 1740s.

The *Jason* and the *Southwell* were actively involved in priva-teering and the slave trade and both of Pocock's detailed pen and ink portraits include unique vignettes depicting the actual purchase of slaves on the coast of Africa (Bristol Museums and Art Gallery).

In the distance to the far left is Cook's Folly. Above Sea Mills in the centre and within Leigh Woods on the Somerset side of the river is the manor house of Abbots Leigh. This was demol-ished in 1811 prior to the building of Leigh Court for Philip John Miles in 1814 on a different site nearby.

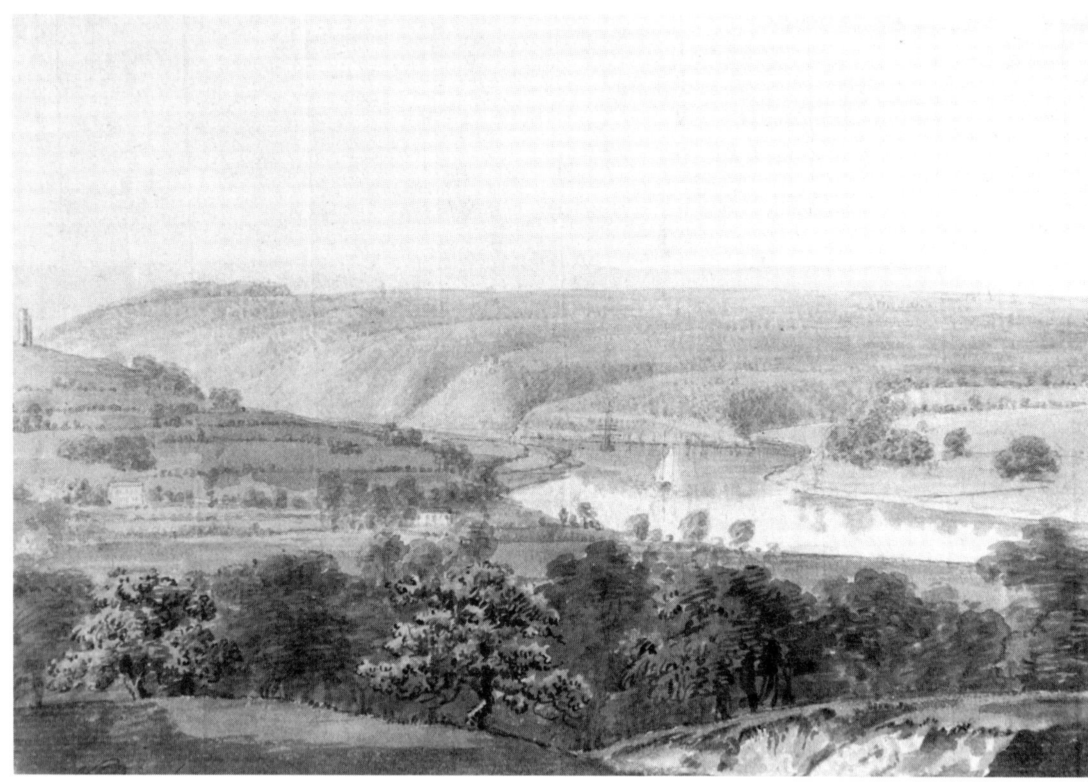

20 Nicholas Pocock 1740-1821
King Road from Portishead Point   1787
Watercolour   425 x 580 mm   Bristol Museums and Art Gallery K1801

KING ROAD PROVIDED GOOD ANCHORAGE and relative shelter whilst vessels awaited the right tide and wind to proceed up river or down the Bristol Channel. Many vessels also took on or discharged cargo, passengers and crew at King Road and perhaps discharged the pilot if a long delay was expected. In this watercolour, which may at first look more like a hasty smuggling operation, Pocock is describing the fearful problems of landing at Portishead Point as well as the risks, here narrowly averted, of getting a large vessel too close to a lee shore.

Pocock exhibited a picture at the Royal Academy in 1788 with the title *Portishead Point*, which it is likely to have been this watercolour. The composition is derived from a well-known shipwreck scene by the French artist, Claude Joseph Vernet. Intriguingly, Sir Joshua Reynolds, the President of the Royal Academy, had commented on the first painting that Pocock had sent to the Academy, saying that it lacked 'union between the clouds, the sea and the sails' and recommended that Pocock follow Vernet's example. Evidently, it was advice that Pocock followed promptly and an influence that he assimilated with ease.

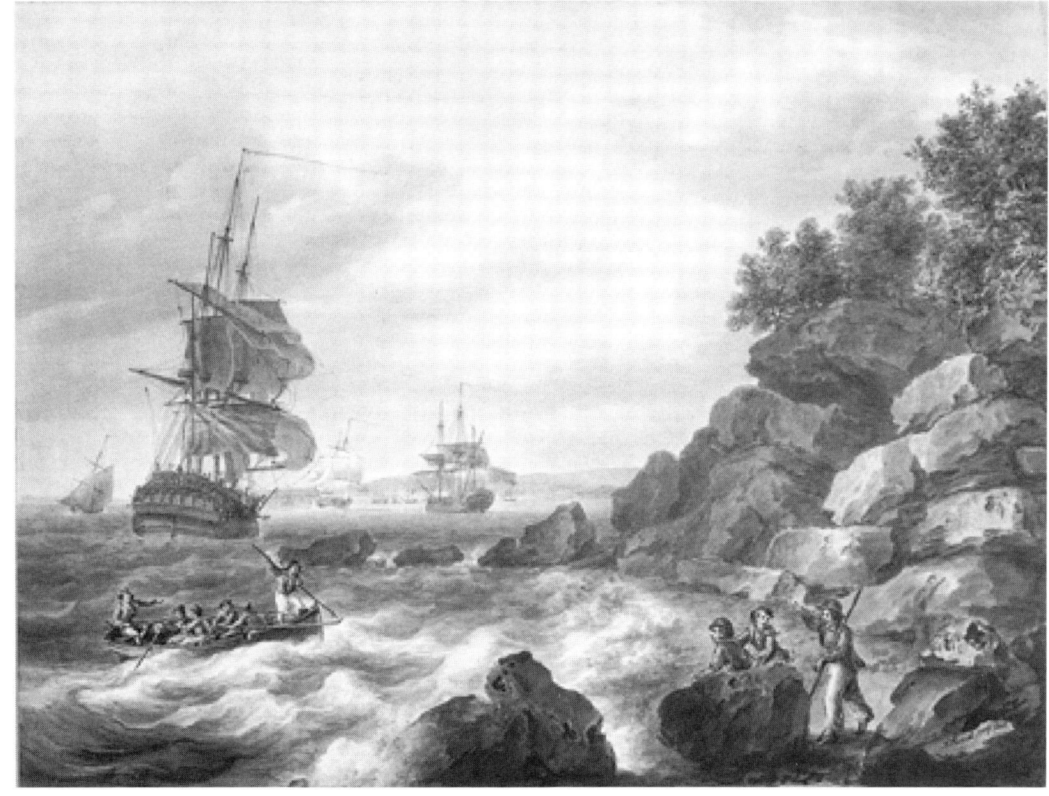

21 James Blackamore op. 1780s
Proposals for the development of Clifton c.1787
Pen, ink and brown wash   560 x 1105 mm   Private collection

THIS IS NOT CLIFTON AS IT ONCE WAS, but Clifton as it was once
meant to be. This drawing confirms the remarkable boldness of
the developer's vision for Clifton in about 1787, in the middle of
that brief decade of peace between 1782 and 1793. As yet, there
is no other evidence for any other unified plan for Clifton on
such a grand scale. The terraces shown here were mostly to be
begun in 1789 or 1790. None was completed as shown and the
outbreak of war with France in 1793 was to bankrupt most of
the builders and developers.

James Blackamore, a surveyor and architectural draughts-
man, was the artist of this careful drawing. In a ground plan for
a Bristol project of 1781, he signs himself as 'of Bath' and it
may be that he worked intermittently for the architect, John
Eveleigh, in that city. It is known that Eveleigh was designing
terraces in Clifton in the later 1780s and Windsor Terrace, as we
see it here, is close in style to Eveleigh's Camden Terrace in Bath.
But it was probably the commitment of William Watts that was
central to the development.

William Watts was a plumber. He amassed a fortune
through his invention of a new method of making lead shot at
his shot tower on Redcliffe Hill. Watts then sold his patent and,
perhaps inspired by Sydenham Teast's nearby Redcliffe Parade,
was tempted to invest in the development of Clifton. He can be
linked to the initial idea for the grandiose two-part Paragon
that we see breaking the skyline in this view, but it was
Windsor Terrace and in particular the vast vaulted abutment
beneath it, that swallowed up his fortune. He was declared
bankrupt in 1794. Only half of the great crescent shown here
was completed and its curve is almost imperceptible today.

St Vincent's Parade, which, like Windsor Terrace, may be to
John Eveleigh's design, can be seen in exaggerated perspective
running out from the Hotwell. It was to be built to only half
that length.

22 detail of 21

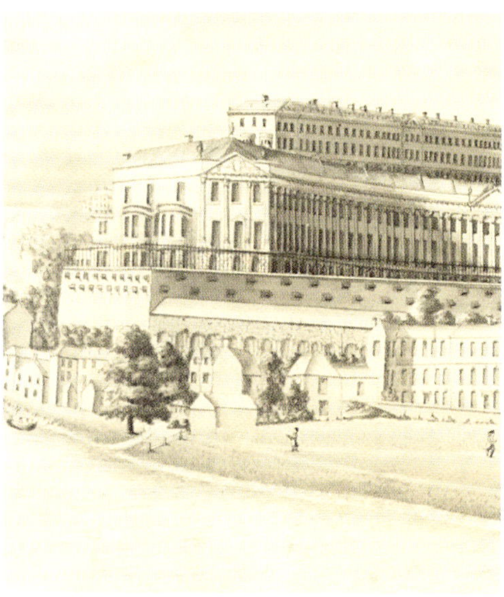

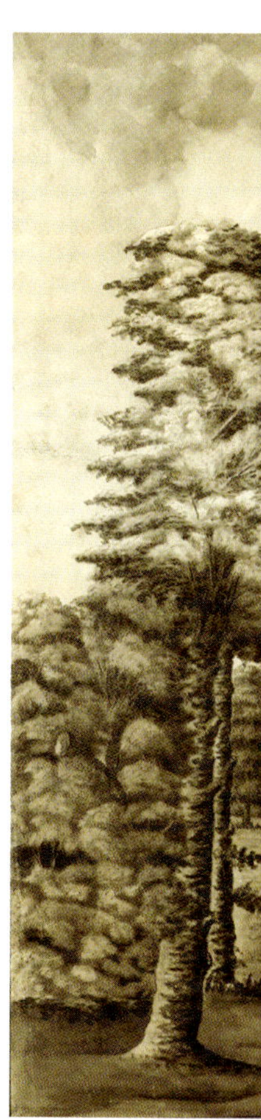

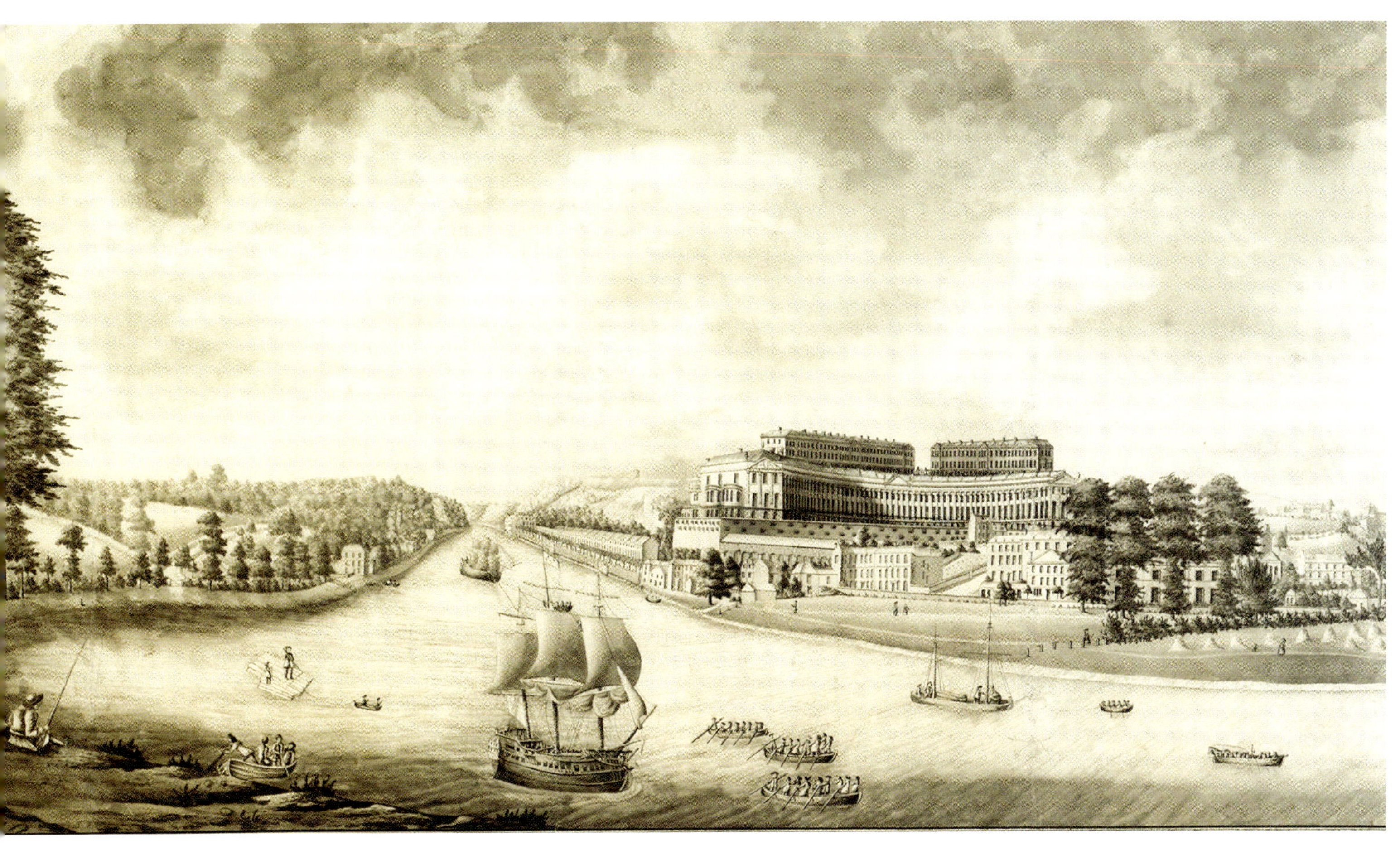

23 Phenedus Daniel after William Bridges
Plan and elevation of a bridge across the Avon Gorge   March 1793
Pen, ink and watercolour   350 x 500 mm   Bristol Museums and Art Gallery Mb107

THERE HAS BEEN AN UNDERSTANDABLE TEMPTATION to ridicule William Bridges's extraordinary design, but there is little doubt that the plans were prepared with serious intent. They were noted by a local newspaper in January 1793 and engraved and published and mentioned in a guidebook in the same year. It would have been the outbreak of the war with France, rather than the damning observations of an engineer, that sunk the proposal without further mention.

William Bridges is otherwise unknown. His architectural style was oddly baroque and out of date. The engraver of the printed version, signed P D, was Phenedus Daniel, an engraver and watchmaker of Clare Street in the heart of Bristol. The thoughtful variety of uses to which the enormous structure would be put included a granary, a chapel and even a museum. The wheels in the central arch were windmills that would provide power for the cotton manufactory and for the cranes for the stone and coal warehouses and the granary. William Bridges appears no more aware than William Vick, the progenitor of the bridge, that such a stone bridge, or indeed any kind of bridge across the Avon Gorge, was far beyond the wit of man at this time.

William Vick was a wine merchant and one of the principal supporters of the Jacob's Wells theatre. When he died in 1754, he left £1,000 to the care of the Merchant Venturers with the intention that the money should grow by compound interest, until it reached £10,000, a sum 'he had heard would be sufficient' for building 'a stone bridge across the Avon from Clifton Down to Leigh Down'.

There was no economic justification for such a bridge in 1754, nor indeed until long after the bridge was built. It would only link the open downland of Clifton, where the houses were then on the farther eastern slopes, with the private estates of Leigh Woods and Abbots Leigh. William Vick's will actually acknowledged that his idea might prove 'unuseful or improper'. In such an event, he asked that £6,000 be spent on a hospital for foundlings and illegitimate children. His concept of the bridge was not a matter of whimsy, but more probably the product of a belief, inspired by the Avon Gorge itself, that the grandeur of nature could always be matched and even enhanced by the genius of man. It reflected a self-confidence, borne of the Age of Enlightenment, which we have largely lost.

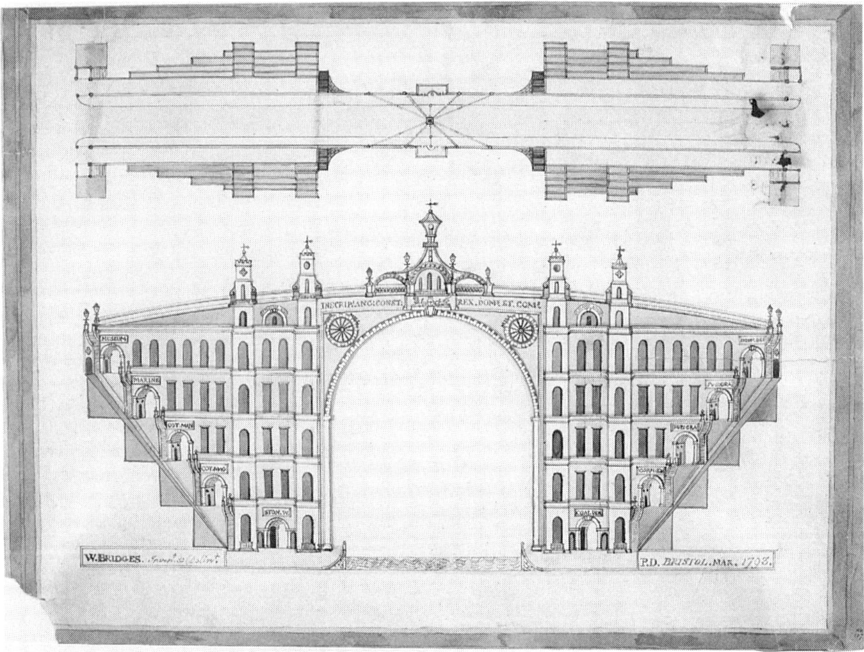

24 Samuel Hieronymous Grimm 1733-1794
'Clifton… from the Road near Bedminster' 12 August 1788
Pen, ink and grey wash 135 x 188 mm Bristol Museums and Art Gallery Ma3703

IT IS 1788 AND THE DEVELOPMENT, heralded in James Black-amore's drawing (21, 22), has yet to begin. The western slopes of Clifton are still bald and empty. The steep incline of the hill is very evident in Grimm's drawing. With hindsight, we see the bankruptcy of Windsor Terrace's developer as inevitable and it is hard to judge by what combination of vision, courage, fool-hardiness or greed William Watts was driven.

Samuel Hieronymous Grimm was born near Berne in Switzerland. He came to England in 1768 and exhibited at the Royal Academy's very first exhibition the following year. One of Grimm's most important patrons was the antiquarian collector, Dr Richard Kaye, Dean of Lincoln. Grimm travelled extensively with Dr Kaye and in July and August 1788 and in August and September 1789 they visited Bristol, staying, in 1789, in the lodging house of Mrs Rossignol in Sion Row (now Sion Hill), Clifton.

Grimm's scholarly curiosity was indefatigable. His Bristol subjects in the British Library's collection include diligent drawings of medieval churches, but also a giant anthill, an enormous tub of live turtles and a hurdy-gurdy player. Some studies, such as those of Hung Road (29-31), are unique records of their subject. No other visiting artist has made such an important contribution to the visual history of Bristol.

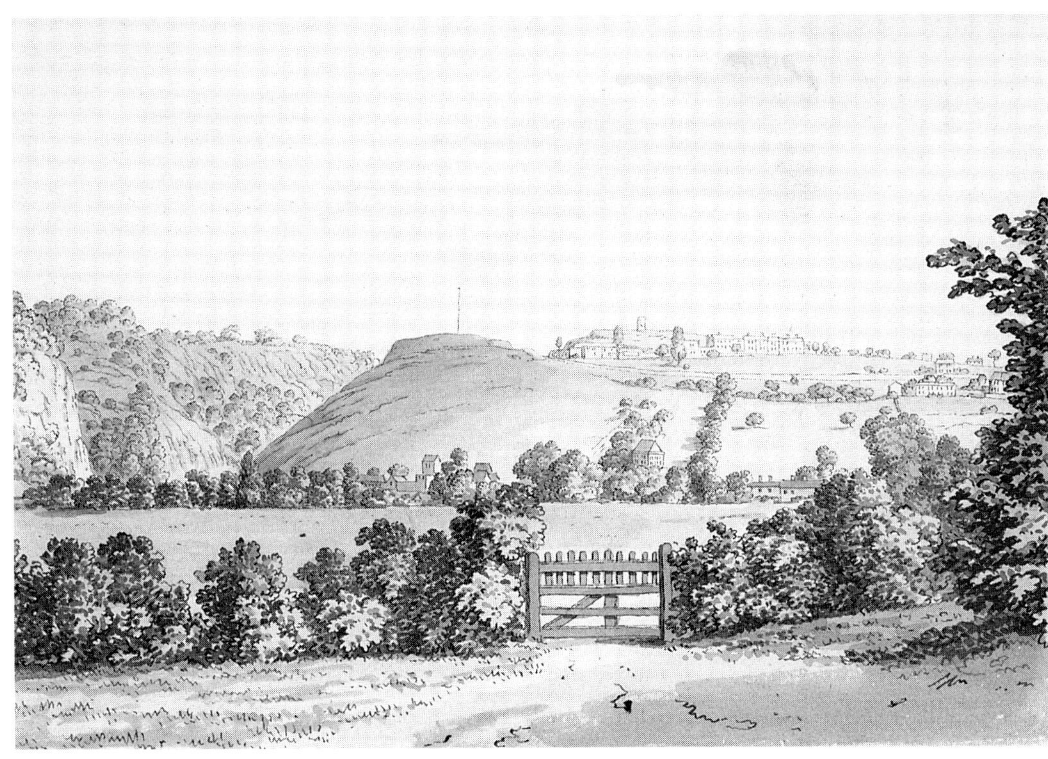

25 Samuel Hieronymous Grimm 1733–1794

'Projection of the S. part of St Vincents Rock…abounding in autumnal Hiacinths' 17 September 1789
Pen, ink and grey wash   135 x 190 mm   Bristol Museums and Art Gallery Ma3707

THE TITLE IS TAKEN FROM GRIMM'S CAREFUL INSCRIPTION at the top of the drawing. The words are testimony to the fame that the Avon Gorge and the Downs had enjoyed since as early as the sixteenth century as a site of special botanical interest.

The autumn hyacinth, *Scilla autumnalis*, is now better known as the autumn squill. It was long believed that the building of the Clifton Suspension Bridge, which springs from the projecting point on which the diminutive figures stand, had obliterated this rare plant. In 1888, however, some plants were rediscovered in the Avon Gorge and a tale of pioneering conservation emerged.

J.W. White in his *Flora of Bristol*, 1912, relates that, some eighty years earlier, Brunel had been warned by Mrs Glennie, wife of his principal engineer, of the destruction he was about to cause. Brunel then ordered his workmen to remove turf that contained bulbs to a safer and apparently almost inaccessible spot. In 1995 an unsustainable colony of only twelve plants remained. Bristol University Botanic Garden has since undertaken the propagation of seeds from these plants with the intention of giving the colony a helping hand. Today the Avon Gorge is classed as one of the top three botanical sites in England.

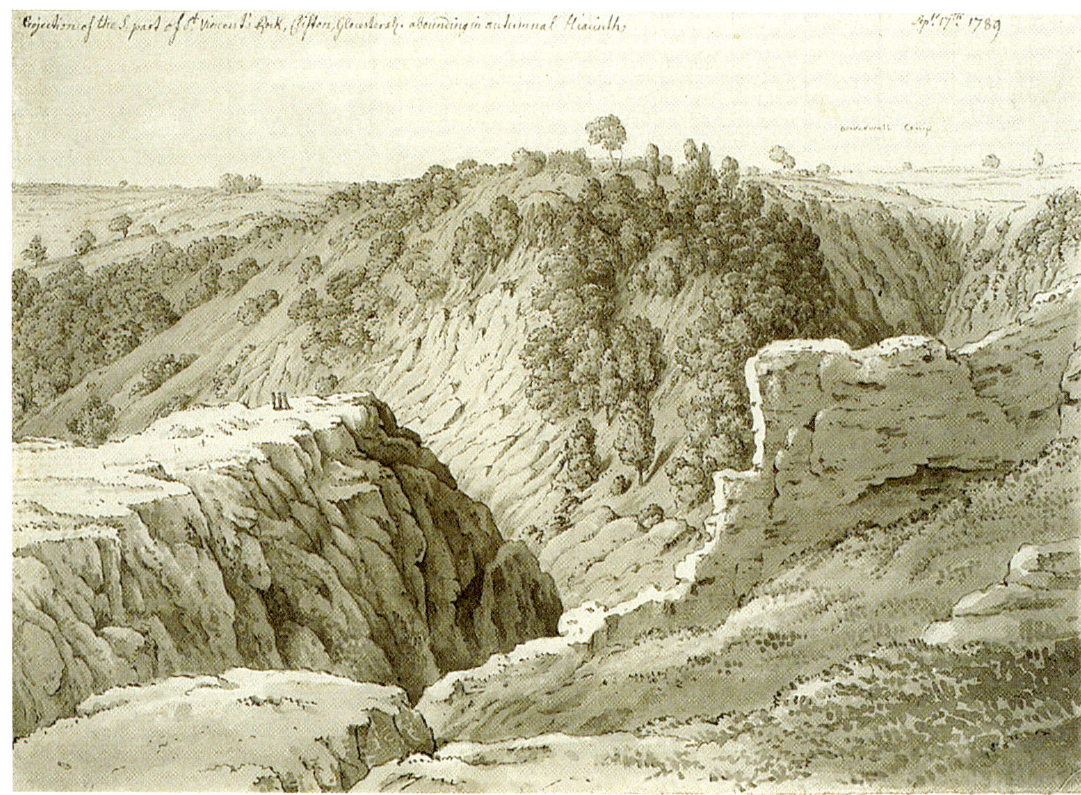

26 Samuel Hieronymous Grimm 1733-1794

'E. View of the Windmill & Camp at Clifton…from my window at Mrs Rossignols …Septr. 12th 1789'
Pen, ink and grey wash 135 x 190 mm Bristol Museums and Art Gallery Ma3701

THE ARTIST DRAWS THE VIEW FROM HIS ROOM IN SION HILL, where he was lodging, diligently recording the popularity of the Downs for riding. In 1793 *Shiercliff's Guide* advised that 'Some ladies also take great delight in riding upon Durdham Down… and the best lady attending the Hot-well, if she does not chuse to ride a single horse, will not refuse riding behind a man… and numbers of what they call double horses are constantly kept for that purpose. In this manner they often go on parties of pleasure to King's Weston…'

Sometimes there was also music to entertain both visitors and residents. In 1808 Rolinda Sharples' mother, Ellen, looked back on the summer and recalled:

Often we rambled amongst the rocks at Clifton, listening to the bands of musick placed at different distances on the summit of the high rocks: the almost perpendicular precipices below looking tremendous. The variety of rocks, woods, and the river Avon winding at their base, the company strolling in every direction on the hills, the diminutive people and objects below; all these seen in the twilight with the musick, had a sublime effect.

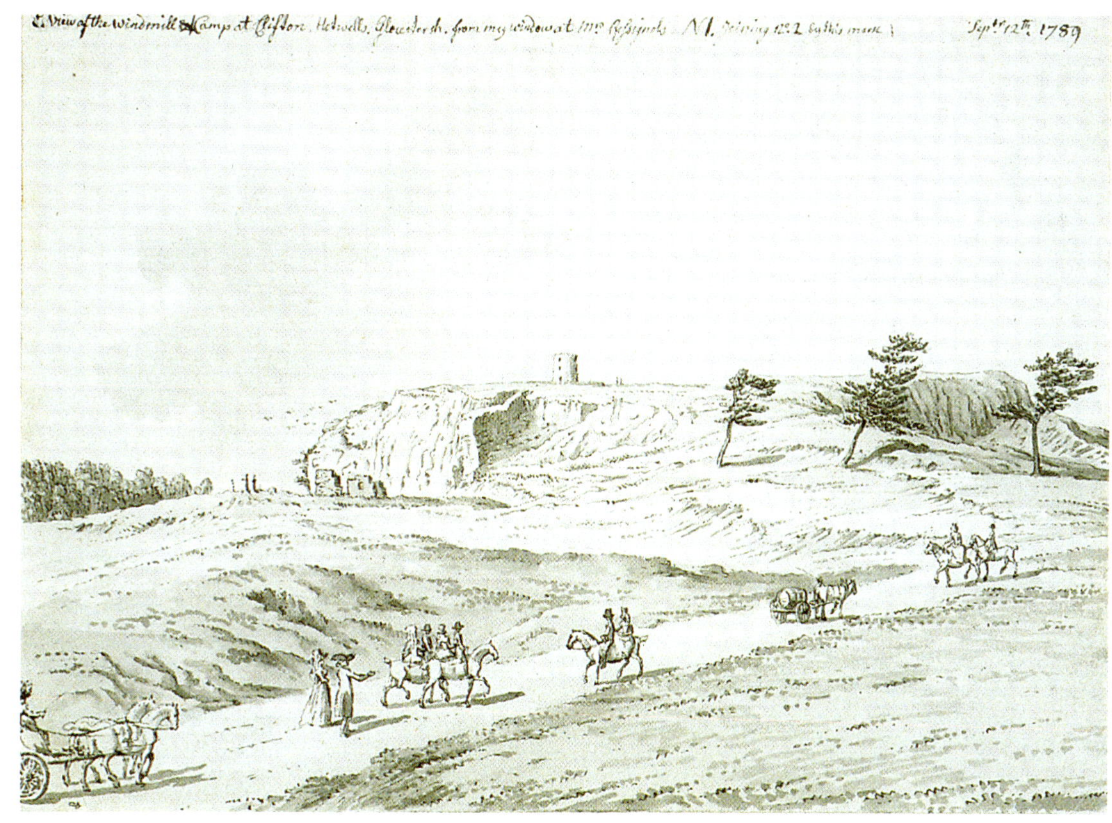

27 Samuel Hieronymous Grimm 1733-1794
'Chasm of St Vincents Rock, below the Windmill.../ Aug 13th 1789'
Pen, ink and grey wash 190 x 135 mm   Bristol Museums and Art Gallery   Ma3711

QUARRYMEN SEND ROCKS HURTLING DOWN THE CLIFF towards the old limekiln at the base, while visitors to the Hotwell perambulate nearby, apparently oblivious of the danger they are in. One contemporary guidebook implied that the quarrying was yet another exciting spectacle and suggested that the explosions and 'the sound of crashing rocks running with thundering peel through the vale...re-echoing on every side of the surrounding cliffs... make it most awfully sublime and grand.'

Towards the end of the eighteenth century the Avon Gorge became famous as a site of great geological interest. Bristol Diamonds, however, had already been celebrated since the sixteenth century, when William Camden mentioned 'S. Vincents rock so full of Diaments'. Camden also noted that they were too plenteous to be valued. The broken geodes or nodules in which the clear quartz crystals appeared were much used by Thomas Goldney in his grotto at Goldney House, Clifton, in the 1740s. They were also one of the most popular souvenirs of a visit to the Hotwell.

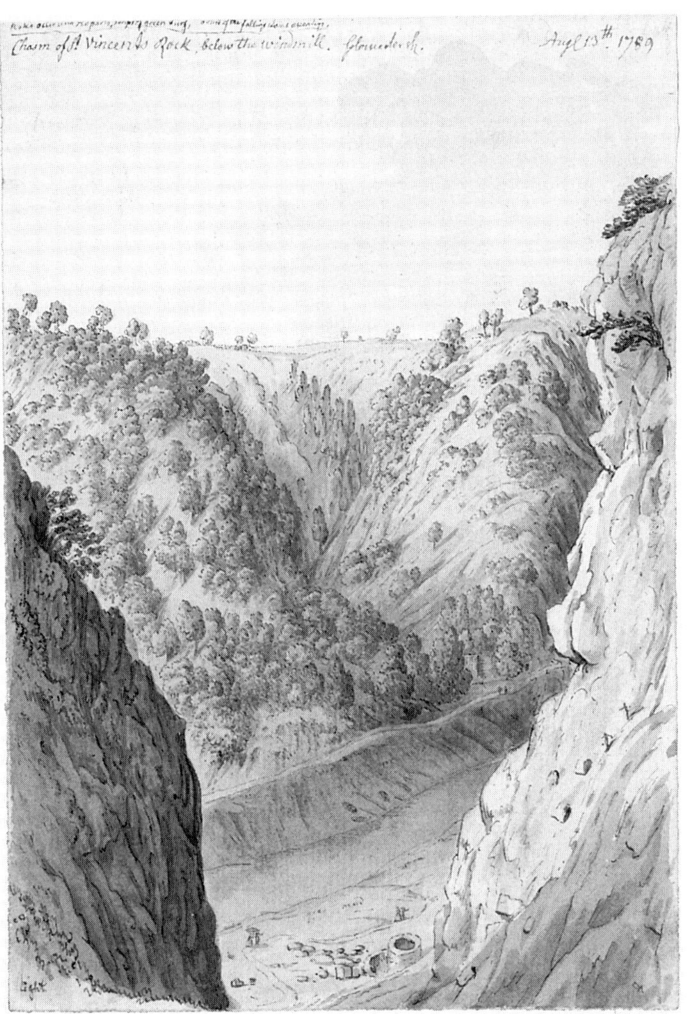

28 Samuel Hieronymous Grimm 1733-1794
The New Hotwell from Sea Walls   July 1788
Pen, ink and grey wash   British Library   Add MS 15540/190

IT WAS A CERTAIN JOHN WALLIS who generously built this wall along the edge of the cliff in 1746 for the safety of the visitors to the Hotwell. The Bristol historian, John Latimer, suggested that Sea Walls, the name for the cliff face and this traditional viewpoint, might derive from 'Wallis's wall'.

Grimm's drawing shows what a well-crafted wall it was. It has long since been rebuilt, but the same footing was followed and many of the original mid-eighteenth-century conical capping-stones, made of blocks of iridescent slag from Bristol's brass and copper industry, were reused. In the distance to the right the turnpike house can be seen below the ruined windmill.

Within the Avon Gorge is the New Hotwell. This second hot spring had been discovered in 1702. It was first leased by the Society of Merchant Venturers in 1731. By the 1750s it was being managed by the Bristol preacher, John Dolman. His decidedly uninspiring *Contemplations amongst Vincent's Rocks* of 1755 tell us that John Wesley, the founder of Methodism, had been a patron for three weeks in the previous year. Wesley himself recorded only that he was delighted that the New Hotwell was 'free from noise and hurry'. Despite such patronage, access continued to be too difficult to allow any sustained success, and, although it continued to be used intermittently until the 1780s, by 1792 the building had become just 'a hovel for the miners'.

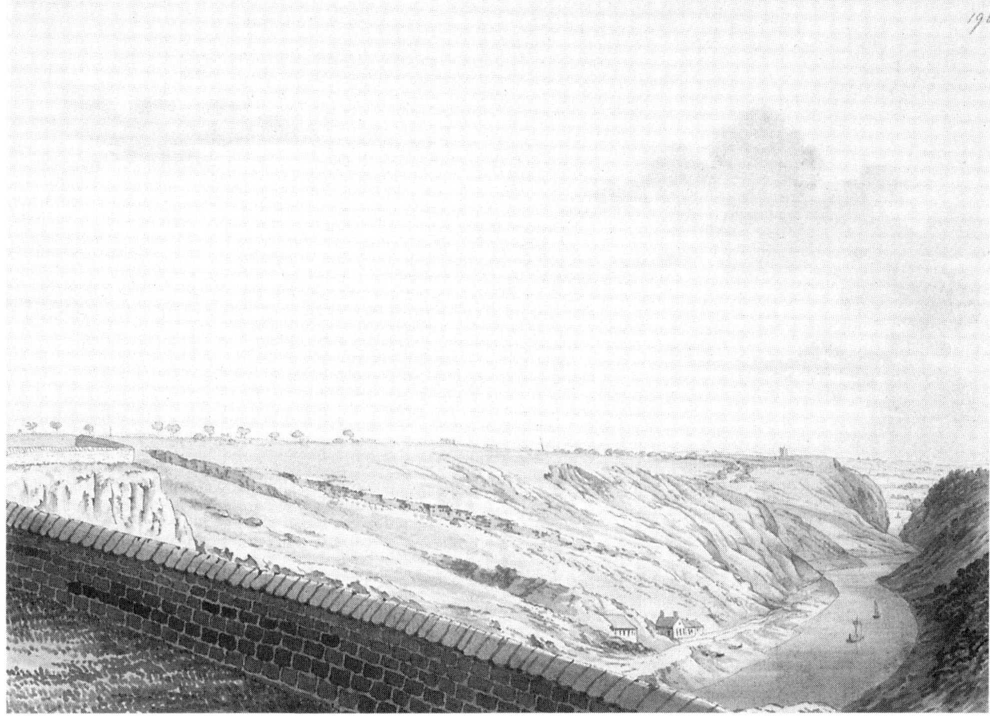

29 Samuel Hieronymous Grimm 1733-1794
Lamplighters Hall and Hung Road August 1788
Pen, ink and grey wash 135 x 195 mm Bristol Museums and Art Gallery Ma3723

GRIMM'S INSCRIPTION ON THIS DRAWING deserves to be quoted in full. 'The passage Inn, vulgarly called Lamplighters Hall, on the Avon near the Hotwells, Glocestersh. with the Hungroad where the Norway Ships unload & send their Cargoe to Bristol by wherries. Augt. 13th 1788.'

The view looks upstream from the Gloucestershire bank past Lamplighters Hall towards Hung Road, that vital if distant portion of Bristol's harbour, five miles downstream from the city. At Hung Road there is a small cliff, against which vessels could lie, tying their masts to chains set into the cliff face and, thereby, remaining upright at low tide.

Hung Road was already much used in the sixteenth century. In 1578 the *Golden Lion*, a ship of at least 500 tons, broke loose from her mooring and was driven onto the rocks. As the tide ebbed she fell over bringing another vessel of about 400 tons with her. It was many weeks before the river was navigable again and two years before the wreck was finally removed.

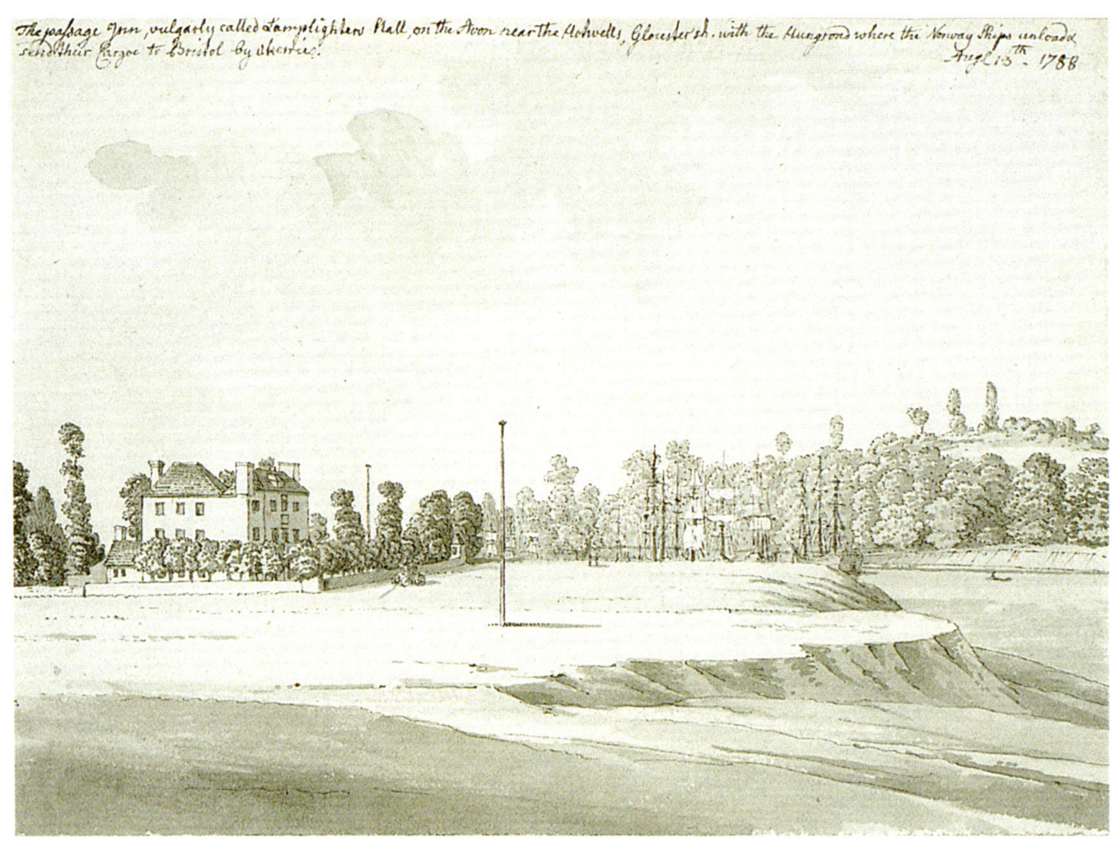

30 Samuel Hieronymous Grimm 1733-1794
'Manner of unloading a Norway Man in Hungroad. / Augt 1789'
Pen, ink and grey wash   British Library Add MS 15546/170

IN 1792 THREE VESSELS LEFT HUNG ROAD FOR NORWAY, probably intending to return with timber and pitch. Two of the vessels were towed manually by Pill hobblers. The third was hauled by the horses of a Shirehampton farmer. When the horses came to overtake the hobblers, the men from Pill refused to slacken their ropes to let the horses past. A vicious fight ensued, which in due course was reported to the Merchant Venturers, who managed both Hung Road and the towpaths.

In his eagerness to record the method of unloading Norwegian timber at Hung Road, Grimm has omitted the chains set into the cliff face, a few of which still survive.
The completion of the Floating Harbour in 1809 was to lead to a hasty decline in the use of Hung Road and by 1813 the Merchant Venturers were informed that receipts for the use of the chains were falling below the costs of maintenance.

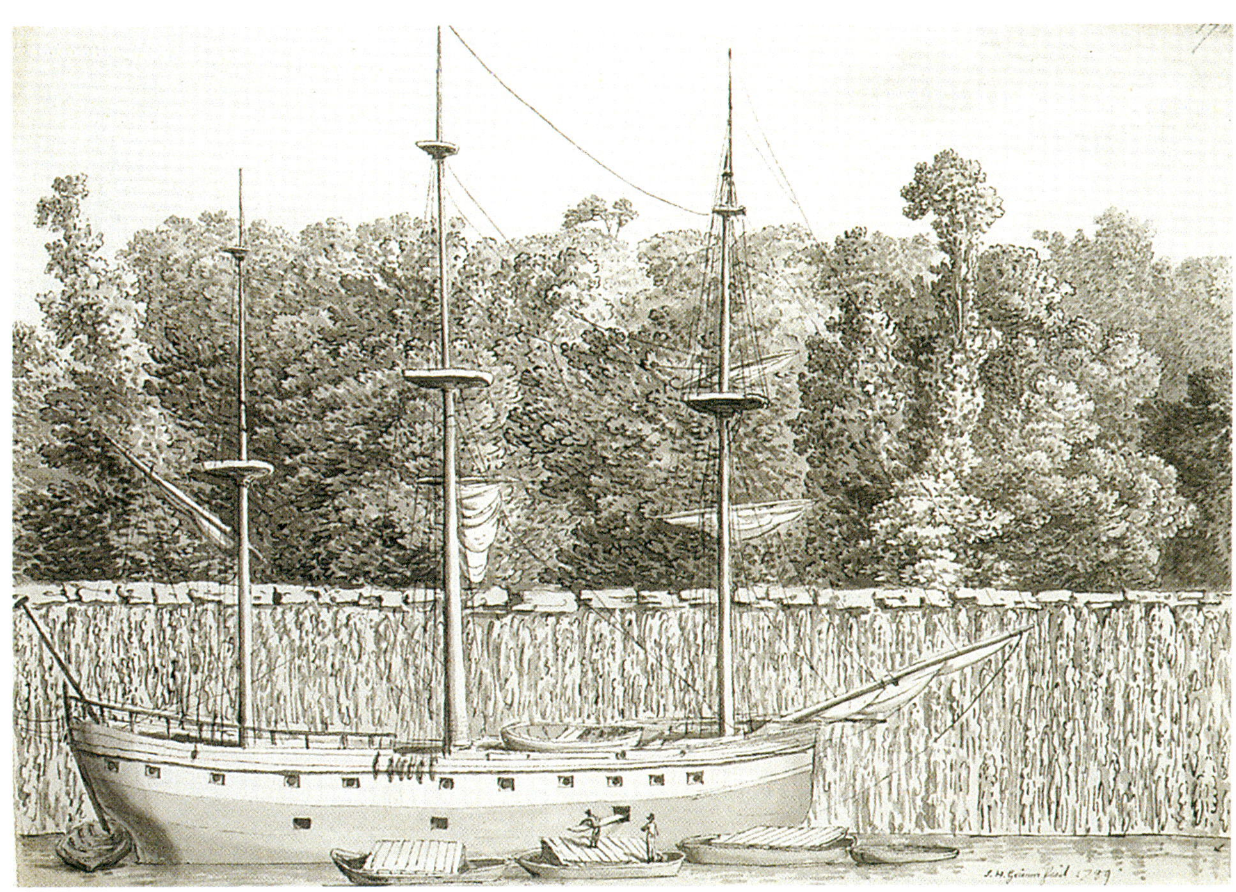

31 Samuel Hieronymous Grimm 1733-1794
  'Mr Bright's pleasure ground at Hungroad, taken from the opposite Bank. Augt 1789'
  Pen, ink and grey wash   British Library Add MS 15546/171

THE CHARMING GOTHICK GAZEBO ON THE HILL survives today, but only just, for although it was restored by Avon Gardens Trust in 1988, it is again on the point of collapse. It is in the grounds of Ham Green House, a largely Georgian mansion owned by the merchant and banker, Richard Bright. One of his sons was Dr Richard Bright (1789-1858), after whom Bright's disease of the kidneys is named.

Ham Green House became an isolation hospital in 1899, at first especially for typhoid patients who were taken there by river. Amongst many specialist sections added over the years was a smallpox hospital built in 1938 but happily never used for that purpose. In 2002 the house and gardens, including the gazebo, were acquired by Bristol Cancer Care Centre, which is at present still in Clifton.

The field immediately to the left, or upstream, of this view was the site of a remarkable medieval industry. It was here between about 1100 and 1250 that Ham Green pottery was produced and exported over much of Europe and as far north as Reykjavik.

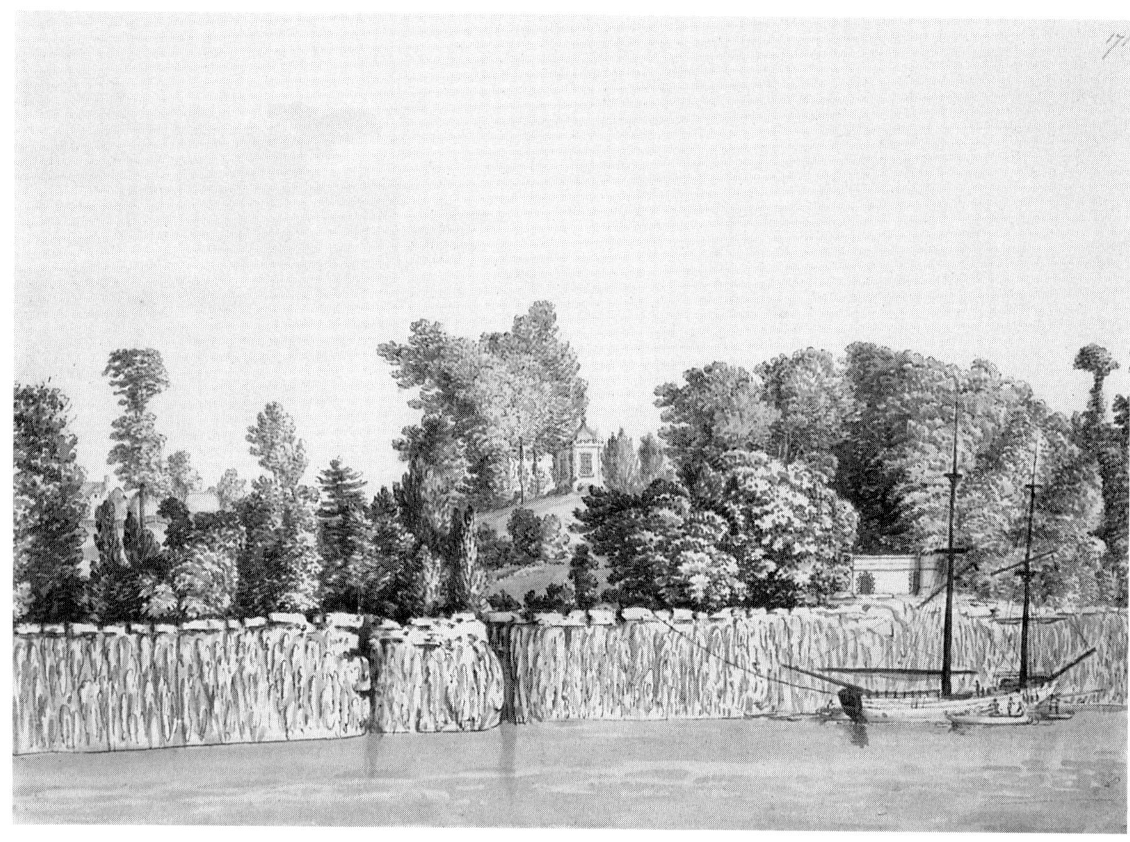

32 Samuel Hieronymous Grimm 1733-1794
Penpole Point July 1788
Pen, ink and grey wash 190 x 265 mm Bristol Museums and Art Gallery Ma3710

GRIMM IDENTIFIES PENPOLE POINT as 'Weston Point' and his inscription draws attention to the two larger ships as 'West-indiamen coming up' the river. They are being towed and are likely to be headed only for Hung Road less than two miles upriver. It is already near high tide for Dumball Island at the mouth of the river has been covered and even the Pill hobblers would not have been able to make headway once the tide had turned against them.

Just five years after Grimm's drawing, the artist-authors of a guidebook, Ibbetson, Laporte and Hassell, mention that on 'the extreme northern point of this knoll is a dial pedestal, which attracted us to the best view we had yet found'. That very tall stone pedestal would have been just behind the artist. Indeed, he may have sat on the iron seat that still surrounds it to make this drawing. The seat was certainly there by about 1820, the approximate date of Francis Danby's drawing (33). The pedestal is probably much older and can be tentatively identified in Kip's engraving of King's Weston, published in 1712. It may be 'the compasse upon Penpole Hill' to the repair of which the Merchant Venturers contributed £5 in 1668.

Today the monument remains, but 'the best view' is needlessly obscured by trees. It is twenty-five years since the *Bristol Evening Post* reported that the Council's press officer had said that the 'undergrowth would soon be cut but he could not give a definite date.' The view could be just as spectacular today, as it ever was. Tower blocks would obtrude but the two great suspension bridges across the Severn and the fine concrete bridge across the Avon, each an outstanding feat of engineering, would now enhance it.

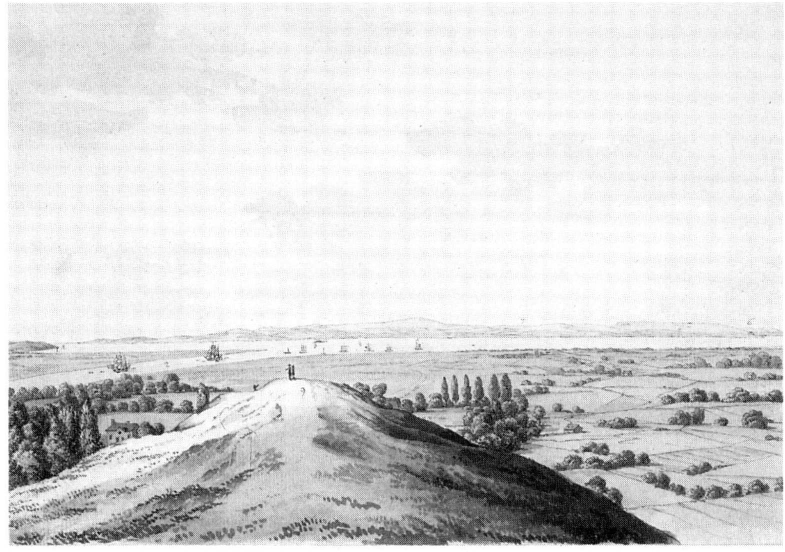

33 Francis Danby 1793-1861
Penpole Point (detail) c.1820
Pencil and watercolour 205 x 320 mm
Private collection

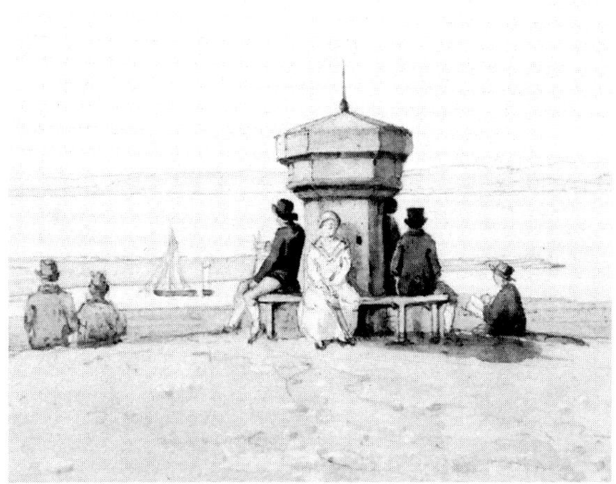

34 Joseph Mallord William Turner   1775-1851
The Avon Gorge and Cook's Folly from Durdham Down   1791
Watercolour   190 x 260 mm   Cheltenham Art Gallery

J.M.W. TURNER was both the youngest and one of the earliest of a succession of major artists to visit Bristol in the 1790s and early 1800s. He came at the age of sixteen in 1791 on his September holiday from the Royal Academy Schools and stayed with the family of a friend of his father's, John Narraway, a leather dresser in Broadmead.

A sketchbook at the Tate Gallery survives from this holiday in which there are drawings and watercolour sketches from nine separate viewpoints in the Avon Gorge – some high, some low and some distinctly perilous. It is no surprise that the Narraways dubbed him 'Prince of the Rocks'. This watercolour could be on a sheet that was once in the Tate Gallery's sketchbook. He was both indefatigable and already very ambitious. A note in the sketchbook suggests that he may even have been considering a series of engraved views of the Avon in the manner of Pocock.

Turner has clambered a short distance down the Avon Gorge to find a composition with trees and foliage that could frame this dramatic view. The circular format and vertiginous viewpoint foreshadow his most mature work and it is almost a relief to note that the young student betrays some uncertainty over the scale of the vessel sailing upriver.

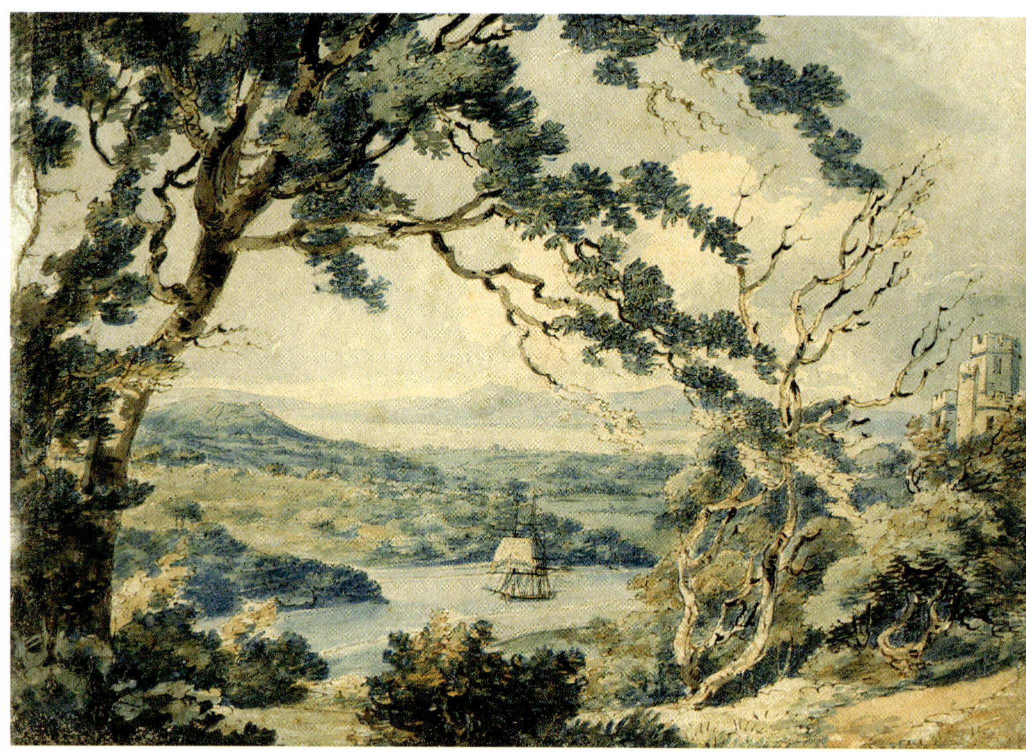

35 Joseph Mallord William Turner 1775-1851
The Avon Gorge and Bristol Hotwell c.1792
Watercolour 360 x 410 mm Bristol Museums and Art Gallery K816

THIS LARGER AND HIGHLY FINISHED WATERCOLOUR, perhaps intended for exhibition, was worked up from drawings made during Turner's visit to Bristol in 1791. Turner subtly encircles the view with stylised foliage, the crisp lines of mast and rigging and a sequence of rhythmic curves that echo the billowing sails. Already, as Andrew Wilton has written, Turner was revealing 'his inclination to construct his scenes as works of art rather than as reproductions of nature.'

Even at high tide, no vessel would have been under full sail as it approached the narrowest point and sharpest corner on the Avon. Turner manipulates the landscape to dramatic effect, but he accurately records the newly built colonnade that brought shops, shelter and a touch of architectural elegance to the Hotwell.

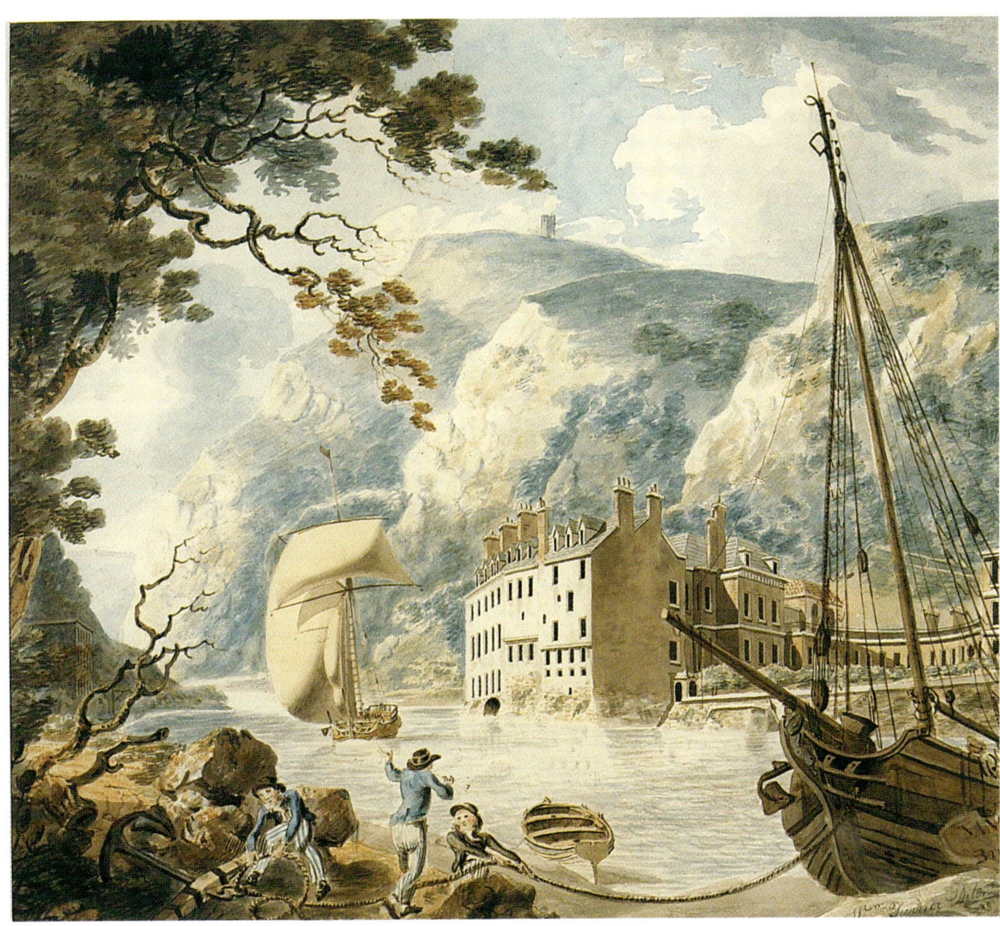

36 John William Upham c.1772–c.1828
St Vincent's Rocks and the Hotwell House   1802
Watercolour   370 x 430 mm   Bristol Museums and Art Gallery K4145

QUARRYING WAS AN ALMOST CEASELESS ACTIVITY in the Avon Gorge throughout the eighteenth century and far into the following century when it was much recorded by early photographers. Travellers were at first encouraged to regard this industry as an exciting drama that enhanced the spectacular scenery of the Avon Gorge and added to its sublime character. Awe and even terror were possible ingredients of the sublime, whether from the overhanging cliffs above you, the vertiginous views below you or from the thunderous explosions of the quarrymen. The sublime was perceived as an extreme form of the beautiful.

J. W. Upham was a West Country artist, specialising in watercolours of Devon and Dorset scenes. He exhibited at the Royal Academy from 1801 to 1811 and was sometime a resident of the fashionable resort of Weymouth, where he died.

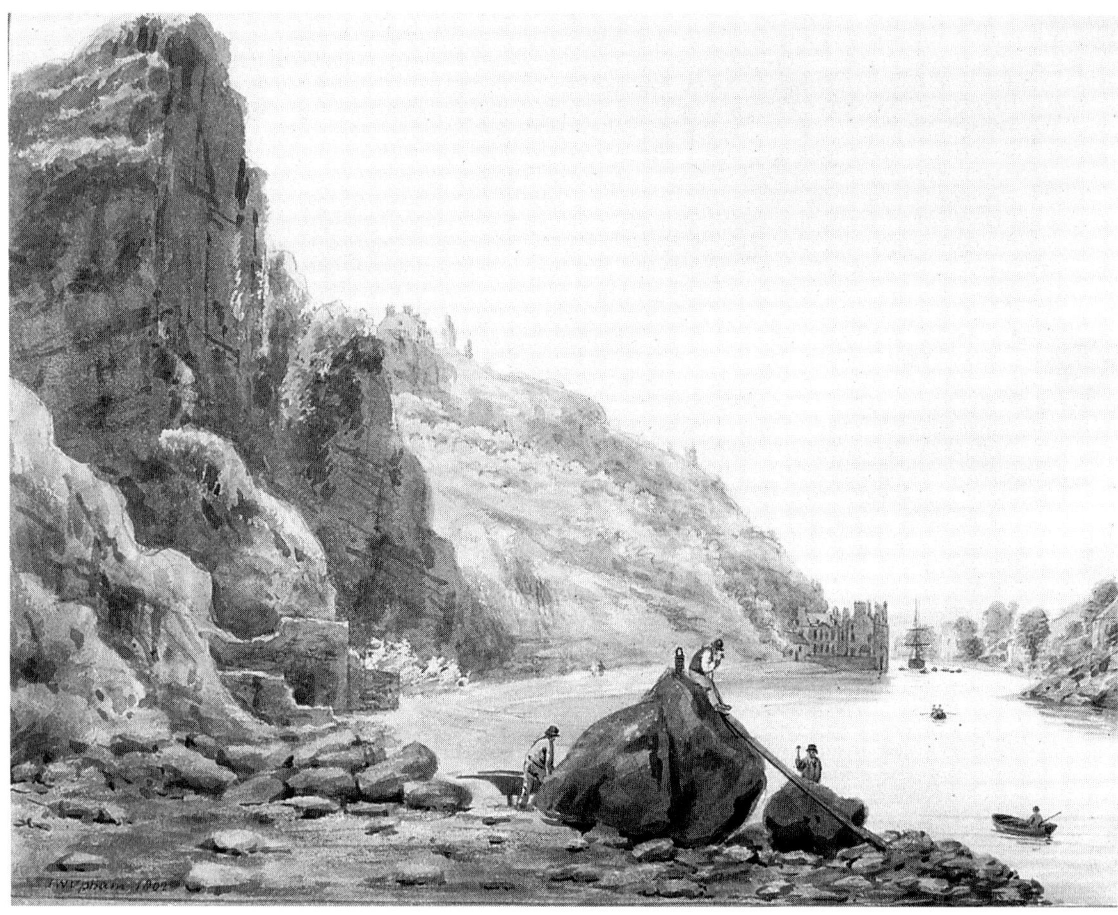

37 William Alfred Delamotte 1775-1863
'blocks of stone blown from the Rocks at Clifton Bristol 1801'
Pencil and grey wash   255 x 362 mm   Bristol Museums and Art Gallery K5120

Towards the end of the eighteenth century the conflicting consequences of quarrying began to be understood. Shiercliff in *The Bristol and Hotwell Guide* in 1793, at first follows his predecessors and acknowledges the sublimity of the explosions and crashing rocks. However, he then goes on to admit that 'if this destructive practice be continued…those sublime wonders of nature the admiration of past ages, whose fame has excited thousands of strangers to visit the Hotwell and Clifton, and been a means of the inhabitants acquiring great wealth, will be wholly demolished.' Robert Southey, the Bristol-born poet and later Poet Laureate, put it more succinctly in 1807: 'The people of Bristol sell everything that can be sold…and here they are selling the sublime and beautiful by the boat load.'

Born at Weymouth, where George III complimented his youthful work, Delamotte moved to London to study under Benjamin West at the Royal Academy. In 1803 he was appointed Drawing Master at the Royal Military College, where he was to teach for 40 years.

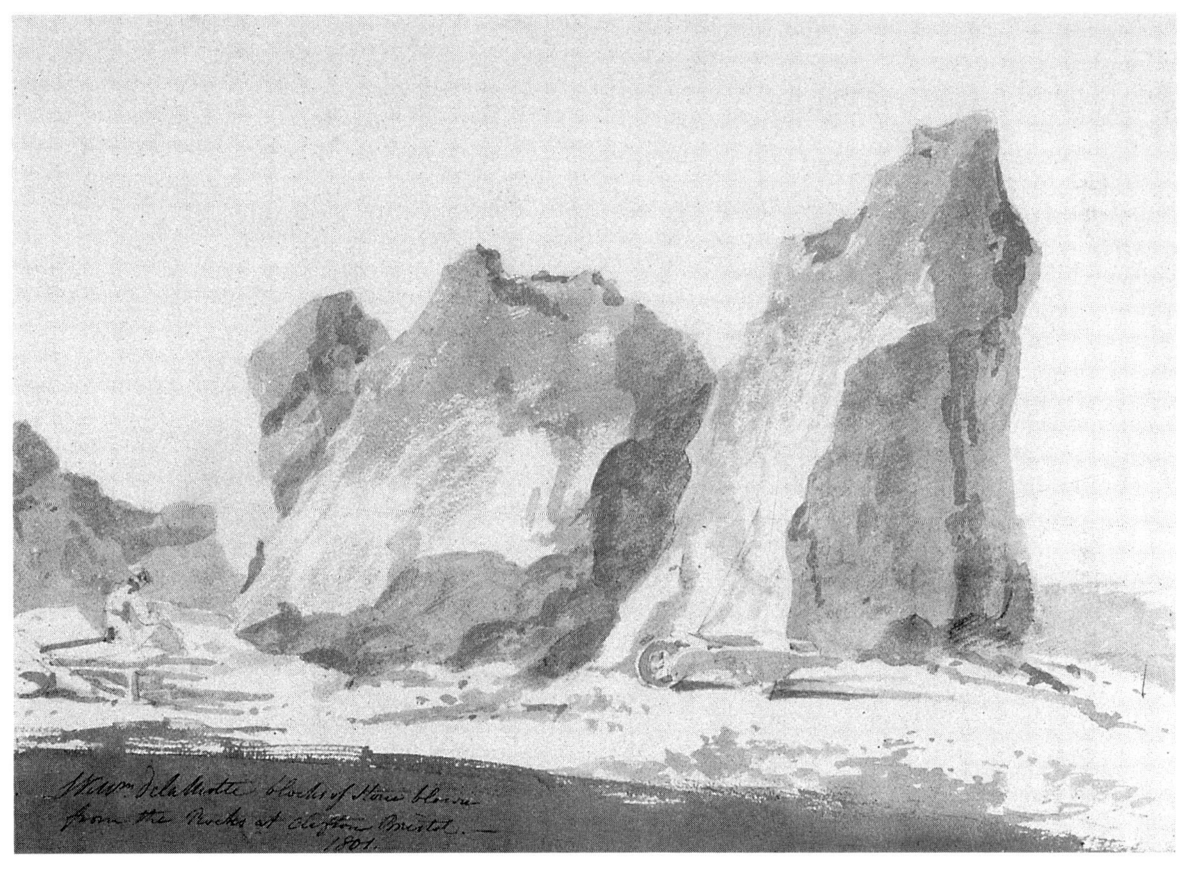

38 Thomas Girtin 1775-1802
St Vincent's Rocks from Nightingale Valley c.1797
Pencil and watercolour 395 x 520 mm Martyn Gregory, London

NIGHTINGALE VALLEY IS ON THE SOUTH OR SOMERSET SIDE of the Avon, immediately opposite St Vincent's Rocks. It is a steep river-less valley running at right angles to the river and up into Leigh Woods.

Within a little more than a decade of Girtin's visit in 1797, the valley was to be the favourite sketching ground of Bristol's resident artists. They were to discover that the views back across the Avon Gorge presented problems of composition. St Vincent's Rocks all too abruptly closes off the view. In this watercolour Girtin resolved this difficulty by manipulating the scenery. He walked only a short distance up the valley for his viewpoint, but he pushed St Vincent's Rocks into the distance and, most significantly, he invented a winding stream, which he substituted for the steep pathway.

Nightingale Valley gains a quiet enclosed pool, a place of calm, contemplative retreat overlooked by the grandeur of the cliffs and by the ruined windmill. The mill takes on the dignity of an ancient castle ruin. It is tempting to look ahead to J. M. W. Turner's early masterpiece of Romanticism, *Dolbadern Castle, North Wales* (Royal Academy, London) of 1800. It may be that Turner's oft-quoted response to Girtin's tragically early death is apocryphal: 'If Tom Girtin had lived, I should have starved.' There is no doubt, however, that Turner was much inspired by Girtin's imaginative response to landscape.

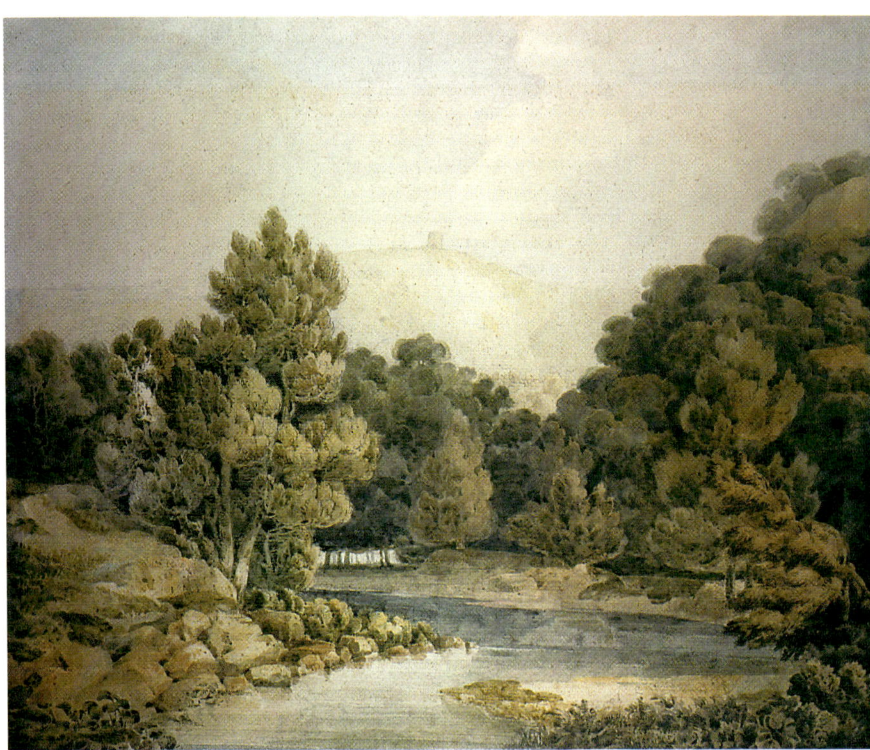

39 John Sell Cotman 1782-1842
St Mary Redcliffe, Bristol; Dawn c.1802
Watercolour 380 x 535 mm © The Trustees of the British Museum 1859-528-117

JOHN SELL COTMAN WAS JUST EIGHTEEN when he stayed in Bristol with the Nortons, booksellers, on College Green, before travelling on to Wales. He had just exhibited at the Royal Academy for the first time and been awarded the great silver palette of the Society of Arts.

His view of St Mary Redcliffe at dawn is a monumental, even sublime, image of early industrial England. It is low tide and the muddy banks are as forbidding as slag heaps. Almost a decade was to pass before the Floating Harbour was completed. The glass kiln to the left and the shot tower to the right of the church are silhouetted against the early morning sky and St Mary Redcliffe's noble tower and truncated spire are enveloped in a grimy haze. It is a scene that reflects Cotman's brooding personality and it is a masterpiece of Romantic painting.

Bristol's local collieries at Ashton, Bedminster, Brislington and Kingswood supplied the city's hearths and industries. The illustrated guidebook, *A Picturesque Guide to Bath, Bristol Hot-Wells, the River Avon…* published in 1793 and written by three artists, Ibbetson, Laporte and Hassell, observed that in Bristol 'The smoke issuing from the brassworks, glasshouses etc. keeps the town in almost impenetrable obscurity.' Industrial pollution can only have increased, but Albert Goodwin at the end of the nineteenth century was almost alone in taking advantage of its pictorial possibilities (109, 110).

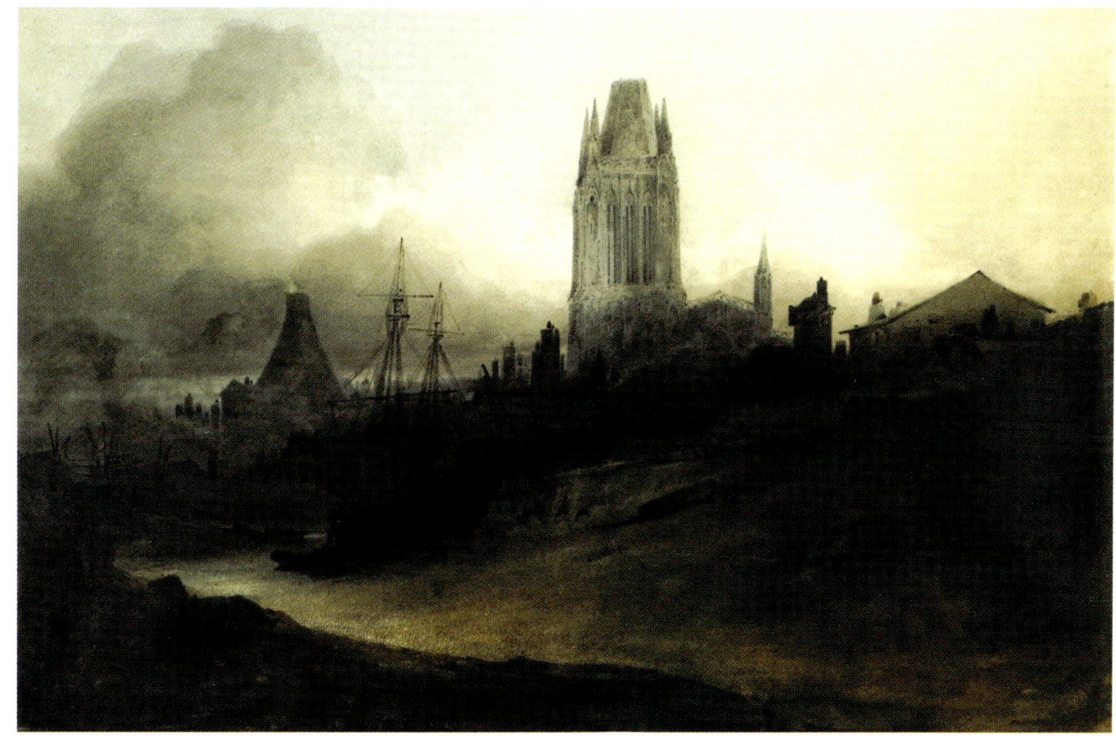

40 John White Abbott 1763-1851
'Part of Bristol & Clifton taken near Rownham Passage.'   September 1795
Pen, ink and watercolour   260 x 370 mm   Bristol Museums and Art Gallery K1378

IN THE MIDDLE DISTANCE ARE HOUSES adjoining the lower part of Granby Hill, with the line of the roofs of Albemarle Row beyond. Thomas Goldney's rotunda on the skyline still has its colonnade, which was soon to be removed.

John White Abbott, a pupil of Francis Towne, was one of the finest of many outstanding amateur artists working at the turn of the century. He showed regularly at the Royal Academy as an honorary exhibitor. He was an apothecary and surgeon in Exeter and, in later life, a country gentleman.

His watercolours are essentially tinted drawings. Even washes of a limited range of colours are laid within sharp ink outlines. There is very careful control of tone so that depth is suggested by a succession of planes. Although his Bristol scenes are strikingly accurate topographical records, they also have a certain detachment. He looks at the busy world of Clifton and Bristol from a distance and from amongst trees, reminiscent of his beloved Devon woods that he drew so often.

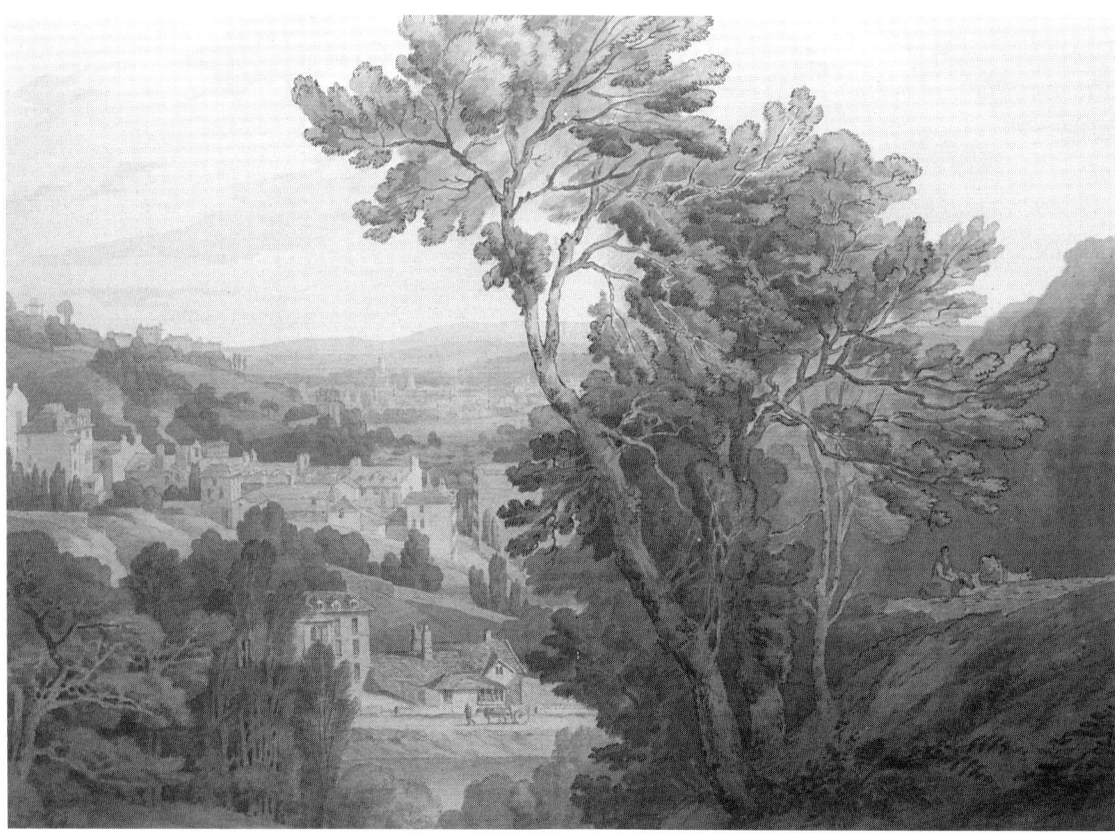

41 John White Abbott 1763-1851
Clifton from Leigh Woods c.1795
Pen, ink and watercolour 260 x 180 mm Courtesy of Agnew's, London

THE VIEW LOOKS ACROSS THE AVON GORGE, probably from the edge of Stokeleigh Camp above the dark recesses of Nightingale Valley. The Clifton houses on the top of the steep slope are Prince's Buildings. This terrace was planned as seven pairs of three-storey houses linked by single-storey annexes. Essentially it was an early sequence of semi-detached houses, a fact that has since been disguised by the raising of most of the annexes to the full height of the houses. Begun in 1789, the terrace was evidently still incomplete at the time of this watercolour.

Above and at right angles to Prince's Buildings is the abrupt end of Royal York Crescent. The first two houses are apparently complete, but the next is roofless. The builders had been ruined in 1793 and, with no purchaser found by 1801, the government had acquired the site for army barracks. Not for the last time, Clifton's residents rose in protest and in May 1809 the government announced the sale of fifteen unfinished houses and at this, the west end, of ten finished houses. The last gap in the crescent was not to be filled until 1818.

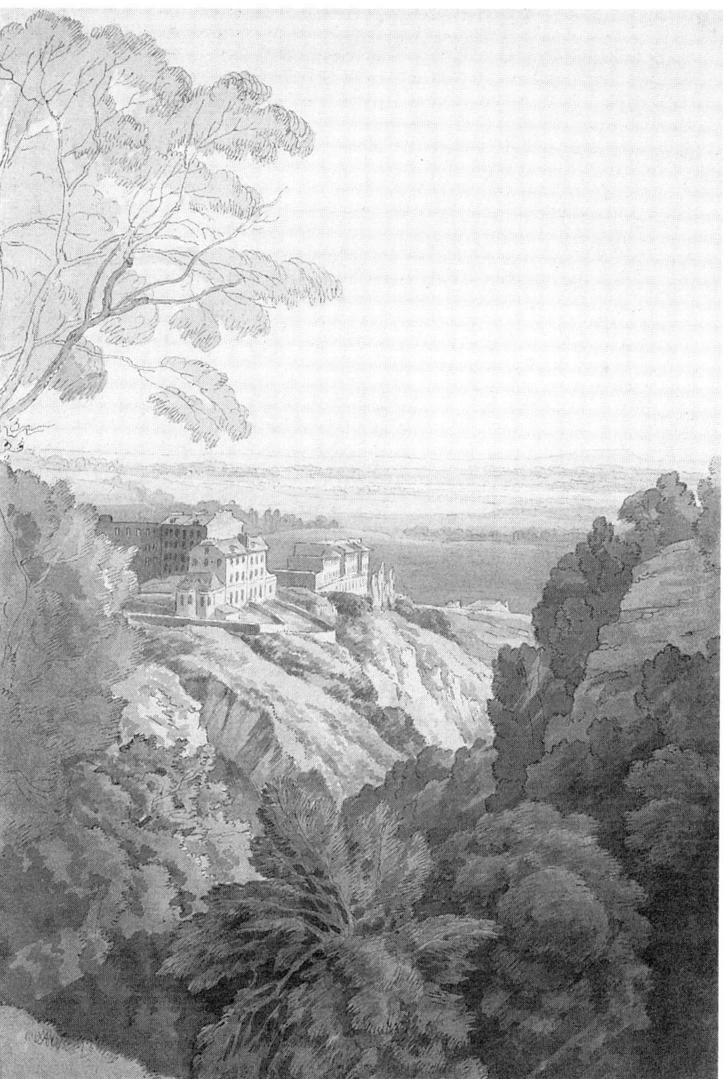

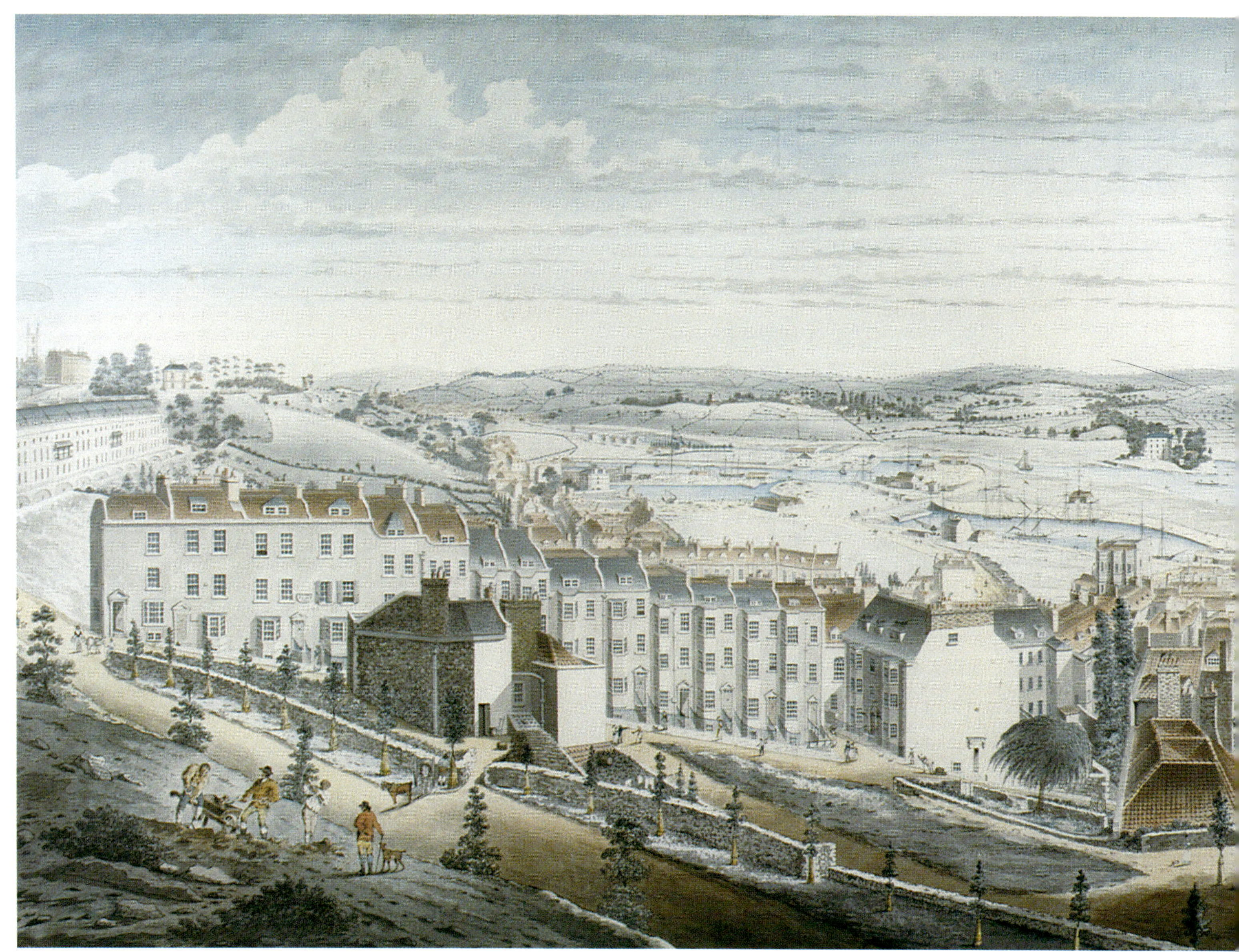

42 Lt Col William Booth 1748-1826
Granby Hill, Clifton 1822
Pen, ink and watercolour 760 x 1315 mm Bristol Museums and Art Gallery K101

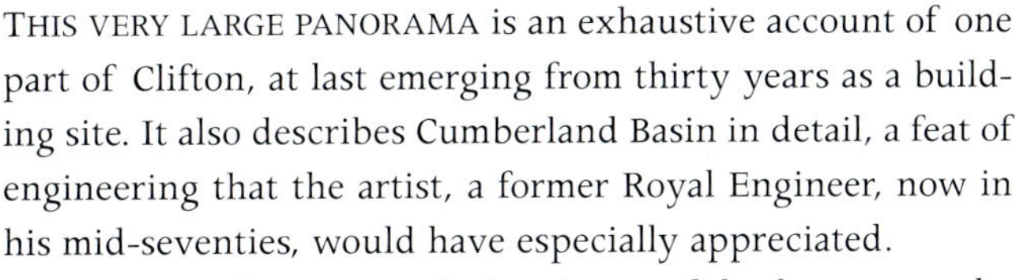

THIS VERY LARGE PANORAMA is an exhaustive account of one part of Clifton, at last emerging from thirty years as a building site. It also describes Cumberland Basin in detail, a feat of engineering that the artist, a former Royal Engineer, now in his mid-seventies, would have especially appreciated.

To get a clear view of the river and harbour over the roofs, Booth has gone to the rear terrace of the Paragon. The road in the foreground, where an avenue of trees has just been planted, leads to Windsor Terrace. Before us is Granby Hill and a plaque on the third house down, No 54, reads 'Granby Place/1791'. The lower part of this terrace has bay windows on four floors and most of it was to be demolished in the 1960s. Beyond is Dowry Parade, built as lodging houses for visitors to the Hotwell in the 1760s.

Above the upper end of Granby Hill is the east end of Cornwallis Crescent. This had been begun in 1791. As elsewhere, several of the various builders went bankrupt two years later. The same happened again in 1809, when the architect, Francis Greenway, also failed. He was sentenced to death in 1812 after forging a promissory note concerning 34 Cornwallis Crescent. Transported instead, he later became the father of Australian architecture. The crescent was not fully completed until 1835.

On the hill above Cornwallis Crescent is the new tower of St Andrew's Church, completed in 1822, the year of Booth's drawing. Before it are Prospect House and Beresford House and to the right is Goldney House with the rotunda from which the colonnade has now been removed.

William Booth had been a professional soldier in the Royal Engineers. His few surviving works are fascinating examples of the serious training in landscape drawing which was once given to both army and navy personnel. His watercolours are impressively matter-of-fact. No foreground foliage frames the prospect, conveniently obscuring complex details. They are panoramic, wide-angled views. One could safely lead an army across his landscapes or target one's artillery with precision.

Booth is said to have retired from active service in 1800. Three years later he was an honorary exhibitor at the Royal Academy. There is a sketchbook of views of Bristol and Swansea in Bristol Museum and Art Gallery dated 1783, but his actual association with Bristol, where he died in 1826, is as yet unclear and his name does not appear in the Bristol directories.

Clifton from Rownham Mead   c.1790
Watercolour   300 x 425 mm   Bristol Museums and Art Gallery M4178

WE HAVE RETURNED TO THE EIGHTEENTH CENTURY to include the picture that best illustrates the meadows from which Cumberland Basin was to be dug.

The houses of Bristol's merchants in Clifton and Clifton Wood look down on the lodging houses in Paradise Row and Dowry Parade. These two terraces flank the nearest building, the New or Lower Long Room. This was the Hotwells' second assembly room and a symbol of the spa's success. Here, from 1785, a Master of Ceremonies presided over weekly public breakfasts, cotillions and balls. The Lower Long Room was to become a school following the 1870 Education Act and was finally demolished in 1963 to make way for the Cumberland Basin flyover, named Plimsoll Bridge.

Trade and industry barely invade the scene. Only the ships' masts on the right mark the site of Merchants' Dock. Haymaking is in progress. There is no hint of the ambitious schemes for the Clifton terraces, so many of which were initiated in 1789, nor of the demise of the spa itself, whose reputation was to sink so fast in the early 1800s. The meadow, however, was certainly now under threat. Proponents of different plans for the Floating Harbour had already recognised that this land was the key to a controlled entrance to the new harbour. But of this, the amateur artist of this watercolour, perhaps a visitor to the Hotwell, was probably unaware.

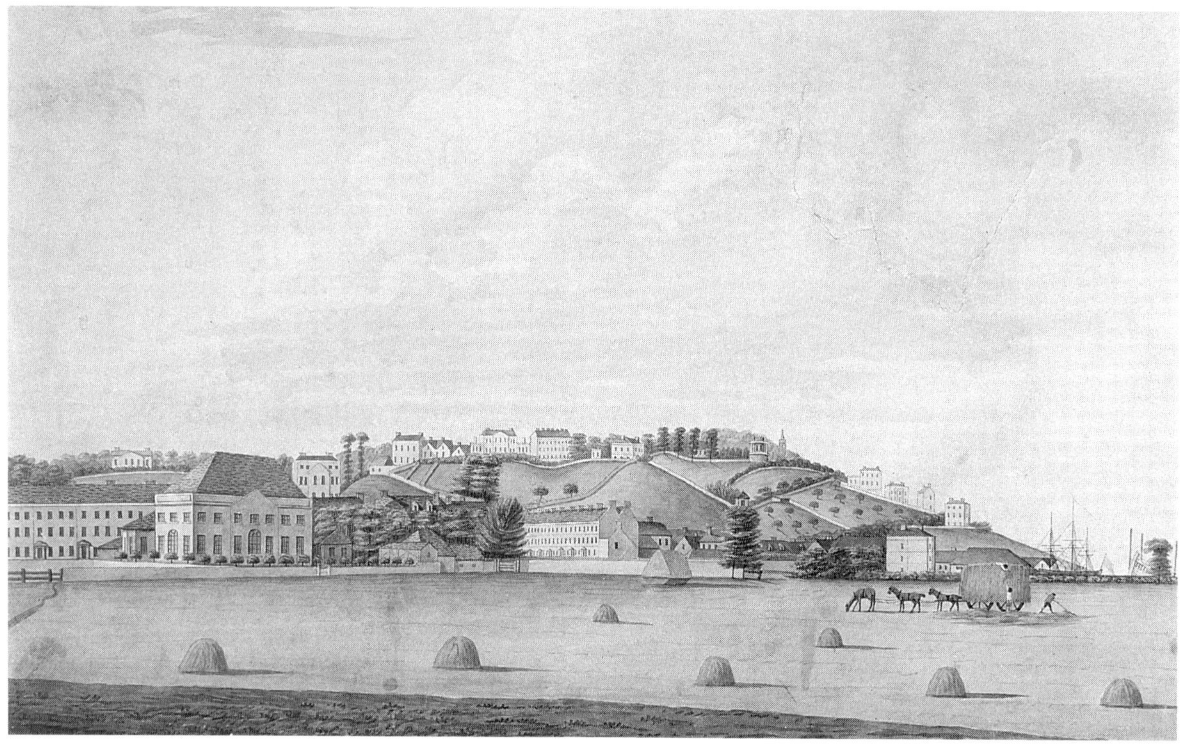

44 George Holmes 1776-1852
View of Clifton from the new dock   c.1808
Pencil and watercolour   285 x 380 mm   Bristol Museums and Art Gallery K2356

THE CONSTRUCTION OF THE FLOATING HARBOUR, 1804-9, is clearly still in progress. There are no gates on the entrance locks and the quaysides have yet to be surfaced. The vessels coming upstream would still proceed on the original course of the river in a great loop behind the viewpoint. Very soon the river would be dammed near the apex of that loop at Underfall Yard and the completed New Cut would carry the tidal flow of the Avon.

On the right the Lower Long Room can again be seen, but it now looks forlorn. In 1816 Dr Andrew Carrick, who was soon to advise the Merchant Venturers on how the Hotwell spa might restore its declining reputation, wrote that 'One of the ballrooms and taverns has long ago been shut up, and the other with difficulty kept open.'

Above is Windsor Terrace, just about to be completed after nearly twenty years. Its stark and vast red abutment seems to confirm both the vision and the vanity of those that invested in it. Higher still is the Paragon. The last of the builders to work on Windsor Terrace was to start on that crescent in April 1809. He too was to go bankrupt.

George Holmes, the artist, had come to England from Ireland in 1798, settling in Bristol in 1802. For some years he seems to have been the only resident supplier of local views to the visitors to the Hotwell. By the 1820s his picturesque watercolours must have looked distinctly dated but he did not deserve Reverend John Eagles' contemptuous words when he wrote that Holmes:

Should twenty years ago have tried
His hand at something else beside.

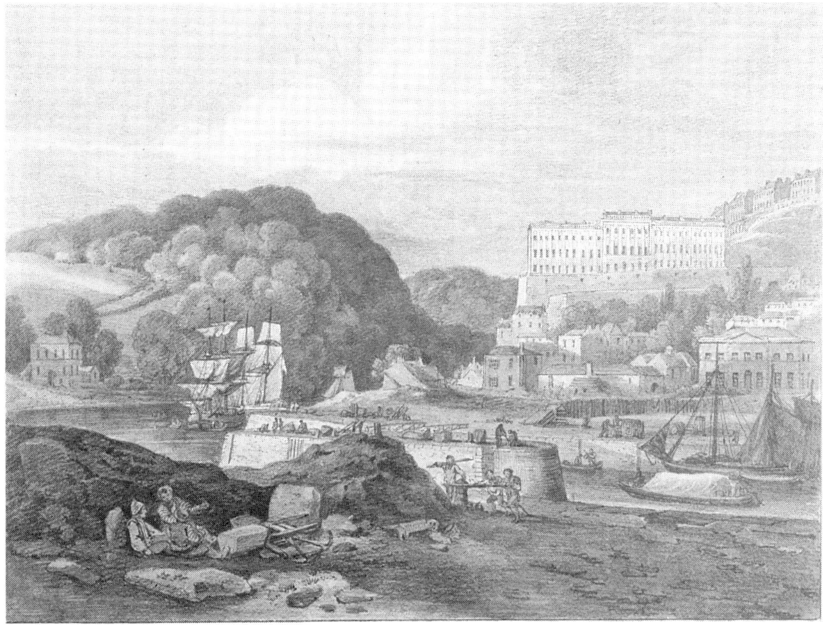

45 Francis Danby ARA 1793-1861
St Vincent's Rocks and the Avon Gorge c.1815
Watercolour and pencil 190 x 298 mm Private collection, USA

FRANCIS DANBY CAME TO BRISTOL IN 1813, aged nineteen. With two fellow artists he had come from Dublin to London to see the Royal Academy's annual exhibition. Danby and James Arthur O'Connor had then walked to Bristol hoping to catch a sailing packet to Cork. Danby was to write that he remained in Bristol because they could raise enough only for one ticket and O'Connor's 'poor little sisters…were orphans and depended on him.' However, John Mintorn, son of a stationer on College Green, gave a more practical explanation. He tells us that the two young artists had succeeded in selling some 'slightly coloured' drawings of the Wicklow Mountains to Mintorn's father, who then commissioned some drawings of the Avon Gorge. 'Thus encouraged, he became strongly attached to a locality affording great scope for the pencil of an artist.'

Danby's earliest Bristol drawings are, indeed, 'slightly coloured'. This example is in exceptionally good condition, very assured and with a stillness that foreshadows some of his most mature work. The viewpoint is from close to the back of the Hotwell House. Morning light emphasises the chasm within St Vincent's Rocks, at the foot of which are the ruins of an old lime kiln.

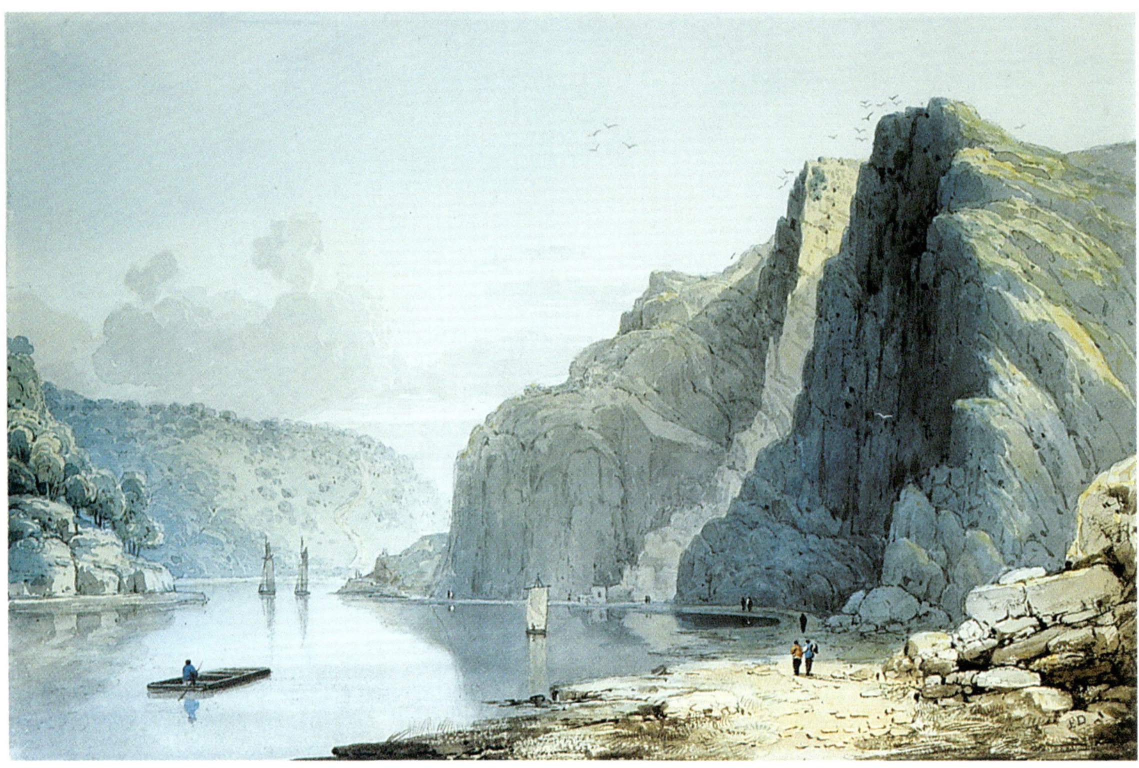

The Avon Gorge from beneath Sea Walls   1820
Watercolour and pencil   137 x 202 mm   Bristol Museums and Art Gallery K2743

THIS WATERCOLOUR IS SIGNED AND DATED 1820 on the stern of the flat-bottomed quarry boat that is moored by the two stone-breakers in the foreground. It is the only dated watercolour from Danby's years in Bristol and demonstrates how radically his style and technique had developed.

In comparison with the earlier tinted drawing, opposite, drawn outlines are now almost absent. The colours are brighter and applied with a stipple technique, using opaque body-colour, rather than transparent washes. The more spectacular or picturesque aspects of the Avon Gorge are played down. Instead it is the incidental details, such as the figures and the vessels with their slack sails, that have become a central feature. To the still reflections in the water, Danby has added warm evening sunlight and the shadows of moving clouds.

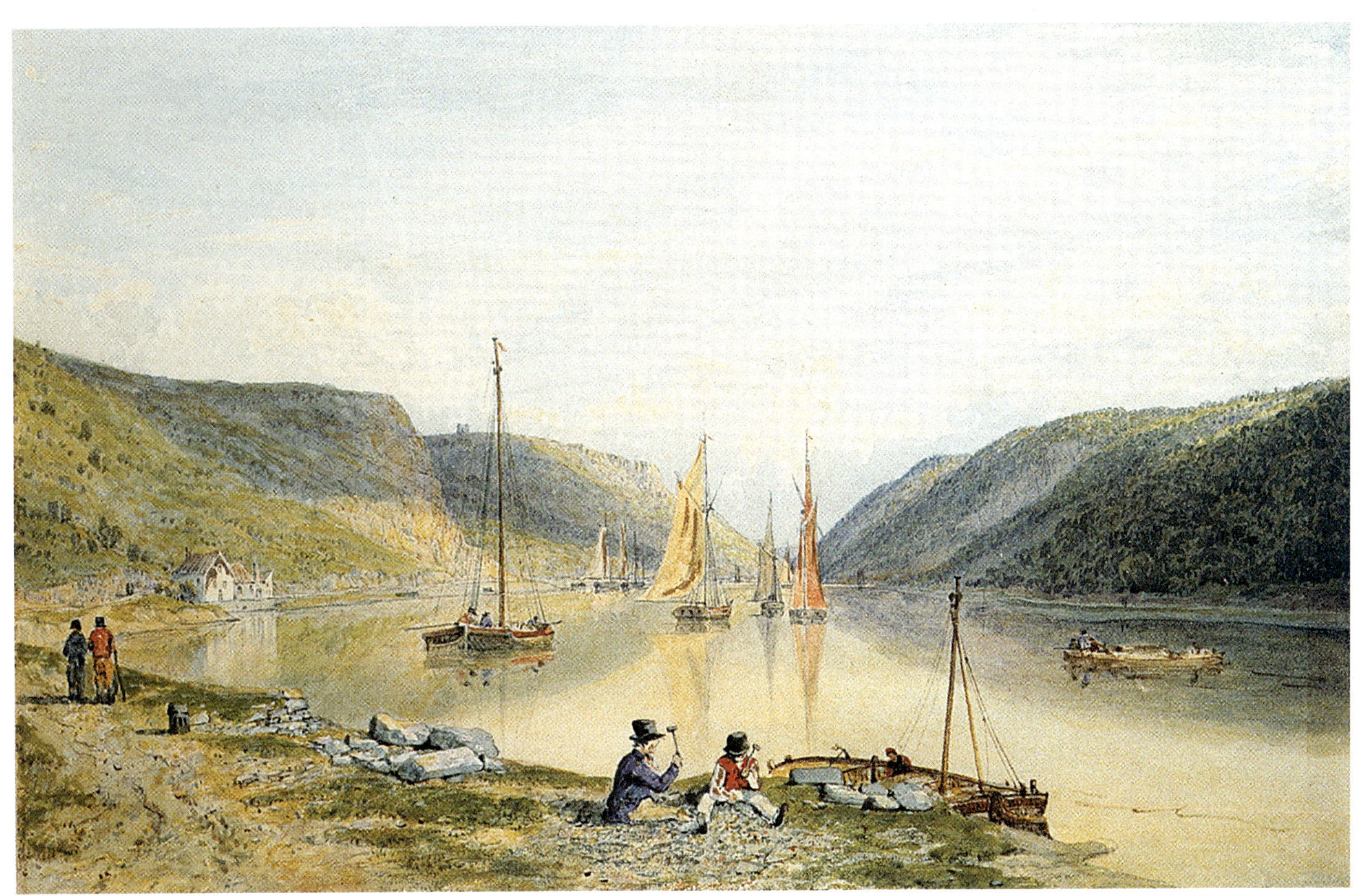

47 Francis Danby ARA 1793-1861
Rownham Ferry c.1820
Watercolour and bodycolour   267 x 467 mm   Bristol Museums and Art Gallery K184

ROWNHAM FERRY IS THE DIMINUTIVE BOAT in the centre precariously carrying both people and horses from the Somerset bank. It is to land by Rownham Tavern on the left near the entrance to Cumberland Basin and the Floating Harbour.

There is a careful and revealing study for this watercolour in the British Museum. In the study, which is even more lacking in significant features, the towpath takes up still more of the picture space and the trees are almost in the centre. Here, in the finished watercolour Danby has shifted the panorama to the left. More significantly, he has now set the distant trees and buildings against darkening clouds, transforming a meticulous topographical drawing into the depiction of an oncoming storm. Less successfully, he has borrowed his foreground figures from the pages of W. H. Pyne's *Microcosm*, a book designed to supply artists with appropriate figures for their landscapes.

The determined naturalism of this unconventional view almost certainly owes much to Danby's increasing contacts with other Bristol artists and amateurs and to their links with such important London artists as John Linnell and William Mulready.

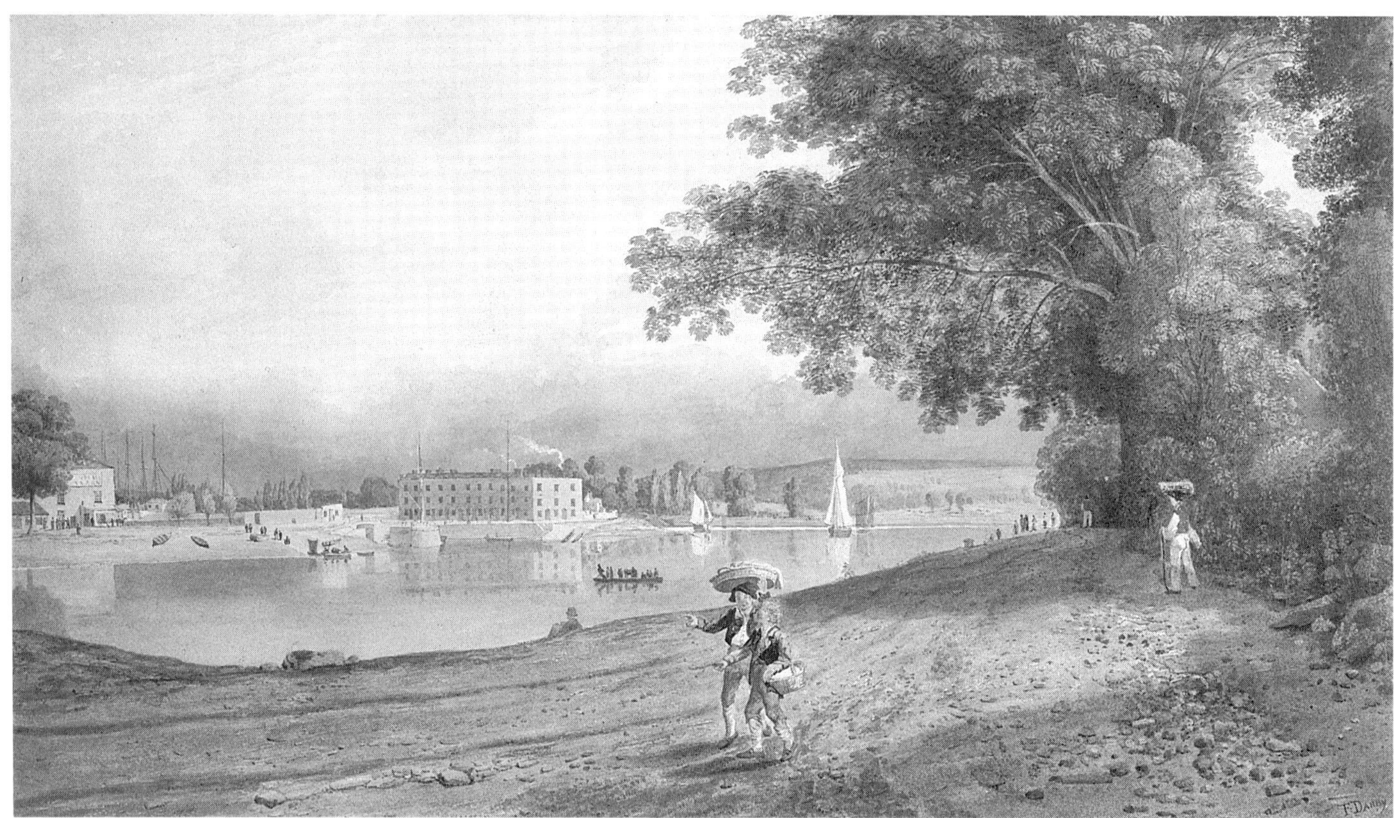

48 Francis Danby ARA 1793-1861
The Avon Gorge looking towards Clifton c.1821
Watercolour and bodycolour 482 x 736 mm Yale Center for British Art, Paul Mellon Collection

IT IS UNUSUAL TO SEE THE AVON depicted at low tide, its muddy banks revealed. Danby breaks the parallel lines of the banks and water's edge with the early-morning shadows cast by St Vincent's Rocks. The sails of the two vessels, one in shade and one in light, together with the swooping gulls, help to articulate the vast empty space before us.

It is from the summit of the farthest and sheerest of the two cliffs that the Clifton Suspension Bridge now springs. No other drawing so expressively describes the enormity of the concept of a bridge from this point.

In the centre the Old and New Hotwell House stand side by side. The New Hotwell House, completed in 1822, was part of a valiant and ultimately unsuccessful attempt by the Merchant Venturers to revive the fortunes of the spa. So too was the building of the new road, which is so prominent in Danby's watercolour. In 1819 an Act of Parliament allowed the road from Bristol to the Hotwell to be continued along the river below St Vincent's Rocks and up what is now called Bridge Valley Road. It, too, opened in 1822 immediately after the demolition of the Old Hotwell House. It is likely, therefore, that this watercolour was based on studies made in the summer of 1821.

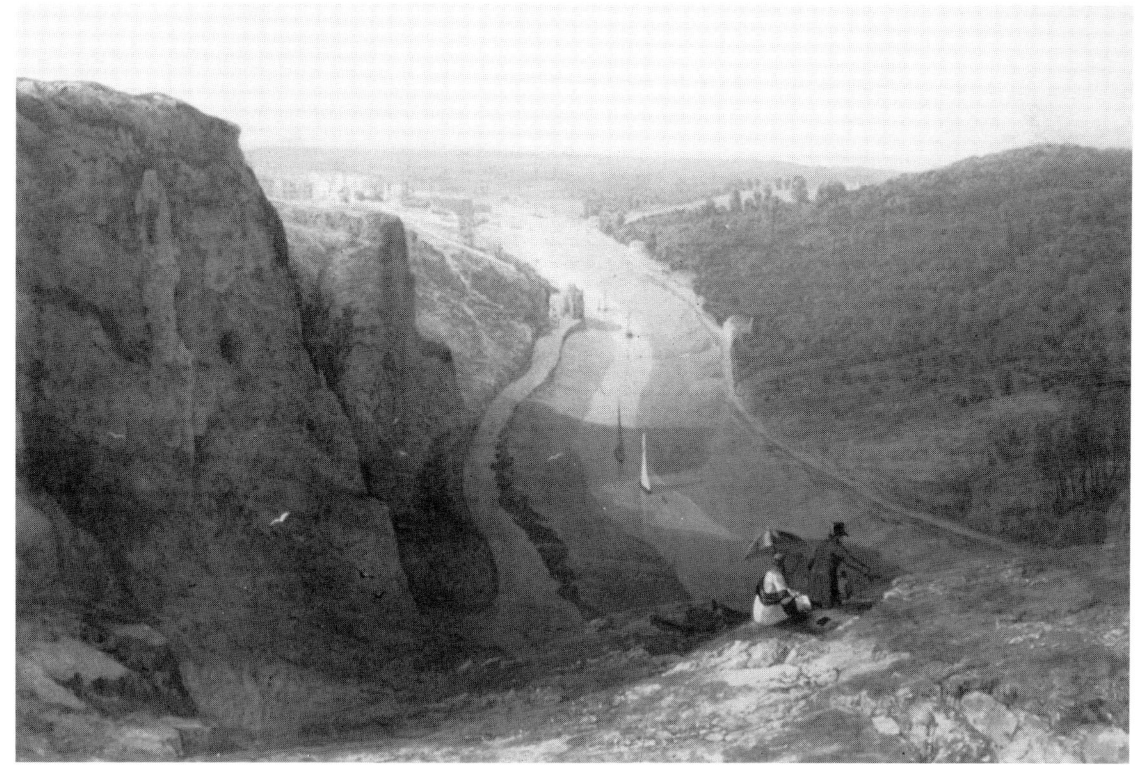

49   Francis Danby ARA 1793-1861
View of the Avon Gorge 1822
Oil 346 x 466 mm   Bristol Museums and Art Gallery K2655

THE VIEW LOOKS DOWNSTREAM from the Somerset bank across the entrance to Nightingale Valley. A couple is just entering the valley, a favourite haunt of Bristol's artists. Two horses on the towpath haul a quarry boat up the river. Sea Walls is in the far distance and immediately below we should see rather stronger evidence of Bridge Valley Road cutting steeply around the bank on the right. The road was certainly completed in 1822. That is also the date below Danby's signature on the trunk of the foreground ash tree. It may be that the painting was based on earlier studies or, more probably, that Danby was determined that nothing should disturb the tranquillity of the scene.

The pair to this painting is a scene at the top of Nightingale Valley in which a man and a woman rest on the grass, each with sketchbooks, surrounded by the luxuriant greens of Leigh Woods. One suspects that the people in these two paintings are friends of the artist. These works are not just records of particular local scenes but depictions of man's delight in nature and of his unusually harmonious relationship with it.

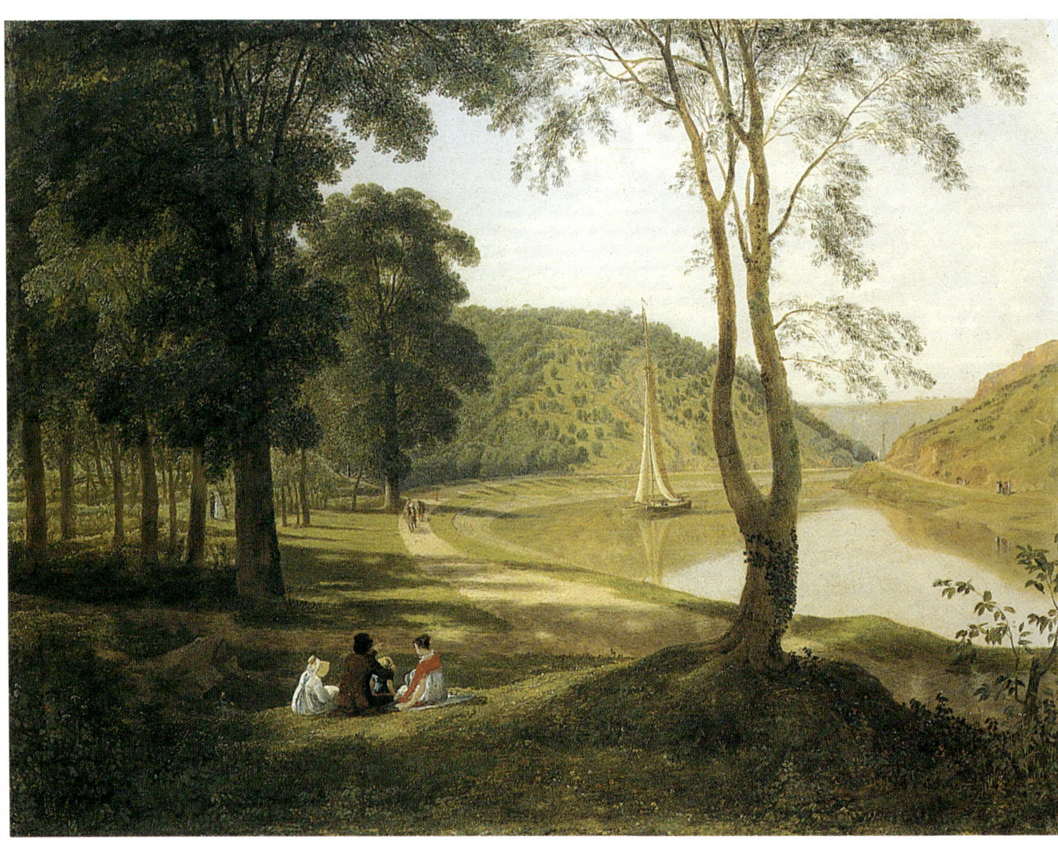

50 James Johnson 1802/3-1834
  The entrance to Nightingale Valley 1825
  Oil 255 x 340 mm Private collection

IN THE DISTANCE ON THE LEFT IS A GLIMPSE of Bridge Valley
Road curving up the side of the gorge on the far side of the
river. We are just a few yards from Danby's viewpoint in the
painting opposite, but deeper into the woods. And it is now low
tide. Beyond the two ladies, the scattered sketchbooks and the
stool, are the slack sails of a vessel sitting on the mud.

Three years separate the paintings on these two pages. The
influence of one artist upon the other may be evident but more
important is the sense of the coherence of the Bristol artists at
this time. They have taken possession of Leigh Woods, sketching and painting together with evident delight. The Reverend
John Eagles, amateur artist and friend of almost all the artists in
Bristol, wrote wistfully from his Somerset parish in 1829: 'I
think of a drawing party in the Woods. I send you a specimen
of a song to be sung by the Stainers Company… For we joke
and we pun and bask in the sun all brethren of the brush.'

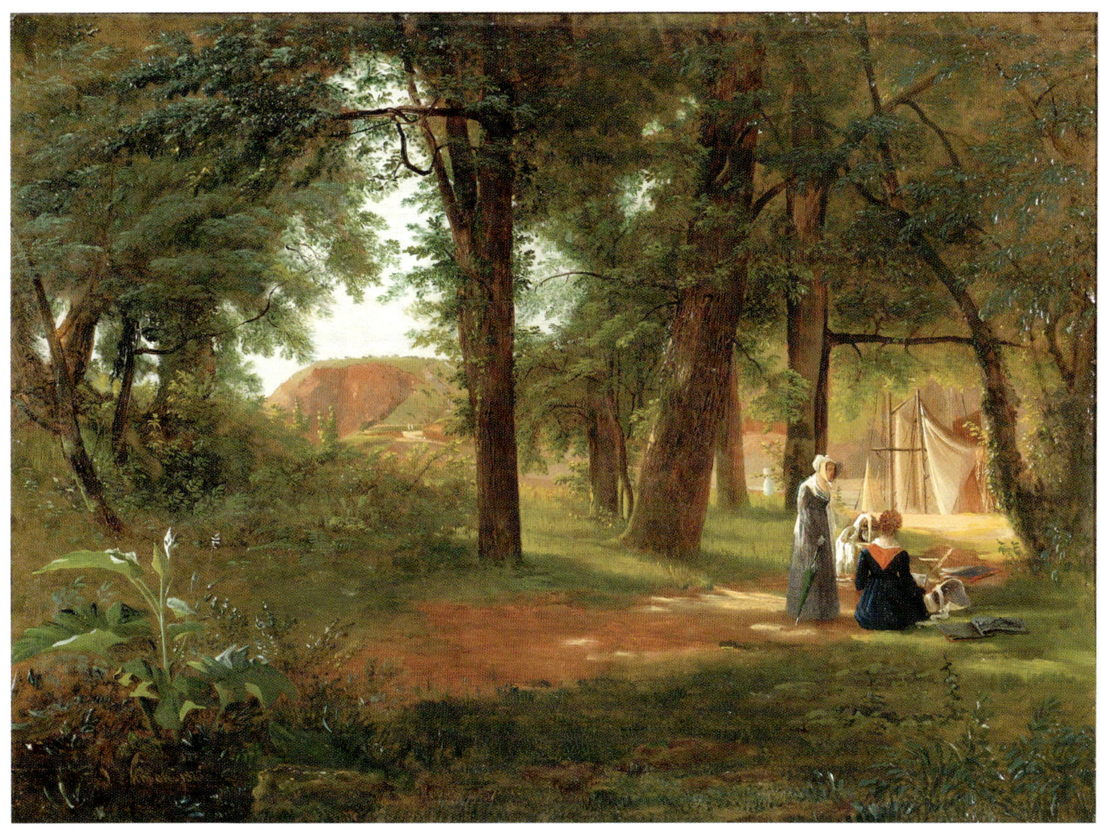

51 Edward Villiers Rippingille c.1790-1859
Sketching party in Leigh Woods c.1828
Pencil and brown wash   175 x 275 mm   Bristol Museums and Art Gallery K3078/30

RIPPINGILLE'S MOST FAMOUS PAINTING, *The Stagecoach breakfast*, hangs at Clevedon Court, North Somerset. Exhibited at the Royal Academy in 1824, it recalls the golden age of Bristol's literary associations some 25 years earlier. Samuel Taylor Coleridge, William Wordsworth, Robert Southey, Charles Lamb and others are gathered together breakfasting at an inn.

Rippingille's drawing of a rather crowded sketching party in Leigh Woods is unlikely to record a specific occasion. Instead, it is probably his first idea for an ambitious oil painting that would commemorate another high point in the history of the arts in Bristol.

We know that Dr John King, a good friend of those poets, strolled in the woods in July 1828 with the two amateur artists, Reverend John Eagles and George Cumberland, and the artists Rippingille, James Johnson and N.C. Branwhite. They talked of Francis Danby and of the phenomenal fame he was then enjoying in London and wondered if such success could have happened if it had not been for his friends and patrons in Bristol. Such a discussion may have inspired this drawing.

It could be Danby who is seated under the oak tree. It is certainly the lanky figure of Rippingille on the ground beside the picnic basket, the empty bottle and the guitar, which he and several of the Bristol artists played. It might have been Danby's flight to the Continent in 1829, pursued by creditors and amidst much scandal, which ensured that Rippingille did not carry on with the painting.

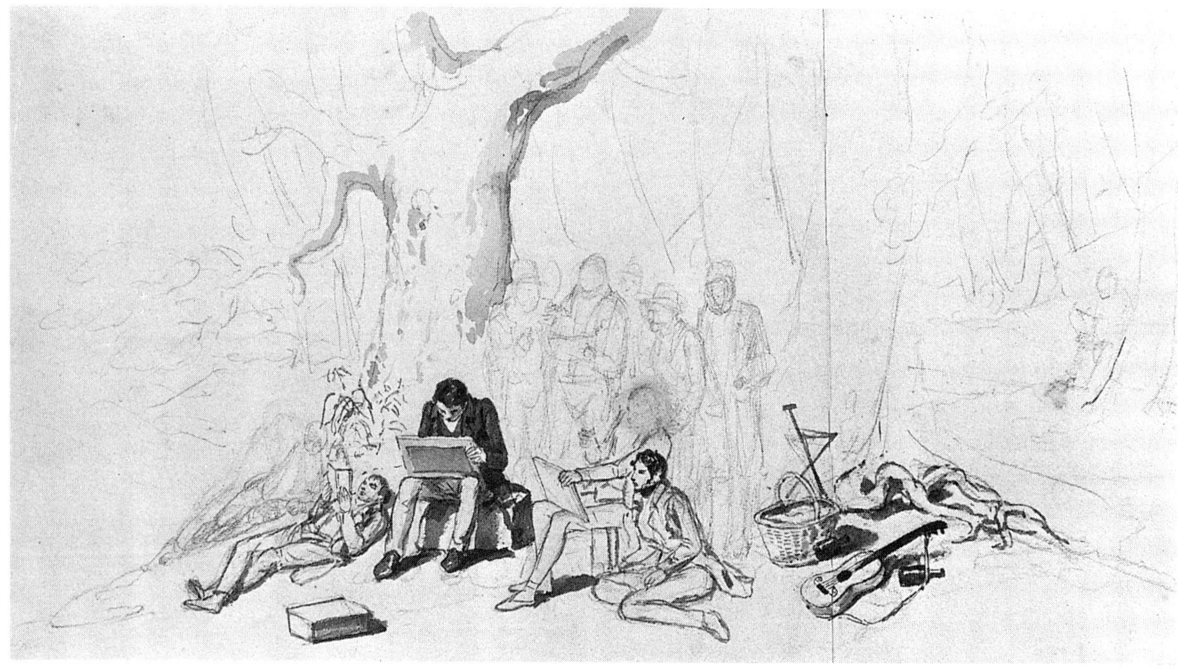

52 Francis Danby ARA 1793-1861
Landscape near Clifton c.1822
Oil 914 x 711 mm
Yale Center for British Art, Paul Mellon Collection

IN THE DISTANCE THE AFTERNOON SUNLIGHT catches the end of
Windsor Terrace, to the right of which the sails and smoking
funnel of a steam packet can be seen at the entrance to
Cumberland Basin. Through the trees and far below the figures,
a vessel's sails mark the course of the river. Francis Danby is
deliberately emphasising the contented detachment of the couple and, presumably their daughter, in their pleasant retreat in
Leigh Woods. His friend, Reverend John Eagles, spoke of
'Those beautiful woods opposite Clifton, separated from it by
the muddy Avon…dividing…the cares and turmoils of a busy
…world from the regions of Elysium.'

Both Eagles' escapism and, obliquely, his classical allusion are
evident in Danby's painting. Eagles endlessly advocated the imi-
tation of the seventeenth-century artist, Gaspard Dughet, and
Danby's scene can be compared in composition and content to
Dughet's paintings of Tivoli near Rome. Tivoli is replaced by
Windsor Terrace, the dramatic falls by the Avon Gorge and the
Virgilian shepherds by Danby's friends. John Sell Cotman (39)
made the connections between the two landscapes, Tivoli and
the Avon Gorge, the subject of his soft-ground etching entitled
Clifton. It is a view, reversed, from almost exactly the same spot
as Danby's painting, but in the foreground is a pensive shep-
herd, dressed for the countryside of ancient Rome, not contemporary Bristol.

52a John Sell Cotman 1782-1842
Clifton
Soft-ground etching 205 x 175 mm Private collection

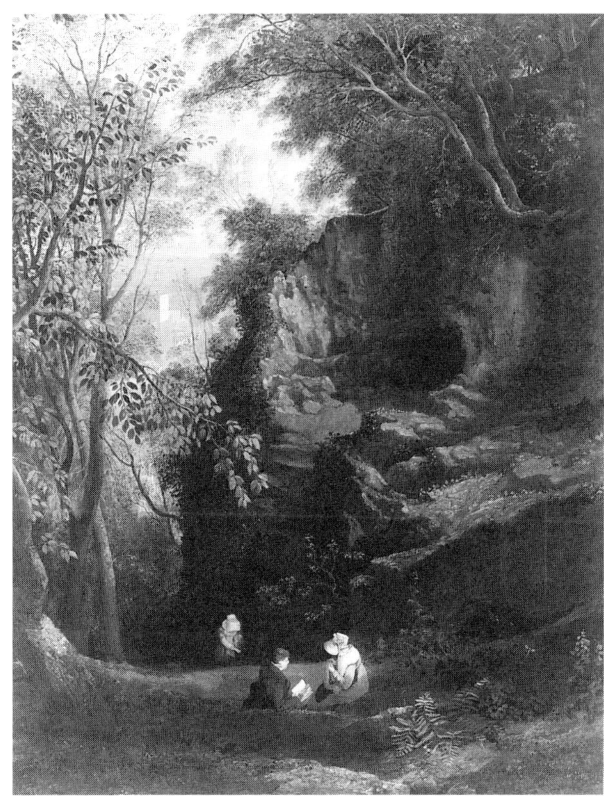

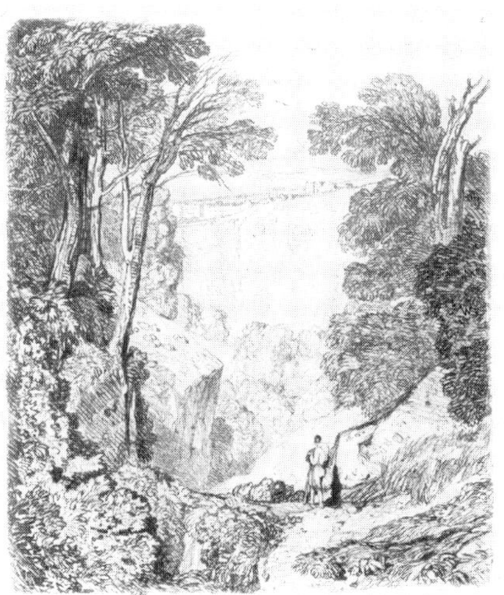

53 Francis Danby 1793-1861
The Avon from Clifton Down   c.1822
Watercolour   168 x 286 mm   Private collection

IN SUPERB CONDITION AND PAINTED WITH A LIMITED PALETTE
but with great freedom and sureness of touch, this is one of the
most moving of Danby's Bristol watercolours.

In the distance the line of trees marking the far side of
Durdham Down is seen against the Welsh hills, which are outlined against the evening sky. To the left the sun catches the
Bristol Channel and, in the centre, Sea Walls and the Great
Quarry, below which quarry boats rest on the mud. Throughout,
the structure of the landscape is clear, and depth and distance
are conveyed with subtle variations of tone and colour. In the
colouring of the open downland there is even the suggestion of
the dew of a late summer evening.

In this view and in the watercolour opposite, Danby studies
the effects of the last moments of sunlight with a sensitivity
and concentration almost without parallel in British painting.

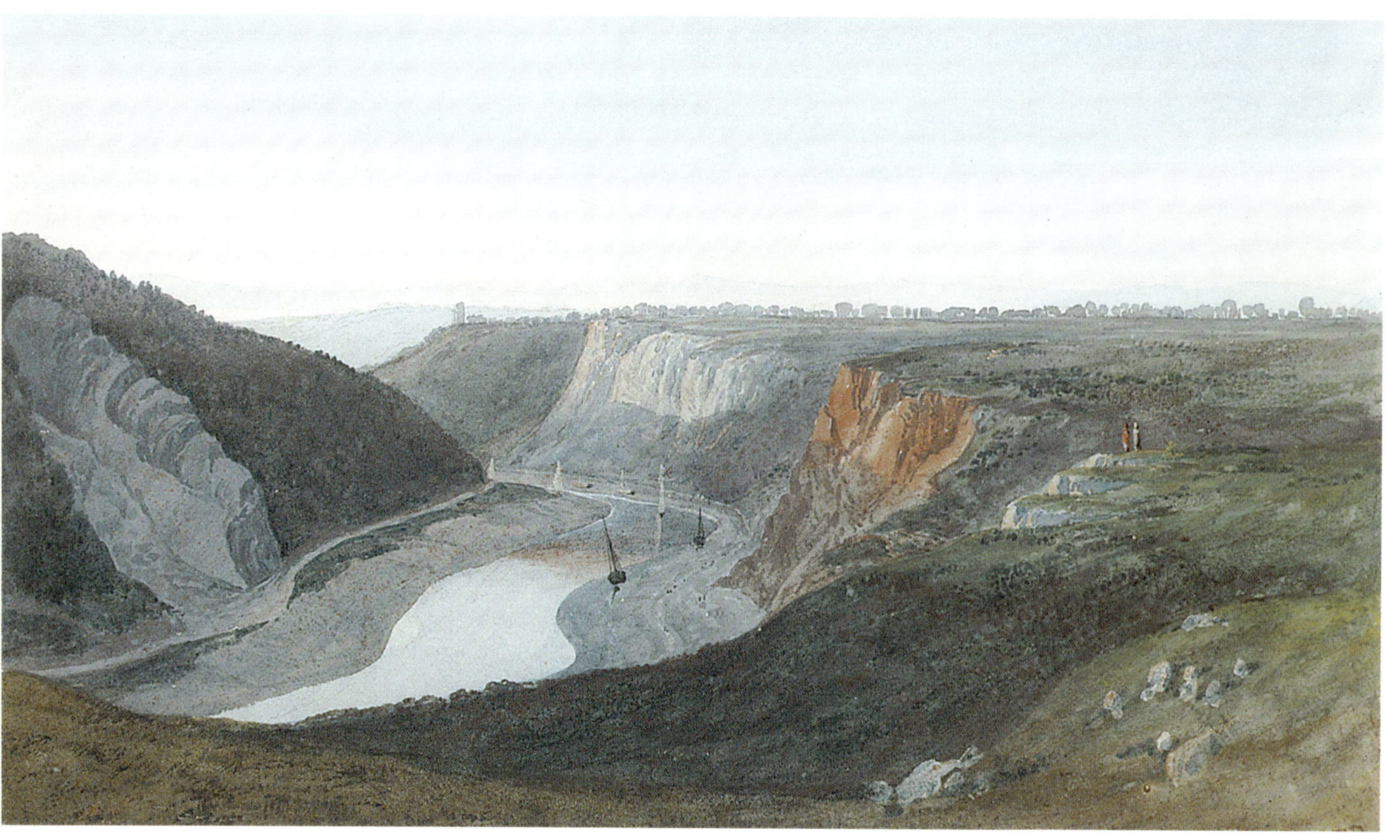

54 Francis Danby 1793-1861
The Avon at Clifton c.1821
Pencil, watercolour and bodycolour 129 x 217mm Bristol Museums and Art Gallery K4658

THIS REMARKABLY FULL AND ACCURATE RECORD of a particular scene and of a precise moment of the day is not dominated by information and observation, but by mood. It is a masterpiece of English watercolour painting.

In the centre are the Old Hotwell House and the avenue of trees before St Vincent's Parade. Sunlight catches the top of a sail and the end of Windsor Terrace. The trees at the bottom of Rownham Hill on either side of the New Inn are a rich, dark tone edging towards black and that flatness of form which comes with dusk. A steam packet is about to enter Cumberland Basin. There is the suggestion of crowded quaysides and Rownham Ferry crosses the full, still river. But against this activity, it is the detached onlooker seated on the bank that epitomises the quiet, calm, contemplative mood of the scene.

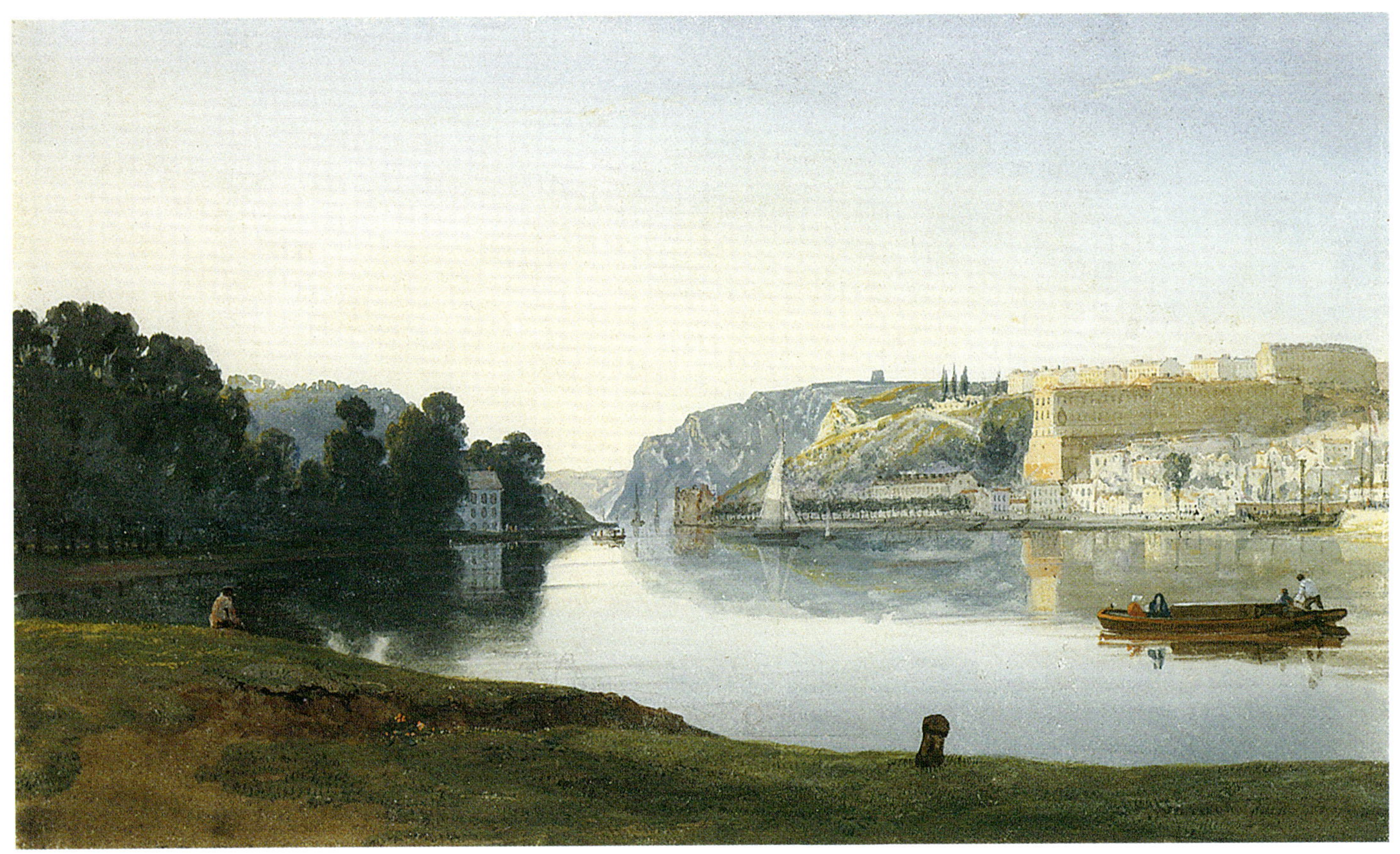

55 Francis Danby ARA 1793-1861
The Avon Gorge, evening   c.1820
Oil on panel   127 x 254 mm   Private collection

THE VIEW LOOKS UPSTREAM FROM THE SOMERSET BANK to the back of Windsor Terrace. The setting sun catches the topmost trees at the very top of Nightingale Valley and, on the opposite side, the upper parts of St Vincent's Rocks. At the foot of these cliffs is the ruined lime kiln, which had featured prominently in many earlier picturesque views of the Avon Gorge. The last remains of the kiln had probably been removed by 1821 during the construction of the road from the Hotwell to Clifton Down.

The uncertain scale of the tiny figures on the path on the left recalls those in some of Danby's earliest Bristol water-colours. But this small oil makes no attempt to dramatise the cliff faces and does not include the Hotwell House. Instead Danby concentrates on the stillness of a summer evening and on the manner in which the evening light exaggerates the character of the opposing sides of the Avon Gorge. The heavily wooded south side, softly contoured, dark, receding and with an element of mystery is set against the brighter but barren heights of St Vincent's Rocks. The dense shadows on one side are relieved by the fires on the two vessels. This activity, together with the figures on the towpaths, emphasises the stillness and the onset of dusk.

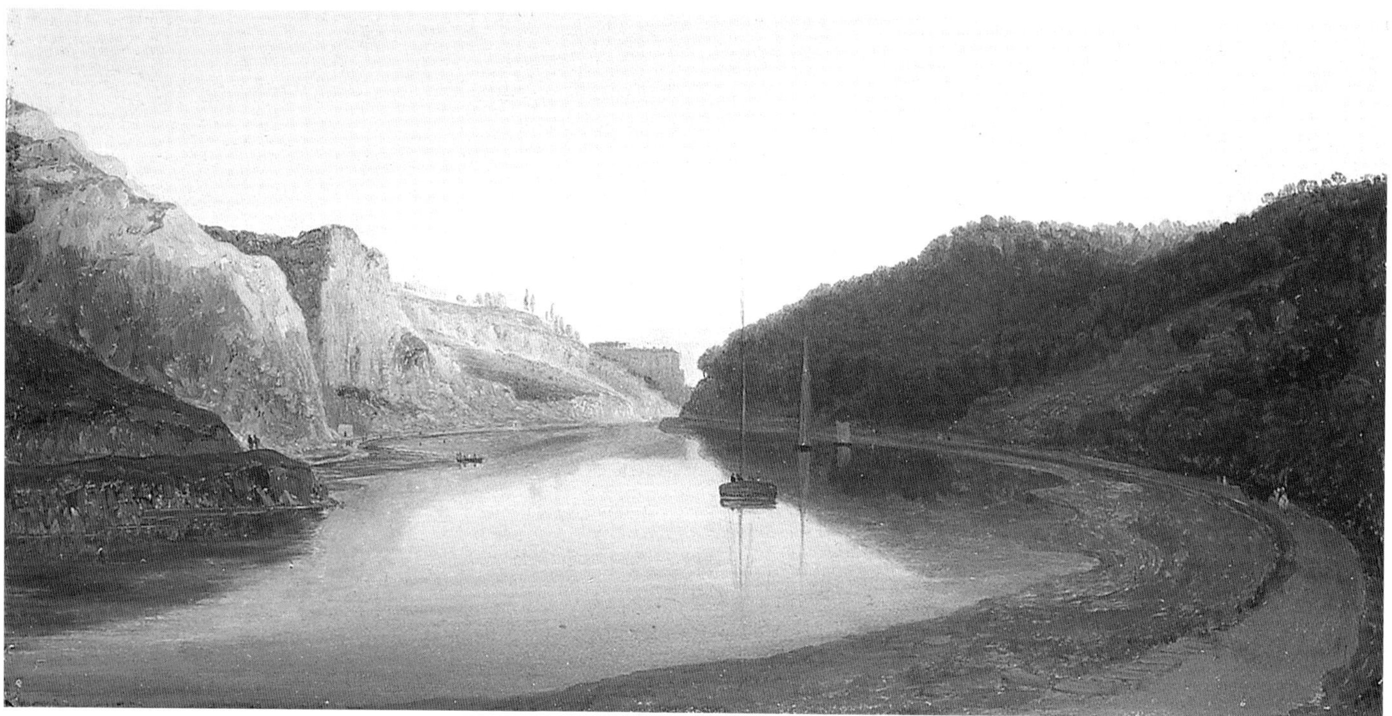

56 Francis Danby ARA 1793-1861
The Avon Gorge c.1823
Oil   241 x 352 mm   Private collection

THE ARTIST LOOKS DOWNSTREAM TOWARDS THE GREAT QUARRY, the central cliffs of Durdham Down, midway between the two better-known rock faces of Sea Walls and St Vincent's Rocks.

This study has a breadth and immediacy in the handling and observation suggesting that it may have been painted on the spot. However, we know that in 1828 Danby worked again on this picture to 'improve the poor figures' and it is possible that much of the foreground, including the strong reflections, may have been over-painted at this time.

Danby was fascinated by both dusk and dawn and the moments that precede and follow them. Some years later he admitted that his larger 'deep toned pictures' were hard to sell and acknowledged that he would have to curb his instincts. 'I think I am almost cured of painting dark pictures, <u>but I shall ever like them best</u>.'

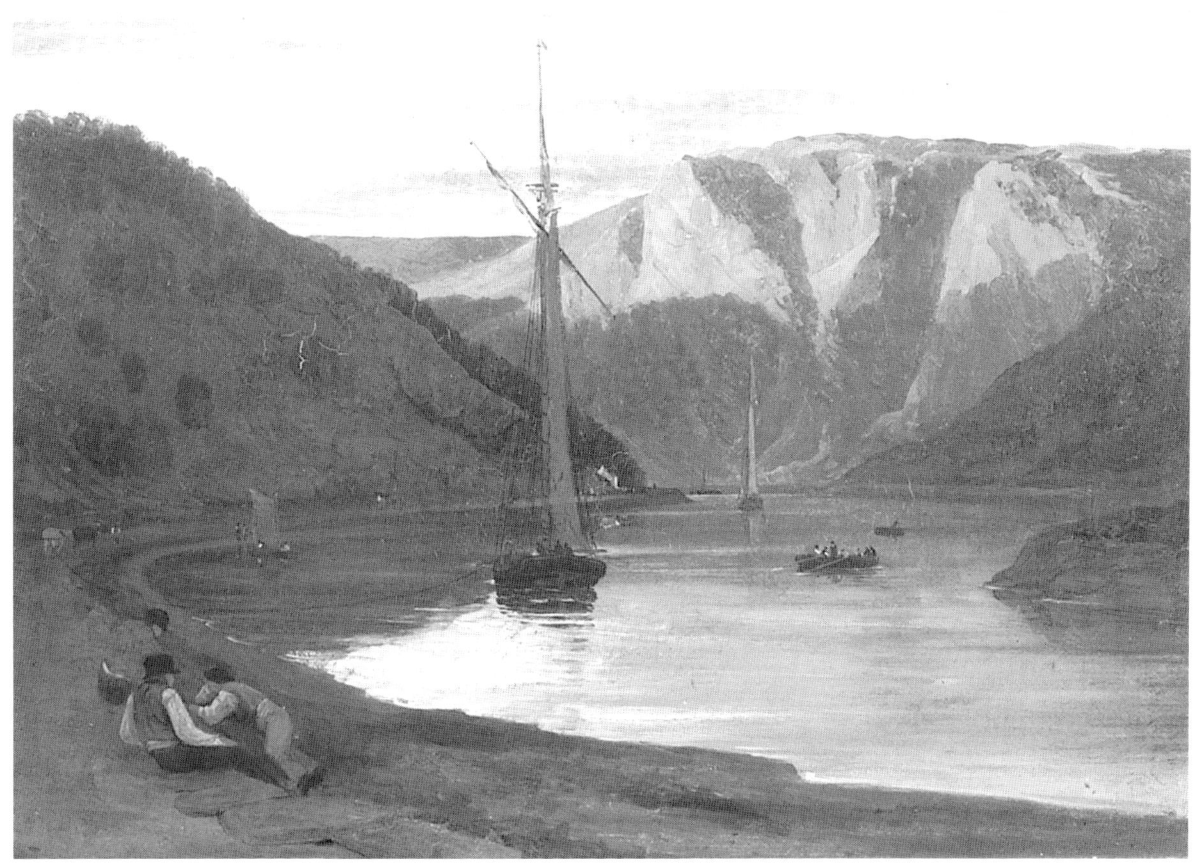

57 James Johnson 1802/3-1834
Canon's Marsh and Bristol Cathedral 1823
Watercolour 190 x 365 mm Bristol Museums and Art Gallery K846

TODAY, WE WOULD BE STANDING BENEATH THE CRANES by the Bristol Industrial Museum looking across to the headquarters of Lloyds TSB. Thankfully, the noble thirteenth-century tower of the Cathedral still commands this view.

The walled ship-building yard in the centre was a recent addition to the timber wharves of Sea Banks, but the yards glimpsed to the right along St Augustine's Reach were developed in the later eighteenth century.

Amongst the Bristol artists, James Johnson was the most strongly influenced by Francis Danby, even following Danby, unsuccessfully, to London. Like Danby, he also painted ambitious imaginary landscapes in oil, but his fragile genius is best seen in a series of architectural views of the interior of St Mary Redcliffe. Son of a local publican, he suffered intermittently from a severe mental illness and was to die after throwing himself from the window of an asylum. When Danby heard of his death during his own self-imposed exile in Switzerland, he wrote: 'Of all young men I ever knew, he had the most honour, love and feeling.'

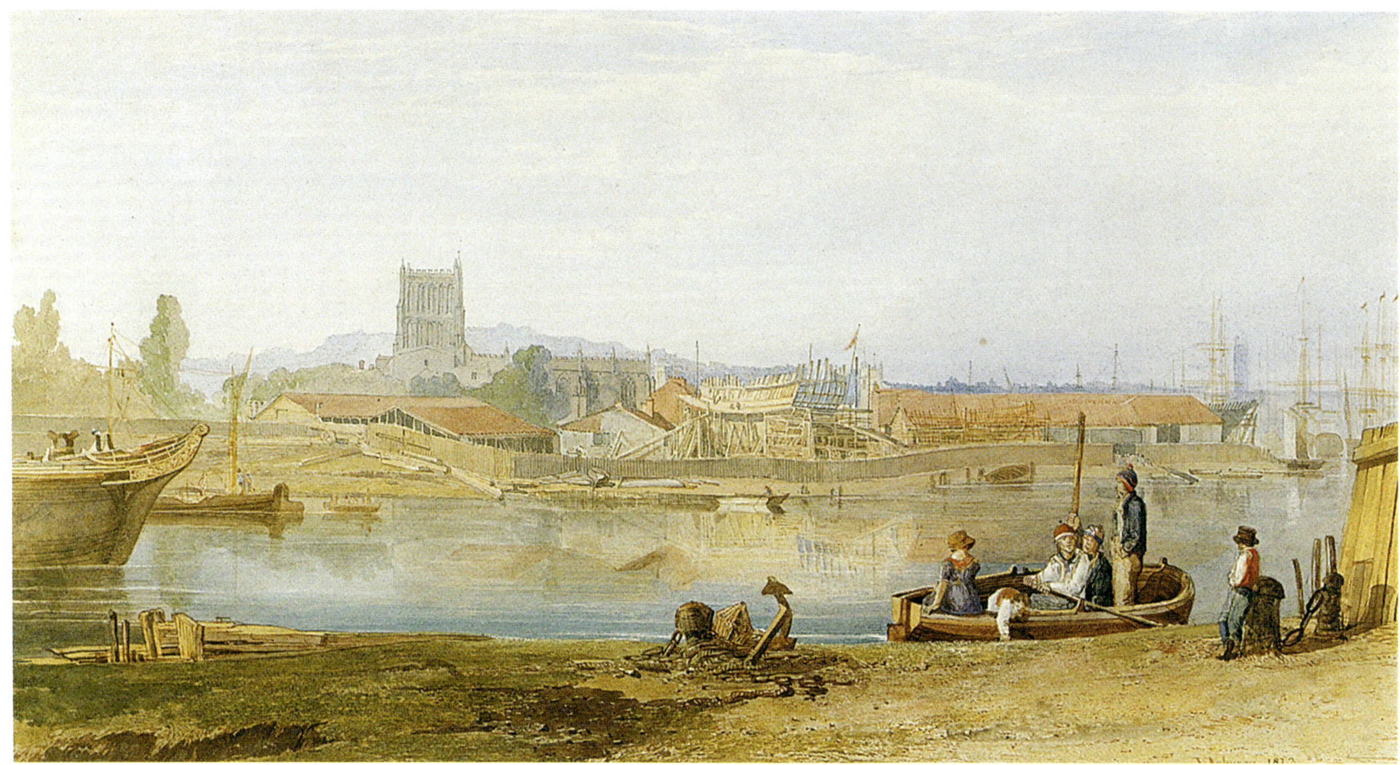

58 James Johnson 1802/3-1834
The Floating Harbour from Wapping with Canon's Marsh, St Mary Redcliffe and the New Gaol c.1823
Pencil and watercolour 130 x 265 mm Private collection

TODAY, THE *GREAT BRITAIN'S* car park would be just behind us.
It was then an open meadow – hence the stop-gate on the right
to keep the cattle from straying. The long, low buildings below
the trees contained a ropewalk. Next are the great prison walls
and two wings of the New Gaol, built 1816-1820, and of which
only the entrance gateway now remains. Beyond, the chimney
marks the site of Acraman's iron works on Bathhurst Basin. On
the left above Sea Banks is the tower of St Mary Redcliffe,
grouped with a pyramid of ships' masts and drying sails, all
drawn with the slightest and most delicate of washes.

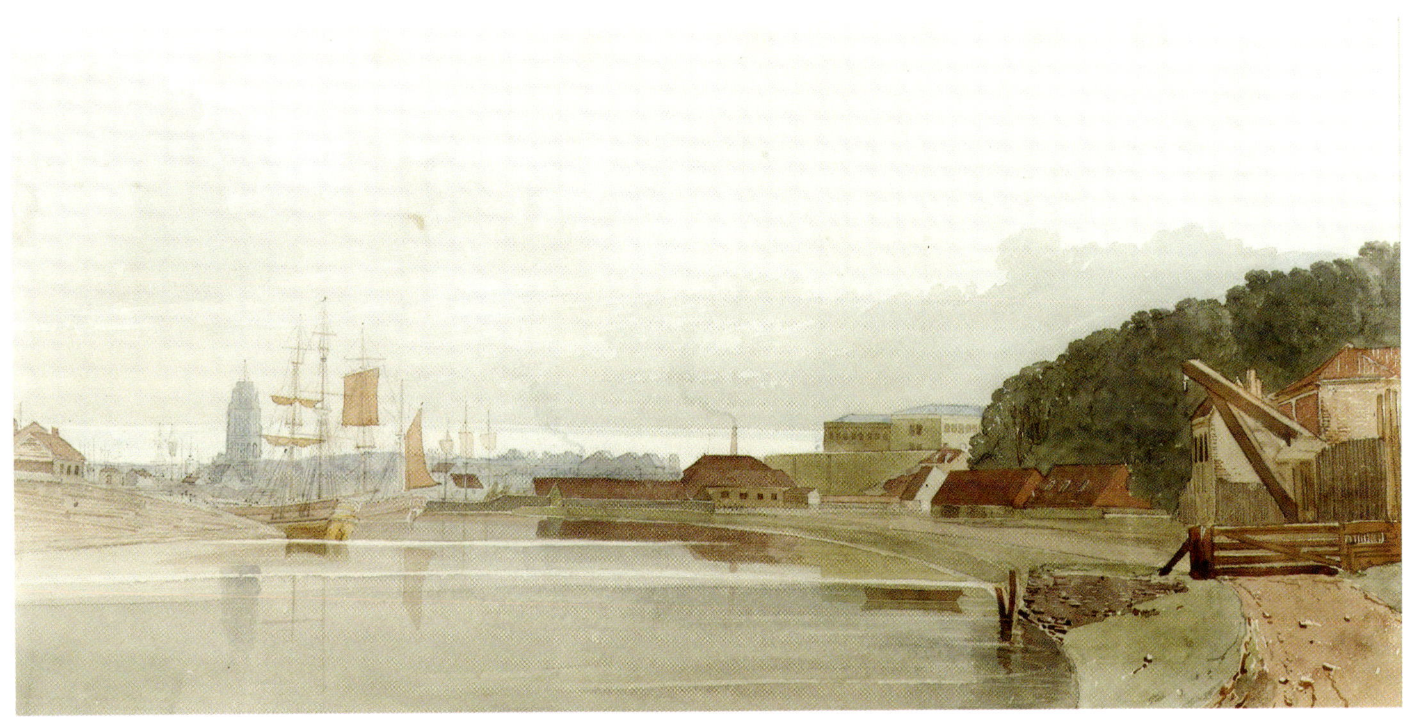

59 Samuel Jackson 1794-1869
Bristol Bridge and St Nicholas' Church   1824
Watercolour 228 x 198 mm Bristol Museums and Art Gallery M2176

ONLY BARGES AND SAILING VESSELS that could drop their masts, as we see here, could proceed up-river beyond the bridge. The sails on the far side are of coastal vessels moored at Welsh Back, where fish and vegetables, especially, were unloaded near the oyster-women's shelter.

The building of the new bridge, opened in 1768, necessitated the removal of a city gateway and the rebuilding of the nave and chancel of St Nicholas' Church. Samuel Jackson's watercolour is a most elegant tribute to James Bridges, the architect of both the church and the bridge, one in a classical or Palladian style, the other an early example of Georgian Gothic. Very sadly for Bristol, James Bridges, also the architect of Bristol University's Royal Fort, was so frustrated by bitter disputes over alternative plans for the bridge that he left Bristol for the West Indies in 1763. William Paty completed both the bridge and the church, designing the tower and spire himself.

The domed tollhouses were to be the cause of vicious riots in 1793 in which fourteen people died. The tollhouses and the fine balustrades were removed when the deck of the bridge was extended in the 1860s. Today, one can still enjoy Bridges' original arches when passing under the bridge en route for Temple Meads station by ferry.

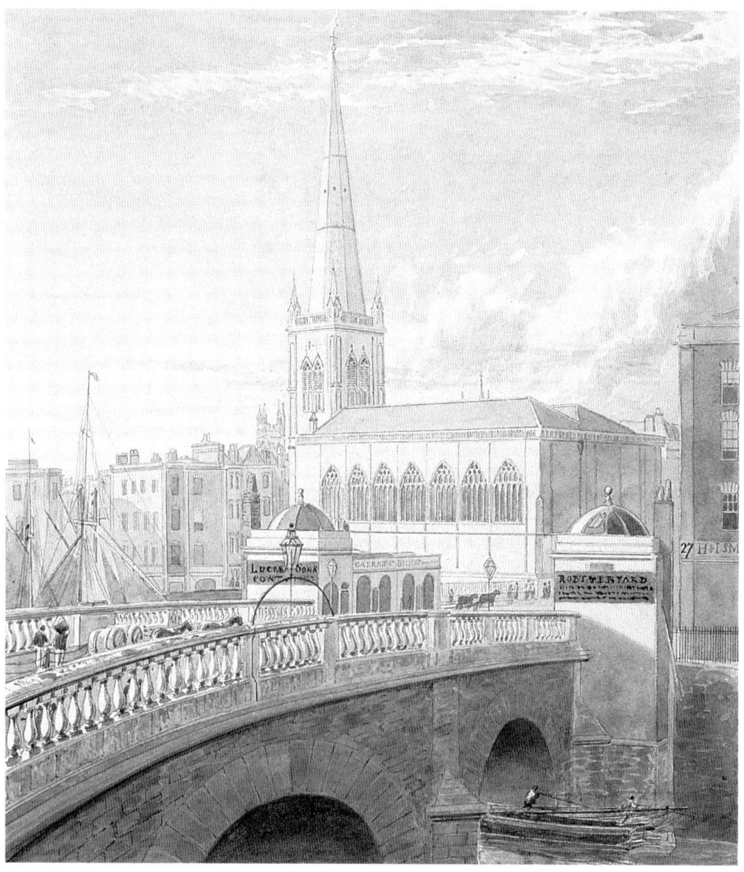

60 Samuel Jackson 1794-1869
The entrance to Bathurst Basin from the New Cut   c.1825
Watercolour   179 x 274 mm   Bristol Museums and Art Gallery M973

WHEN PLANNING THE FLOATING HARBOUR, William Jessop wisely took advantage of the Malago river, which flowed through Bedminster. Just before it ran into the Avon, he widened it greatly, creating the triangular Bathurst Basin and providing a second entrance to the Floating Harbour from the New Cut.

The New Cut, seen here at low tide, had been dug out primarily to divert the tidal flow of the Avon from the Floating Harbour. The steam packet companies, whose regular services from Bristol began in 1822, soon discovered that their vessels could come up to this jetty, letting off and taking on their passengers close to the centre of Bristol without having to pass through any locks.

On the far left is the wall of the New Gaol and the balconied Bathurst Hotel, much later irrelevantly called the Smugglers and now renamed the Louisiana. Carolina, where several Bristolians had plantations, would have had more relevance. The capstans for opening the lock gates are shown, together with a hand crane. The lock was to be filled in during the last war to avoid the risk of the accidental draining of the Floating Harbour if the gates were bombed. By the chimney on the right are Acraman's iron works and above is a former sugar house that was then in use as a bonded warehouse for West Indies produce.

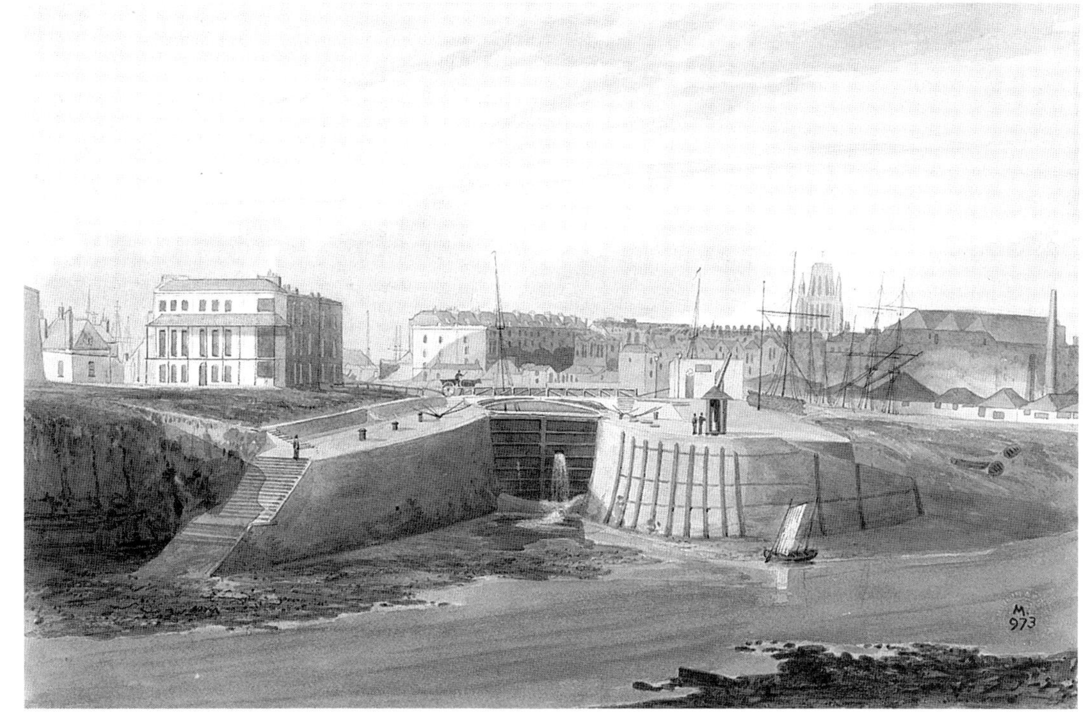

61 Samuel Jackson   1794-1869
Cumberland Basin from Rownham Hill   c.1825
Watercolour   162 x 296 mm   Bristol Museums and Art Gallery M970

SAMUEL JACKSON seems to be almost deliberately mapping the complexities of the western end of the Floating Harbour, completed in 1809. The old course of the Avon passed Rownham Hill in the foreground, continuing up the muddy channel on the right marked by the two sailing vessels. It then looped around Rownham Mead crossing the middle distance horizontally below the trees and thence to Bristol. It was to be dammed at the very centre of this view and a channel, the New Cut, was dug. This carried the tidal waters and flow of the Avon and can be seen continuing diagonally into the distance.

The Junction Lock at the far end of Cumberland Basin is the lock in which Brunel's *Great Britain* was so nearly disastrously wedged in 1844. The southern or right hand of the two nearer locks was rebuilt and widened by Brunel in the 1840s. The northern entrance lock was replaced by a larger lock at a very different angle, cutting the corner and making the entrance bend, previously at right angles to the river's powerful currents, much easier. It was opened in 1873 and is still in operation.

To the south of the locks are Cumberland Buildings, built soon after the completion of the Floating Harbour, but demolished in the 1850s and succeeded by the Dock Master's House.

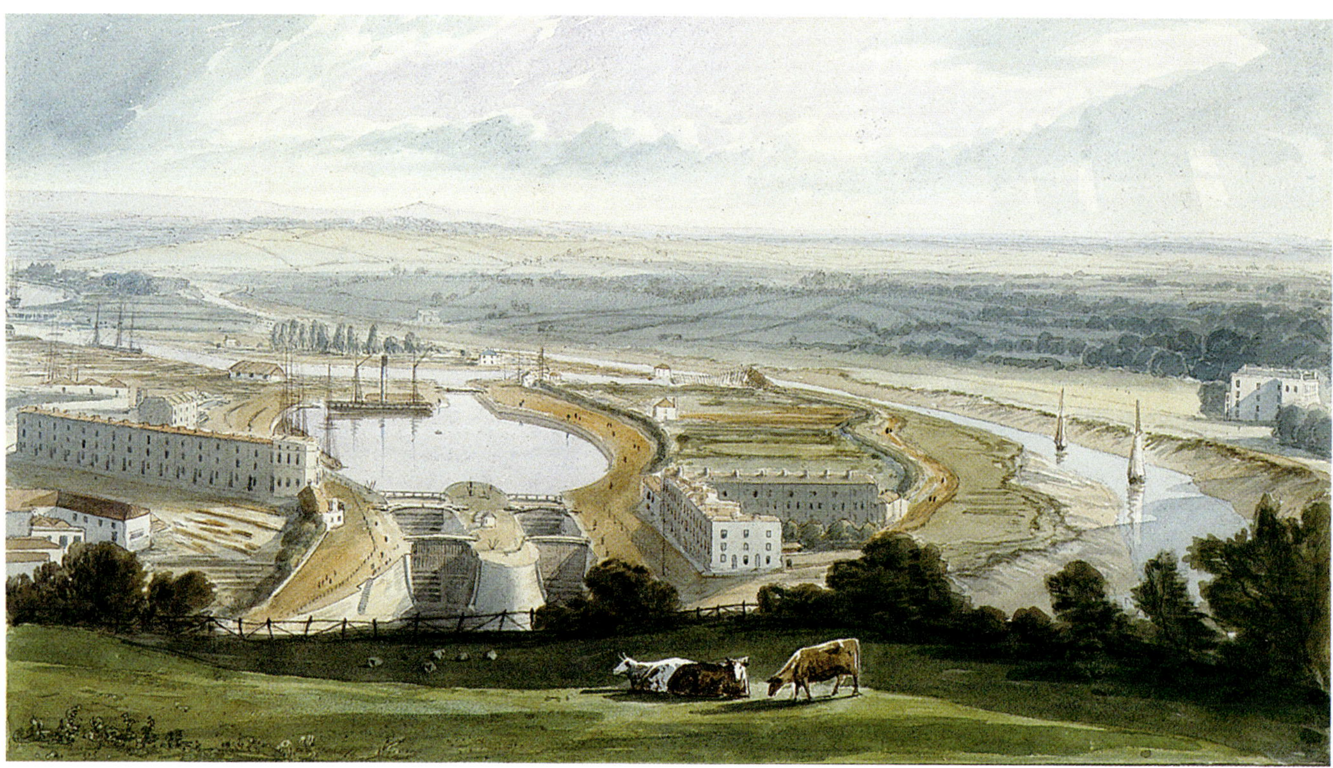

62 Samuel Jackson 1794-1869
Clift House near Cumberland Basin   c.1825
Watercolour   162 x 245 mm   Bristol Museums and Art Gallery M977

SAMUEL JACKSON'S CAREFULLY BALANCED composition and his impressive control of even washes of colour contribute to the sense of an almost soporific summer afternoon.

Clift House in the centre succeeded Red Clift Yard, the short-lived shipyard where J.M. Hilhouse built men-of-war for the Admiralty in the 1780s. The frigates *Termagent, Diomede, Serapis, Nassau,* and *Melampus* were all constructed here on the former site of Mr Warren's glasshouse (4).

In the years before the creation of the Floating Harbour, George Bush, the sugar merchant, lived at Clift House. George Weare Braikenridge, the first owner of this watercolour, recorded Mr Bush's particular hospitality in the manuscript catalogue to his collection:

A long and wide Tea Room was erected close to the water's edge so that a conversation might be kept up with any person on the deck of the Vessels and whilst Bristol sent out so many superb West India Ships, it was Mr Bush's polite custom to invite persons who had an interest in such vessels to come to the Clift that they might enjoy the pleasure of seeing them come up the River on returning from a long and perhaps dangerous voyage.

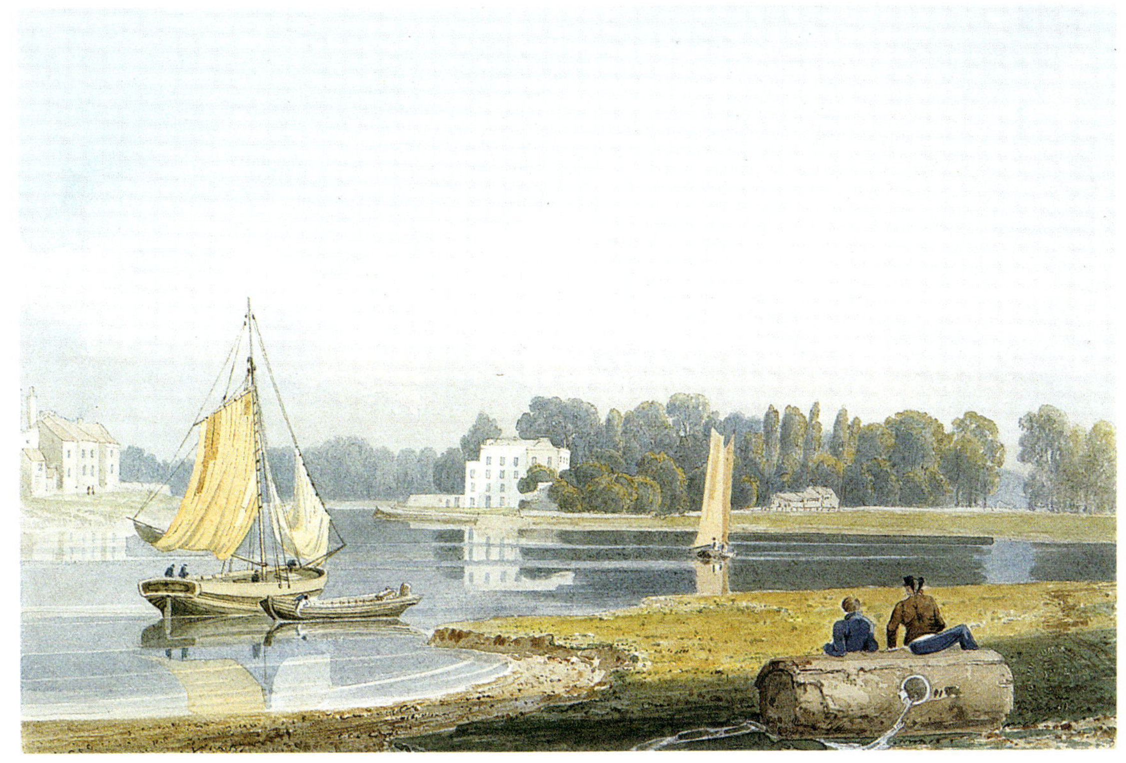

The Avon Gorge from near Sea Walls looking towards Clifton c.1823
Watercolour 117 x 184 mm Bristol Museums and Art Gallery K1501

NO WATERCOLOUR MORE DRAMATICALLY ILLUSTRATES the differences between the opposing sides of the Avon Gorge and the effects of quarrying. The south or Somerset side is heavily wooded. Much of that woodland had been carefully managed since late medieval times with rights of controlled coppicing, for example, being leased to a Bristol baker. The brutal scarring of the quarries on this south side was largely of more recent date. On the opposite side, Durdham and Clifton Downs are almost treeless and there is still little evidence of scrub, despite a decline in the number of sheep grazing the common land of the Downs in the early nineteenth century.

S.H. Grimm had drawn this same view about thirty-five years earlier (28). Compare the two pictures and the extent of the quarrying becomes dramatically clear. The Great Quarry is in the centre, where the quarry boats wait on the mud, and it is now a very different shape. So too is the outline of St Vincent's Rocks in the distance. Despite popular concern, quarrying was to continue until the later nineteenth century to the considerable benefit of the Society of Merchant Venturers.

The terrace on the skyline is Harley Place, the windmill above St Vincent's Rocks is still a ruin and the Clifton Turnpike, in between, has yet to be rebuilt.

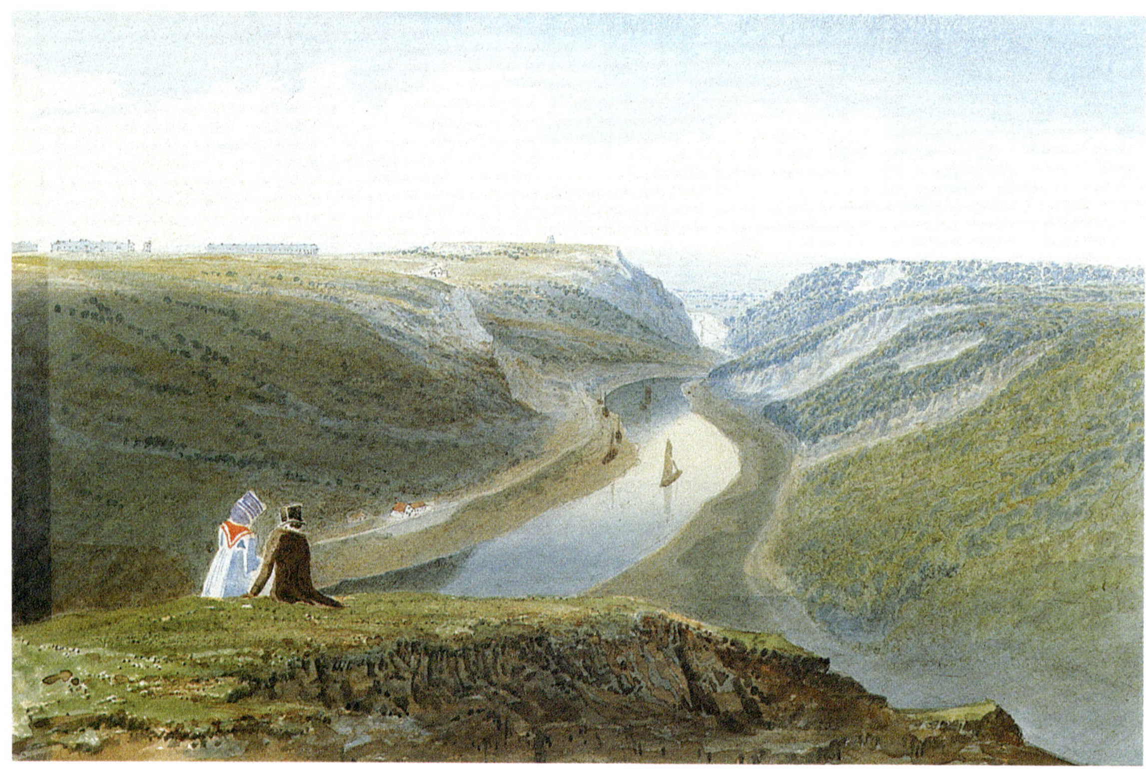

64 Samuel Jackson 1794-1869
Rainbow over the River Avon   c.1825
Watercolour   290 x 447 mm   Bristol Museums and Art Gallery K180

CONSIDERABLY LARGER THAN SAMUEL JACKSON'S other water-colours illustrated here, this is one of a series of ambitious views on the Avon, which Jackson enlivened with such special effects as moonlight, sunset or dusk. Here a dramatic rainstorm moves up the river passing Sea Walls and the derelict New Hotwell (28), now a shelter for the quarrymen.

Unlike so many of his fellow Bristol artists, Samuel Jackson was both born and buried in the city. He turned to art in the early 1820s and was probably, briefly, a pupil of Francis Danby,

of whom he was certainly a lifelong friend. Jackson was princi-pally a painter of watercolours and exhibited regularly at the Old Water-Colour Sociey in London. One obituary notice regretted that he wasted too much of his time 'teaching the unteachable misses and masters in private academies'.

Quiet, unaffected, companionable and humorous, an excel-lent pianist and an able guitar player, Jackson played an impor-tant role in the social life of the Bristol artists in the 1820s and 1830s. He was later to be called the father of the Bristol School.

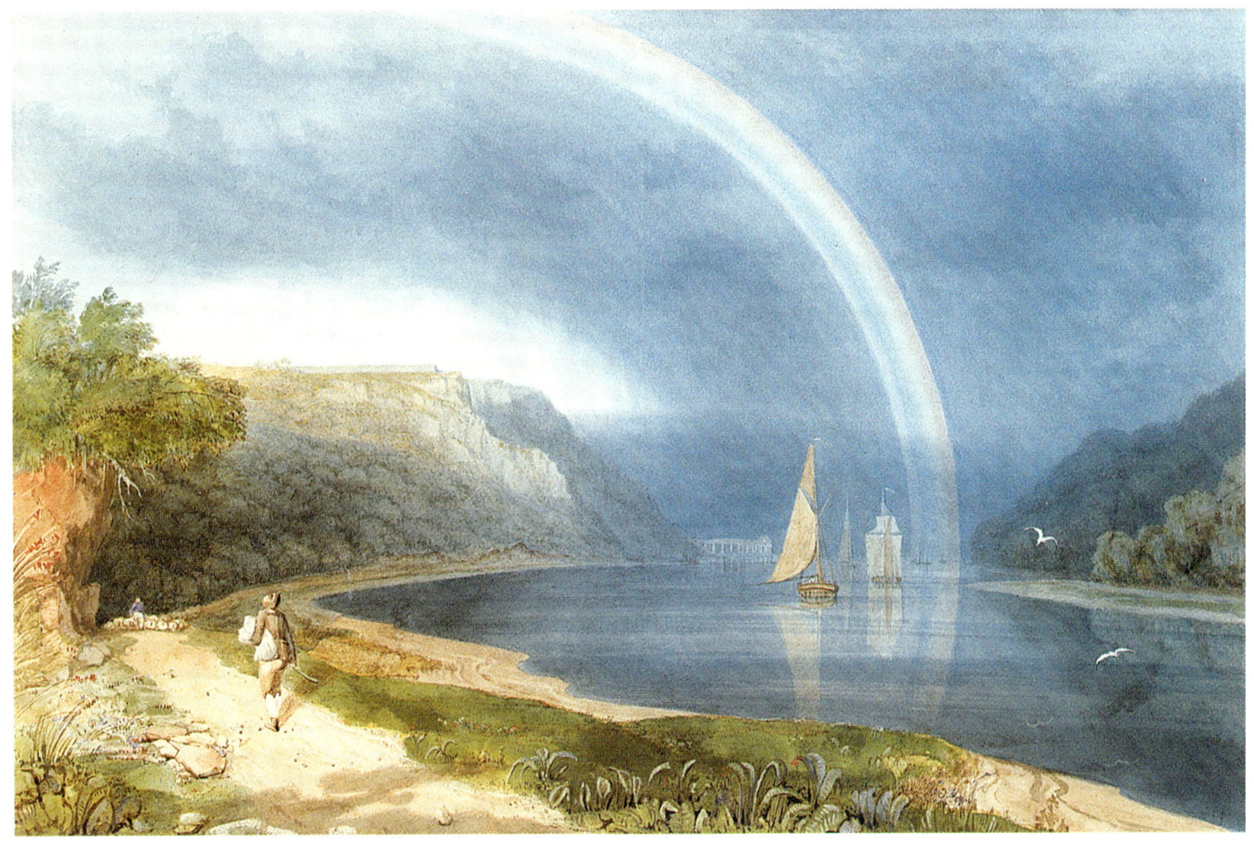

65 Samuel Jackson 1794-1869
St Peter's, Portishead, with Woodhill and the mouth of the Avon c.1835
Watercolour 240 x 345 mm Private collection

WOODHILL, WHICH HIDES PORTISHEAD POINT, is on the left and the mouth of the Avon is on the far right. The outline of the Welsh Hills can be seen across the Bristol Channel.

On stylistic grounds, this watercolour may well date from the later 1830s, a time of serious development for Portishead. The mid-1830s saw the building of new villas, a Marine Baths and Subscription Reading Room, together with new access roads from Bristol and the advent of regular steam vessels from Bristol in the summer.

The problems of navigating the Avon in ever-larger ships had also prompted Brunel's proposals in 1839 for a pier and basin at Portishead. This harbour (100) would have been well to the right of the church tower and close to the site of today's Royal Portbury Dock, constructed in the 1970s.

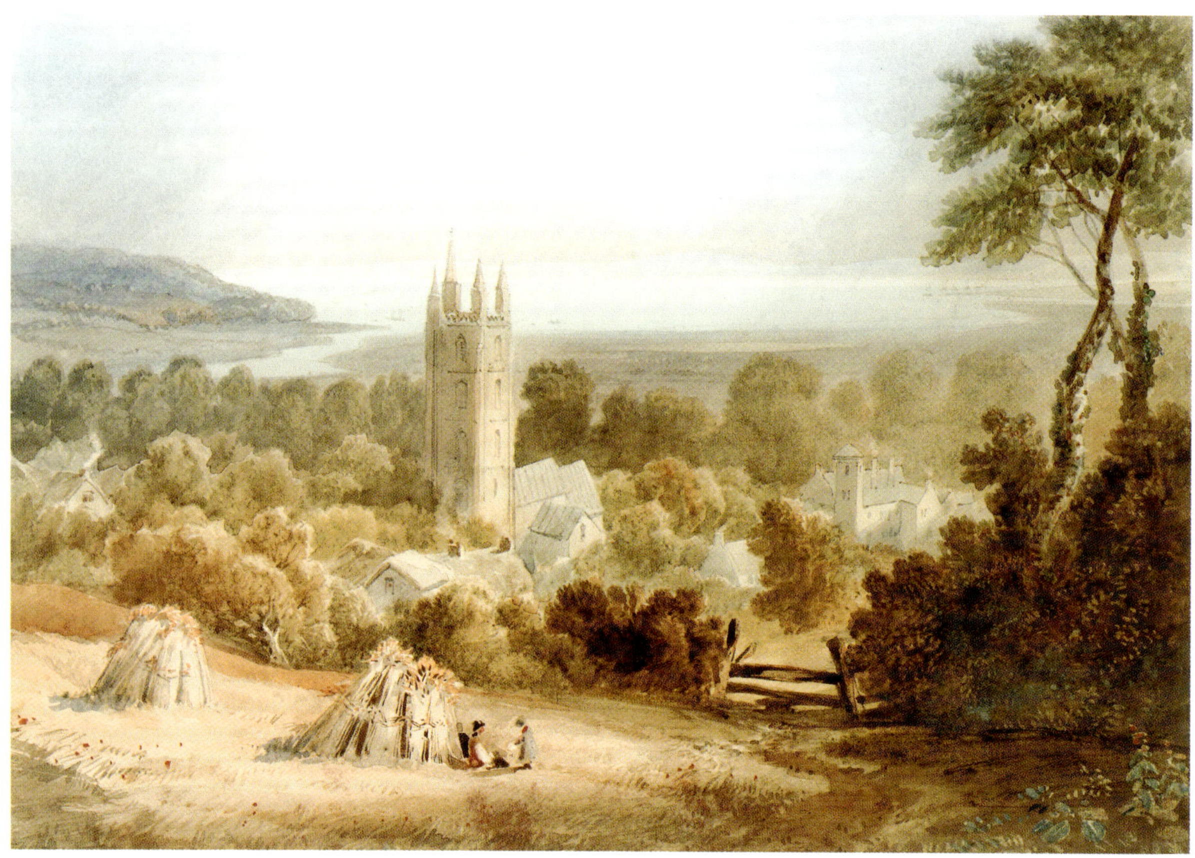

66 Samuel Jackson 1794-1869
Flat Holm lighthouse with Steep Holm in the distance   c.1825
Watercolour   225 x 300 mm   Private collection

PARISH BOUNDARIES HAVE A PROPER RESPECT FOR HISTORY. So, today, Flat Holm and Steep Holm are still within the Bristol parish of St Stephen's, although it is almost twenty years since the Master of the convivial Antient Society of St Stephen's Ringers organised a visit for a symbolic beating of the bounds.

Not until 1891 did the furthest administrative limits of the Port of Bristol contract eastwards from Lundy to Flat Holm and then in 1921 from Flat Holm to the Clevedon Pier light. For centuries the obligation to take a pilot from as far as Lundy had been just recognition of the channel's perils.

The Merchant Venturers first agreed upon the need for a lighthouse on Flat Holm in 1728, but it was a decade before the light, a coal fire, was first kindled. Twenty-five tons of coal a month had to be shipped to the island and the tolls had to be laboriously collected in the ports by agents of successive lease-holders. Finally the Admiralty's Trinity House, having first heightened the tower from seventy to ninety feet, bought out the remainder of the lease in 1823 and installed a full-time keeper. Hence the lighthouse's pristine appearance just two or three years later, when Samuel Jackson visited the island.

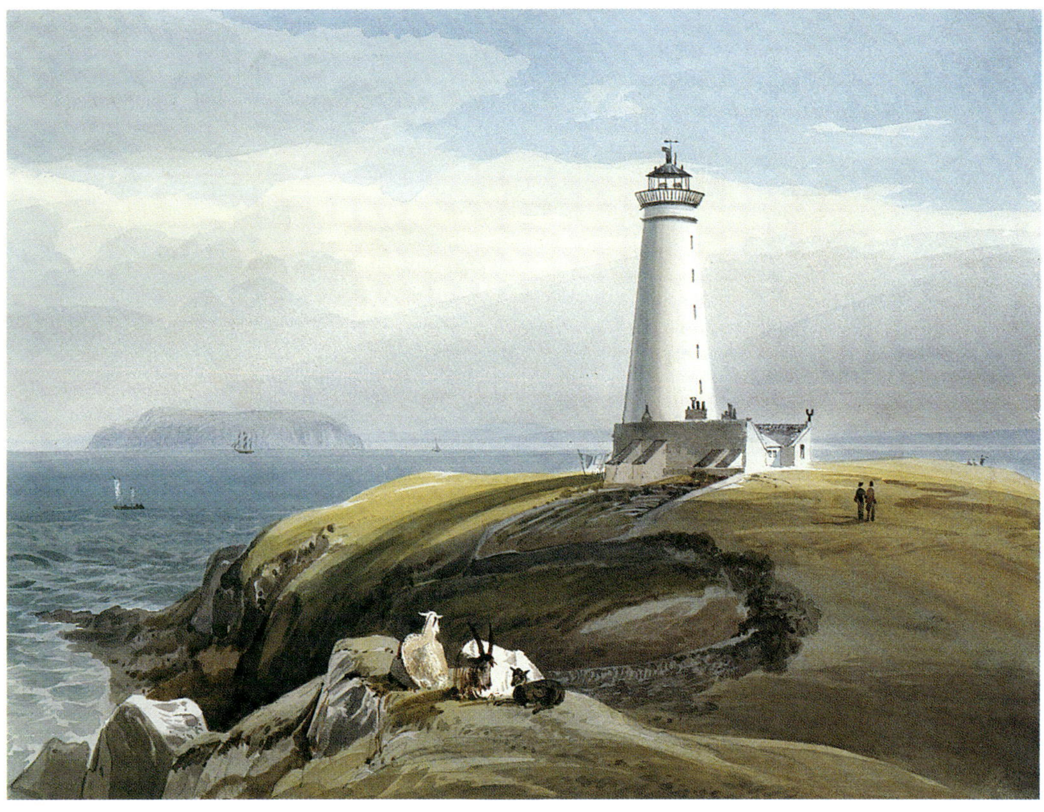

67   Hugh O'Neill 1784-1824
St Augustine's Back from Broad Quay   1824
Watercolour   225 x 185 mm   Bristol Museums and Art Gallery M2917

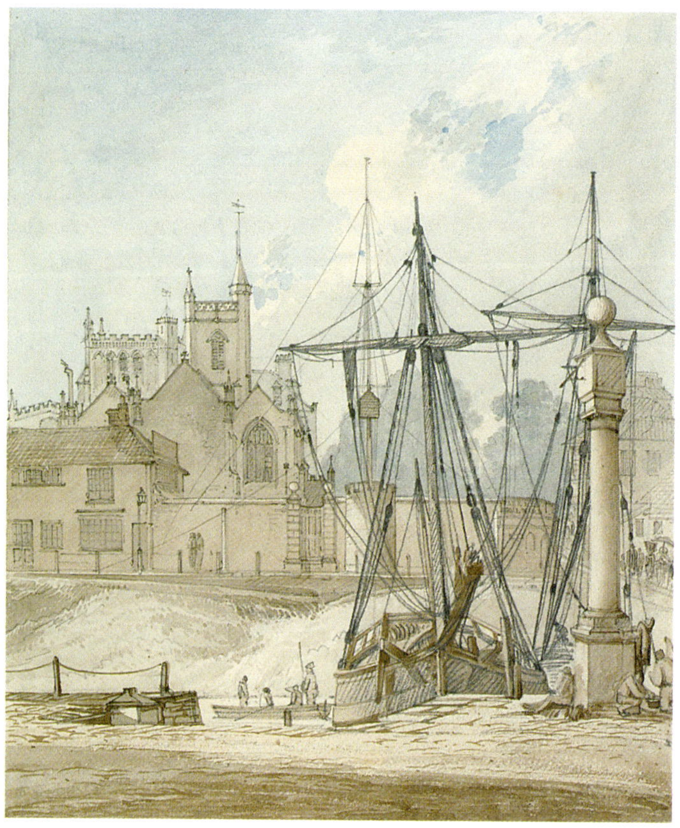

IN THE FOREGROUND IS THE DIAL, an elegant sundial erected very early in the eighteenth century on perhaps the busiest part of Broad Quay. It was not simply ornamental – knowing the time enabled one to anticipate the tide, an especially important consideration in Bristol. There was also strict control of the times at which vessels could discharge their cargoes. An Act of 1559, promulgated in order to contain smuggling, ordered that no vessel was to unload during the hours of darkness. On the grounds of the unique problems created by the range of the tide in the harbour, Bristol quickly secured Letters Patent from the Queen permitting much wider unloading hours.

Across St Augustine's Reach is the church of St Augustine-the-Less, which was blitzed in the Second World War and was finally demolished in 1962. Behind is the tower of the Cathedral, which, as an abbey, had also been dedicated to St Augustine. Beside the entrance to the church's walled graveyard is a castellated tower supporting a tall and complicated signal-mast managed by the Quay Warden.

Hugh O'Neill spent the last four years of his life in Bristol working almost exclusively for the antiquarian collector, George Weare Braikenridge. Braikenridge was to imply that O'Neill's early death was hastened by 'his indolent and irregular habits', but his drawings are precise, patient and accurate. Born in London, he was the son of an architect and worked as a drawing master in Oxford and Edinburgh. He was in Bath from 1813 to 1820, when he moved to Bristol.

68 Hugh O'Neill 1784-1824
St Augustine's Parade from Broad Quay   1824
Watercolour   195 x 165 mm   Bristol Museums and Art Gallery M2918

THE SCENE IS ALMOST A CONTINUATION OF THE VIEW on the opposite page. O'Neill has moved just twenty yards or so along Broad Quay. In the distance is the tower of the Mayor's Chapel on College Green, but it is, once again, the detailed account of the quayside structures that is so fascinating.

G.W. Braikenridge, the collector of these drawings, catalogued the foreground buildings as 'the engine house and Water Bailiffs Office and a Watch House built of free stone and to the left a Landing Waiters moveable box'.

Water bailiffs are first recorded in the thirteenth century and they were originally much concerned with customs duty. By the time of this drawing the Water Bailiff's responsibilities were similar to those of the Quay Warden, but were concerned with Bristol and Redcliffe Backs and the banks of the Avon rather than the main quays. Braikenridge may have understandably confused the offices. It is the Quay Warden's name that is over the right-hand door. This post had been established in 1700 when his responsibilities included controlling the mooring of ships and the enforcement of the specified times for loading and unloading cargo as well as the stringent fire regulations.

A landing waiter was a customs official, who oversaw the landing of goods. His box, on the left, was presumably to protect him from the elements and perhaps also from the deliberately careless movement of goods, for he is unlikely to have been a very popular official.

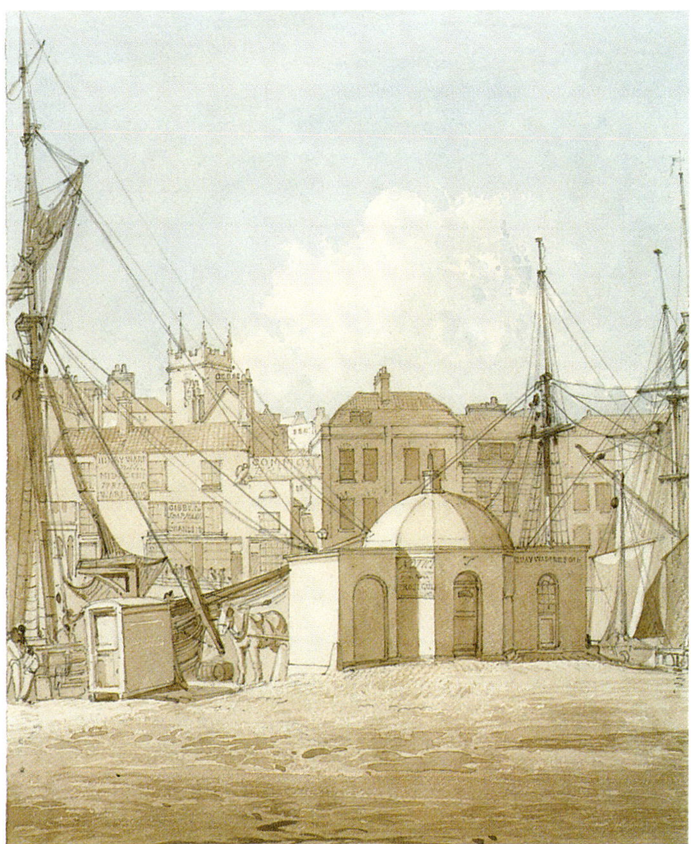

69 Thomas Leeson Rowbotham 1782-1853
St Augustine's Reach from the Stone Bridge   April 1826
Watercolour   183 x 260 mm   Bristol Museums and Art Gallery M2922

THE TWO FIGURES ON THE STONE BRIDGE at the Quay Head look south down St Augustine's Reach towards St Stephen's, St Augustine-the-Less and the Cathedral. They are at the highest navigable point on the Frome, which had been so greatly widenened and deepened in the mid-thirteenth century. It was from the centre of this view that the new half-mile channel for the Frome was dug out so that it no longer ran into the Avon by Bristol Bridge but by today's Arnolfini.

In front of St Stephen's are the tontine warehouses. In 1785 in order to complete the unfinished warehouses, 195 people invested money on the tontine principle. After a specified period of time the proceeds would be divided amongst the investors. Alternatively, the last speculator left alive became the sole owner of the property.

This section of the Frome up to St Augustine's Bridge in the centre of the view was to be filled in and culverted in the 1890s for the Tramways Centre.

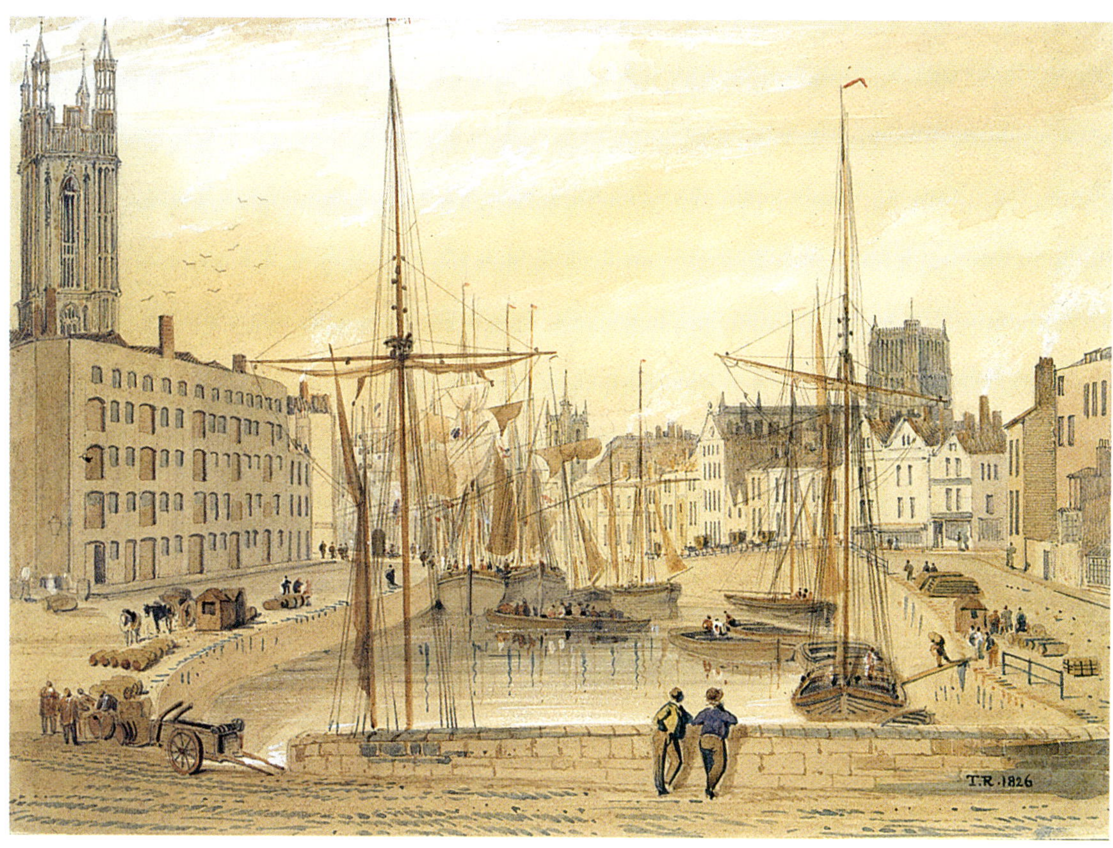

70 Thomas Leeson Rowbotham 1782-1853
Cleaning the Floating Harbour   April 1828
Watercolour   180 x 230 mm   Bristol Museums and Art Gallery M2915

SOON AFTER THE COMPLETION OF THE FLOATING HARBOUR in 1809, it was found to be prone to silting up. One partial solution was to open the lock gates at both Cumberland and Bathurst Basins, draining the harbour into the Avon and the New Cut. By carefully placing a vessel across the Frome, as we see here, a hundred or so men could shovel the mud from the sides into the path of the remaining flow. The problem was to be more successfully alleviated by Brunel in the 1830s (92).

In the distance is St Michael-on-the-Hill rising above the Great House, then home to Colston's School and now the site of Colston Hall. This final section of the Frome was to be covered over in the late 1930s.

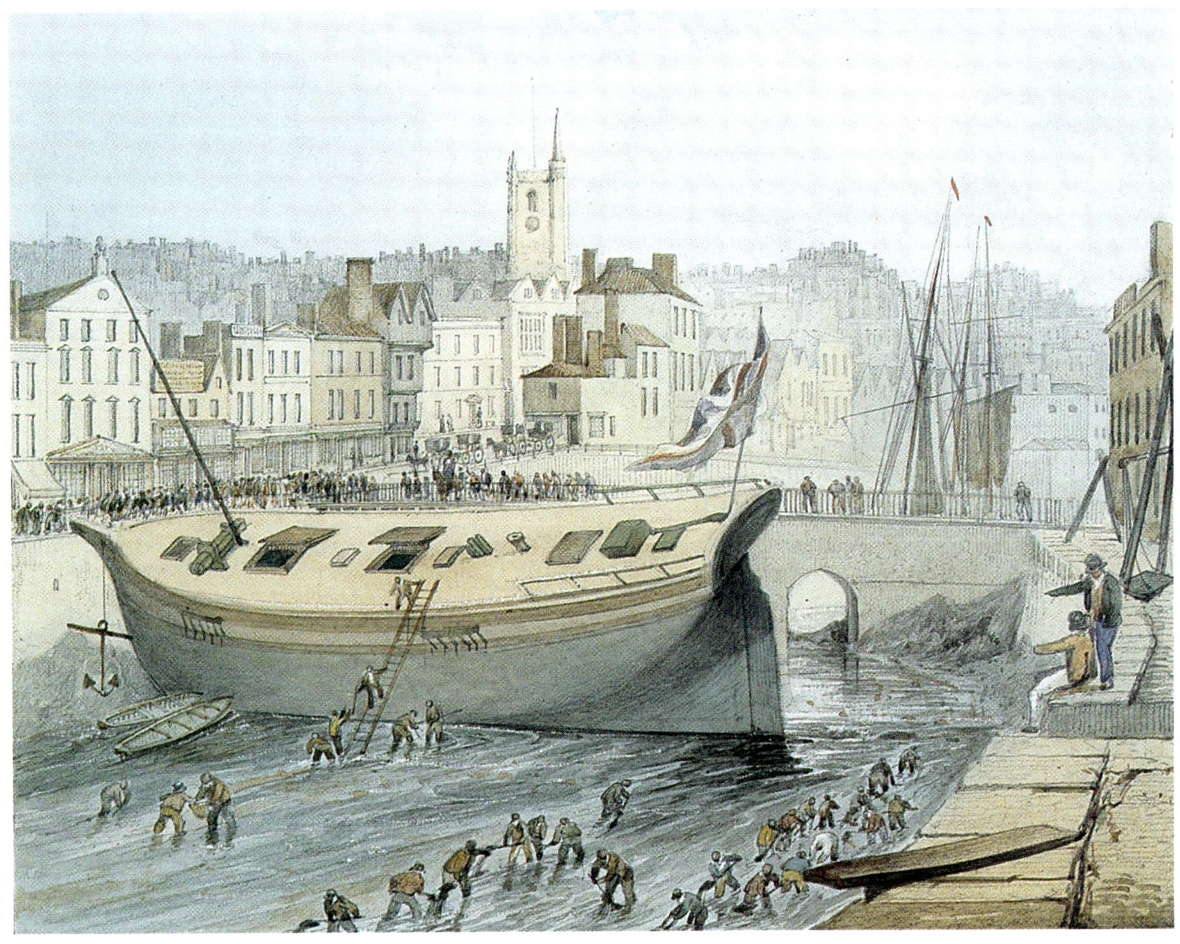

71 Thomas Leeson Rowbotham 1782-1853
Prince Street Bridge July 1828
Watercolour 180 x 230 mm Bristol Museums and Art Gallery M2926

THE ELEGANT TOLLHOUSE'S SORRY TILT was the result of tunnelling deep below it. Since the completion of the Floating Harbour in 1809, pollution became an even greater problem. During the hot summer of 1825 sewage had caused the Frome at St Augustine's Reach to stink intolerably. The bishop was forced to flee from his palace on College Green. The Dock Company was taken to court and obliged to act. A culvert was dug from near the head of the harbour at the Stone Bridge to take the polluted waters of the Frome. This covered channel passed beneath Broad Quay and Narrow Quay before crossing under the harbour, below Prince Street Bridge, and depositing the effluent in the New Cut, where the tide was meant to flush it away.

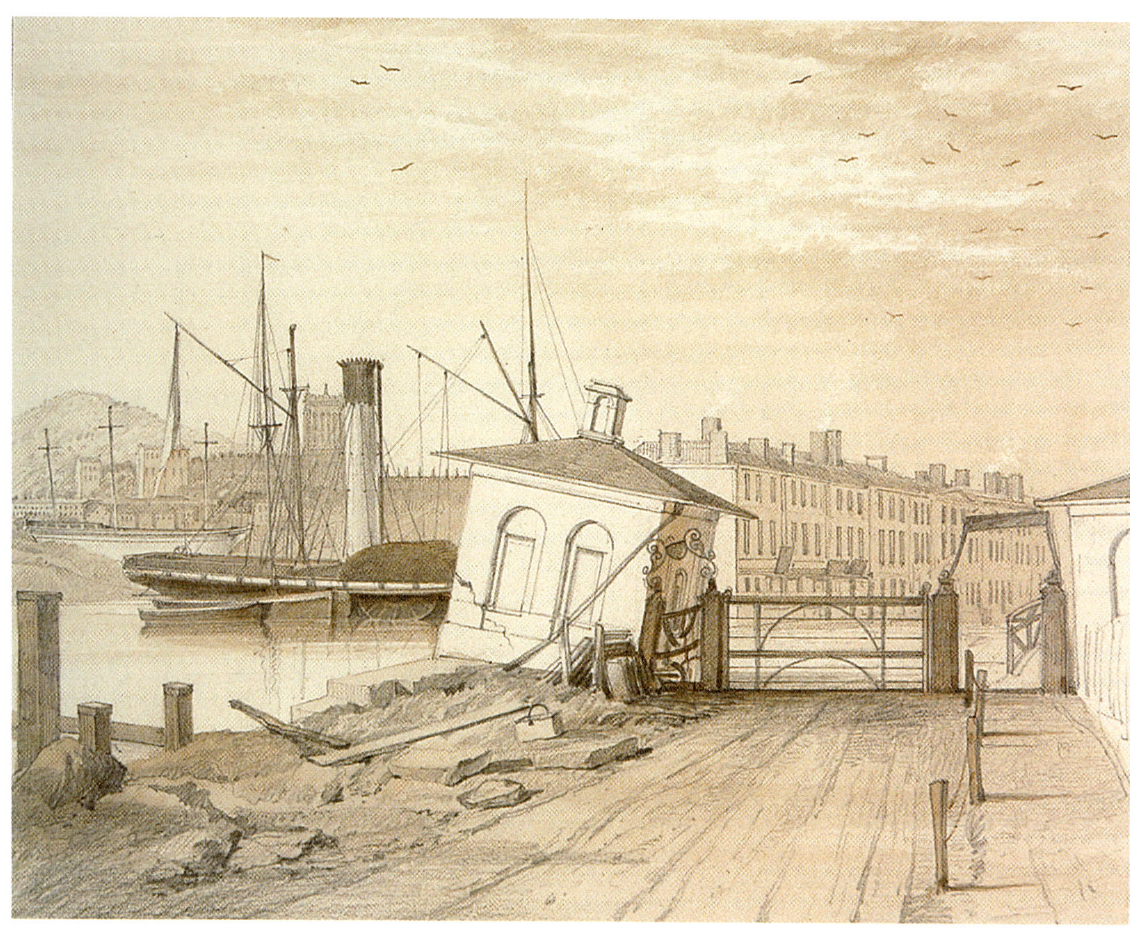

72 Thomas Leeson Rowbotham 1782-1853
The Floating Harbour with Redcliffe Back Ferry   1826
Watercolour   255 x 305 mm   Bristol Museums and Art Gallery K2224

THE TOWERS OF ALL SAINTS', Christ Church, St Nicholas' and St Mary-le-Port catch the evening sun. Coastal traders, many bringing vegetables and fish and fowl for the markets, crowd Welsh Back. A gentleman stands confidently in the ferry on his stately passage from Redcliffe Back towards Queen Square.

Today's Redcliffe Bridge would be behind the viewer, but it was not to be built until 1939. From this modern bridge, Rowbotham's view remains surprisingly intact and the concen-tration of church towers still triumphantly marks the medieval heart of Britain's second city.

In the 1820s only Bristol Bridge, which is obscured by trading vessels in this watercolour, and Prince Street Bridge crossed the Floating Harbour. Within the harbour, the three main ferries were of vital importance. The other two were The Grove Ferry from Guinea Street to The Grove and the Temple Back Ferry to Passage Street.

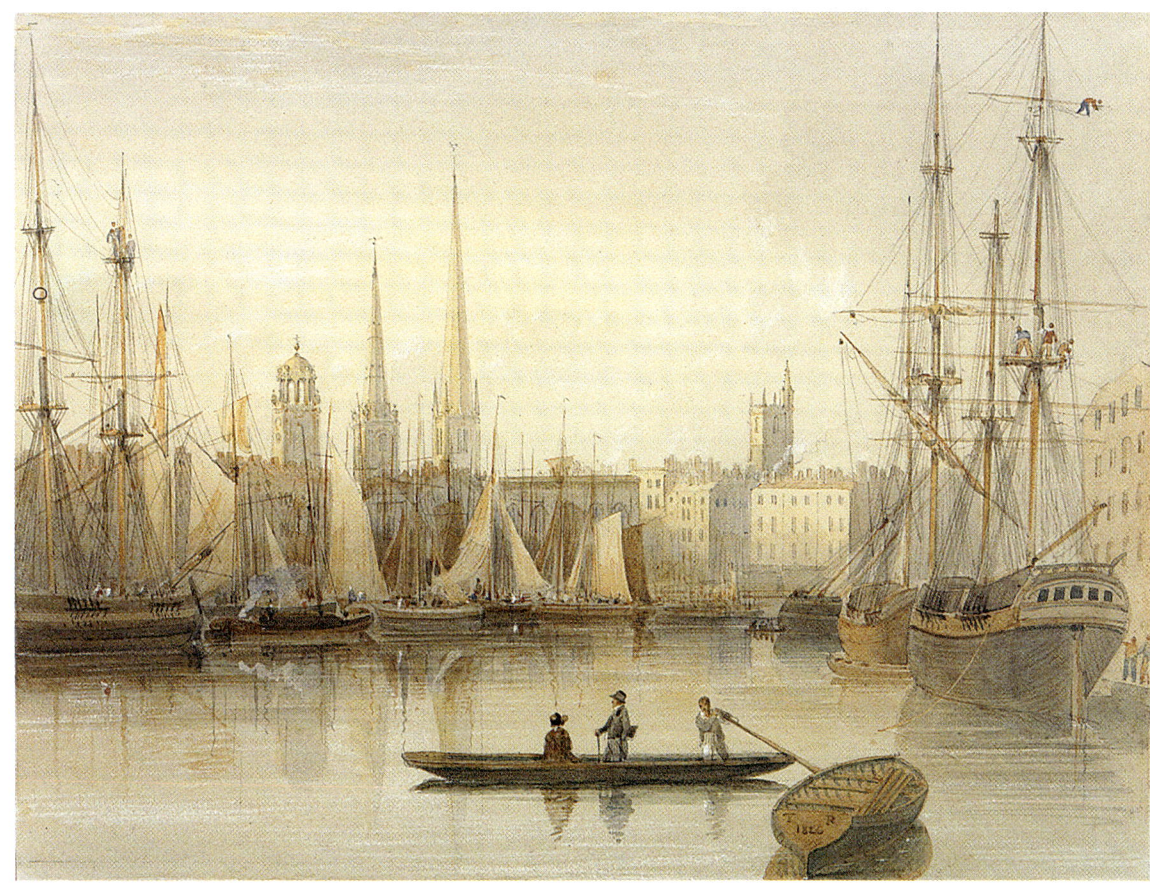

73 Thomas Leeson Rowbotham 1782-1853
Eastern Wapping Dock 2 March 1826
Watercolour 180 x 235 mm Bristol Museums and Art Gallery M2952

THE BARQUE *AVON* IS ABOUT TO BE LAUNCHED. The collector G.W. Braikenridge, owner of all the watercolours by Rowbotham illustrated here, recorded in his catalogue that the *Avon* had been built for the Bristol merchants Gibbs, Son & Bright for trading to the Black River in Jamaica. Logwood, whose red dye was vital to the textile trade, was probably to be the main cargo.

The builder of the *Avon* was William Scott. It was his assistant, William Patterson, who took over the business when Scott went bankrupt, and who was selected in 1836 to build Brunel's *Great Western* in this dockyard. The paddle shaft was to be forged at Acraman's iron works. Their chimney on the far side of Bathurst Basin can be seen on the far left. St Augustine's Reach, which was to be so important to the launching of the *Great Western*, then the longest ship in the world, is behind the viewer.

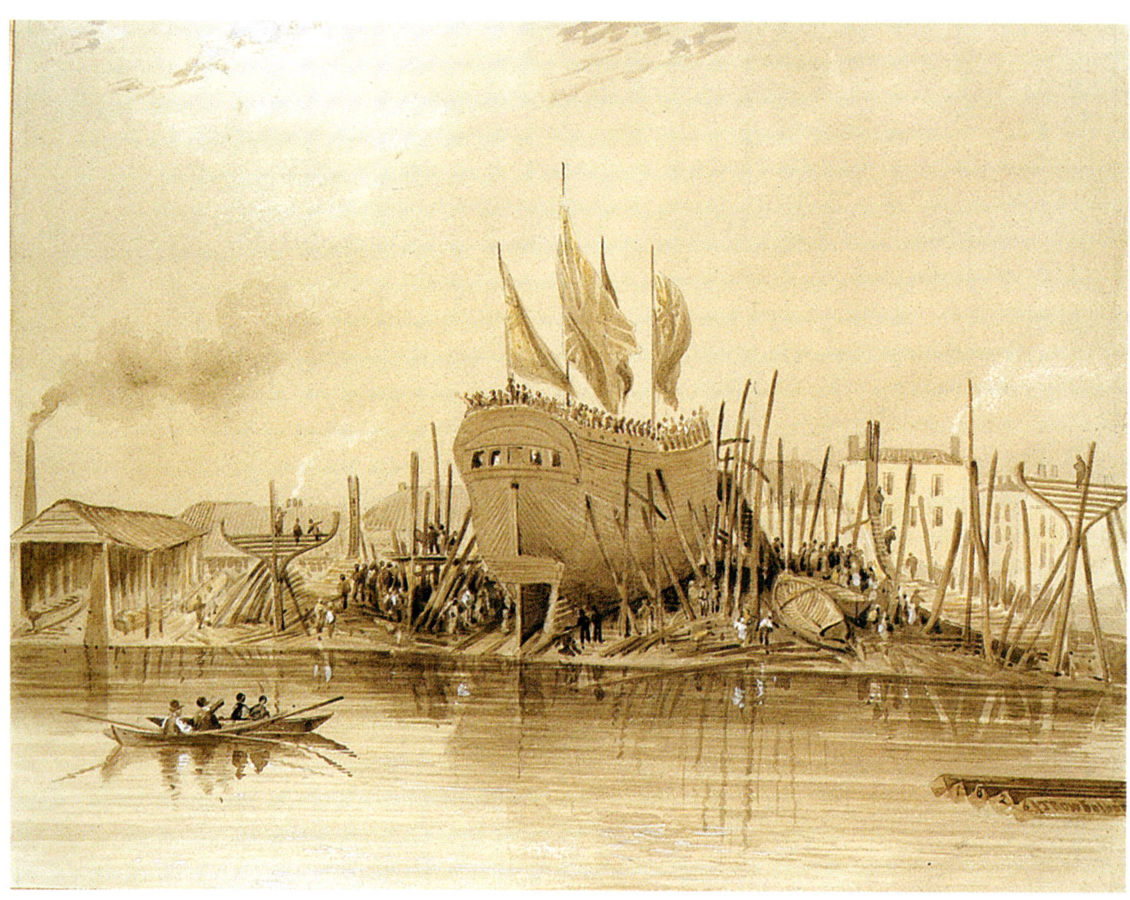

74 Thomas Leeson Rowbotham 1782-1853
Emerald Isle *being refitted near Merchants' Dock*   April 1826
Watercolour   180 x 260 mm   Bristol Museums and Art Gallery M2947

THE *EMERALD ISLE* was once the most powerful paddle steamer visiting Bristol. Built in Liverpool in 1823 with engines of 140-horse power, she was owned by the St George Steam Packet Company in 1827, when, together with the *St George* and the *St Patrick*, she provided a thrice-weekly passage to Dublin via Liverpool.

Rowbotham drew over 250 watercolours of Bristol for G.W. Braikenridge between 1825 and 1829. They cover almost every area of the city, but reveal a particular enthusiasm for the life of the harbour. Here he records his own delight in the sleek lines of this racy steam packet.

Rowbotham was born in Bath in 1782 and he is listed there in 1811 as a teacher of marine painting, cottage figures and landscapes. He later moved to Dublin but had settled in Bristol by 1825. By the mid-1830s, he had moved to London to teach at the Royal Naval School, New Cross. He died in Camberwell in 1853.

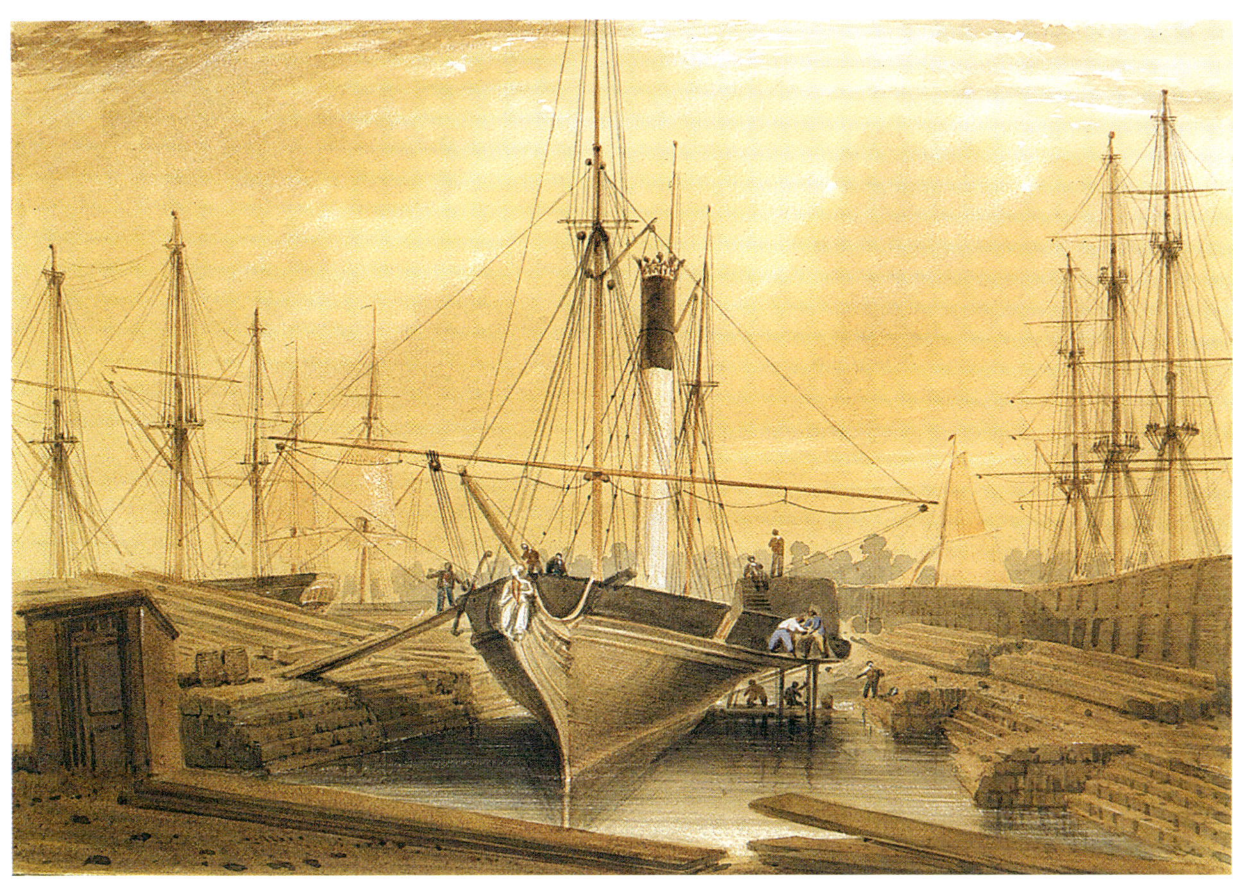

BOTH THE STEAM PACKETS, the *George IV* and the *Saint George*, are in steam and flying the Blue Peter that announces their imminent departure.

The *George IV* was the first sea-going steam vessel to be built in Bristol. Of a modest 126 tons, she was built in George Hilhouse & Co's Wapping yard in 1822. This 'noble vessel… so calculated for the celerity and punctuality of her voyages', as the press reported in 1823, plied between Bristol and Cork via Ilfracombe between March and October.

The *Saint George* of 183 tons had been launched in Liverpool in 1822, the year in which she initiated the Bristol to Dublin route. This steam packet was wrecked in a gale off Douglas, Isle of Man, in 1830. Every life was saved in a heroic rescue in a new and untested lifeboat. The rescue was led by Sir William Hillary Bt., who, six years earlier, had almost single-handedly founded the lifeboat service that was later to become the Royal National Lifeboat Institution.

An equally heroic rescue had already saved the *Earl of Liverpool*, which is moored near the right-hand lock. This merchantman, built in Bristol in 1823 by James Tippett, was homeward bound from New York in a gale, when the last mast was lost close to the rocks near Minehead. It was the *George IV* that saved her and the crew. At enormous risk, the steamer's mate put out a boat and reached the *Earl of Liverpool*. Spars and rigging were cut away and ropes passed between the vessels and the stricken ship was towed to the safety of Penarth Roads.

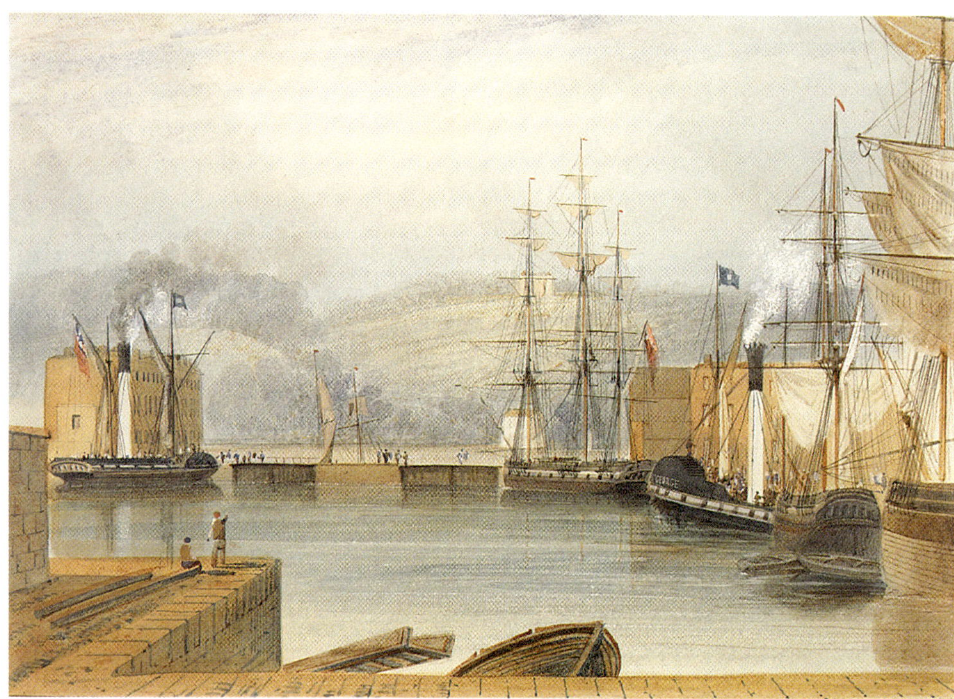

76 Thomas Leeson Rowbotham 1782-1853
Mr Courtney's flight across the Avon Gorge   1826
Watercolour   180 x 240 mm   Bristol Museums and Art Gallery Mb3

ON 22 MAY 1826, Mr Courtney, an American, took a 'flying leap' from the top of St Vincent's Rocks, above the Giant's Cave. The local newspaper, *Felix Farley's Bristol Journal*, reported:

> …the scene presented one of the gayest pictures we ever beheld, the stupendous rocks were covered with gazing multitudes, whose varied dresses formed a striking contrast to the barren stone…at about half past 5, the men were seen tightening the rope, and in a few minutes the adventurous Icarus emerged. He appeared suspended below the rope, in a horizontal position, waving a flag in each hand to represent wings, his descent was most rapid, not consuming more than eight to ten seconds…the immense multitude cheered the hero with loud and simultaneous huzzas…

However, another report tells us that 'owing to some mismanagement he struck his head violently as he came down, and was conveyed to the Infirmary in a state of insensibility'.

Undeterred, Mr Courtney tried again a month later. This time the Merchant Venturers informed him that he could not erect his apparatus on their property. He put his own person in great danger, had been intoxicated on two previous occasions and such an event had 'a powerful tendency to demoralize the lower orders by promoting habits of idleness and Intemperance.' Almost as pompously, John Taylor's *Guide to Clifton* recorded in 1868 that the American was still living locally, but 'in the vale of life and in the depths of poverty.'

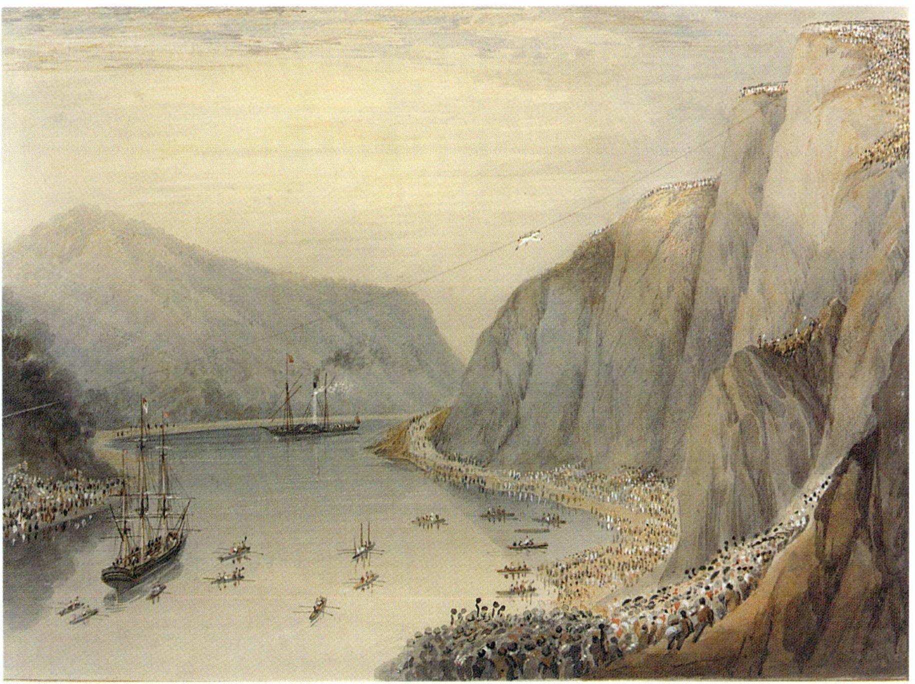

The Avon Gorge from the summit of the Observatory 1834
Oil 690 x 920 mm Bristol Museums and Art Gallery K8

WHEN WILLIAM WEST SHOWED THIS PAINTING at the third Bristol Society of Artists exhibition in 1834, he proudly titled it *From the Summit of the Observatory, Clifton*. It was his very own viewpoint, one that he had, himself, created.

The Observatory had started as a corn mill, erected with the permission of the Merchant Venturers in 1766. It may subsequently have become a snuff mill, until 1777, when, over-driven in a gale, the pivots caught fire and it was burnt out. The windmill became a picturesque ruin and then in 1826 a tool shed for the Committee for the Preservation of the Downs and a shelter at night for the beadle.

In 1828 the Merchant Venturers granted William West a five-year lease to turn the mill into an observatory. By October of that year he had erected a telescope on the tower, which he later replaced with a camera obscura. A successor to that instrument remains in situ today. In 1834 a new twenty-one year lease allowed West to extend the building substantially, including the large circular room to house a revolving telescope, complete with a rotating dome.

William West's scientific interests overshadowed his art. To Brunel's frustration, he took a lively interest in the Clifton Suspension Bridge, visiting Fribourg to examine the new bridge there and advocating, in 1834, a cheaper system of wire cables, which Brunel patiently refuted. In 1839 he was selling 'superior photogenic paper' and displaying 'Various kinds of photogenic drawing' at the Observatory.

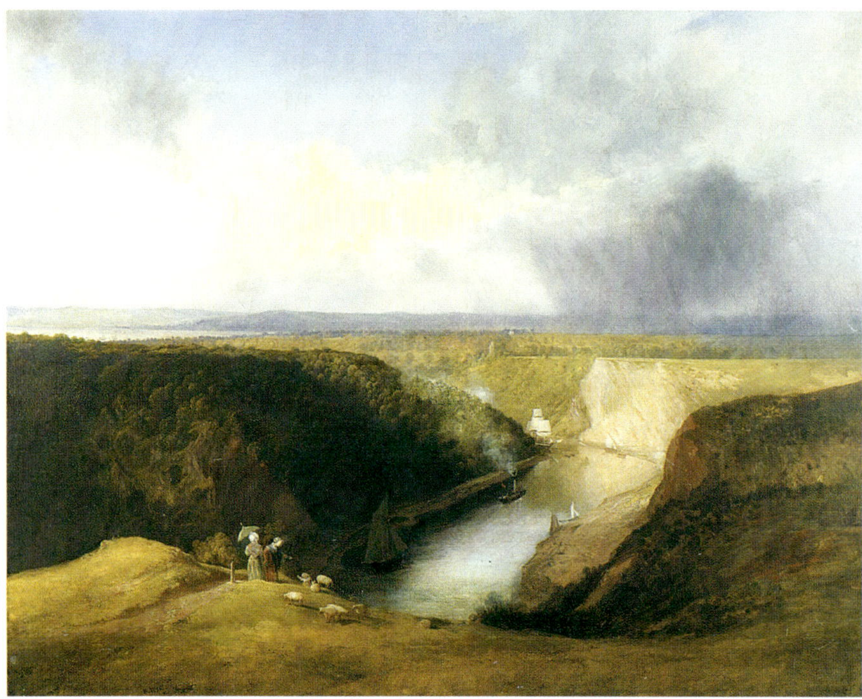

78 Edmund Gustavus Müller 1816-1888
View from the Giant's Cave 1837
Watercolour 188 x 278 mm Bristol Museums and Art Gallery M993

IN THE COURSE OF EXCAVATIONS for the extensions to the Observatory, William West conceived the idea of digging a tunnel that would connect with the Giant's Cave. Two years later, on 4 July 1837, he announced the opening of the 200 feet long passage. This watercolour was executed in the summer of that year and the artist, E. G. Müller, William James Müller's younger brother, must have been one of the earliest visitors.

Today, standing back within the cave and recreating the artist's viewpoint, one finds that the view of Leigh Woods has hardly changed at all. For this we are mostly indebted to George Alfred Wills, who purchased Nightingale Valley and part of Leigh Woods and presented the land to the National Trust in 1909.

Before William West's day Romano-British pottery is said to have been found within the cave, together with ecclesiastical fragments that suggest that the cave was associated with the nearby Chapel of St Vincent, which survived into the seventeenth century, but of which no trace now remains.

In 1977 the Merchant Venturers sold the Observatory, but bound future owners to maintain public access to the camera obscura, which the Society still owns.

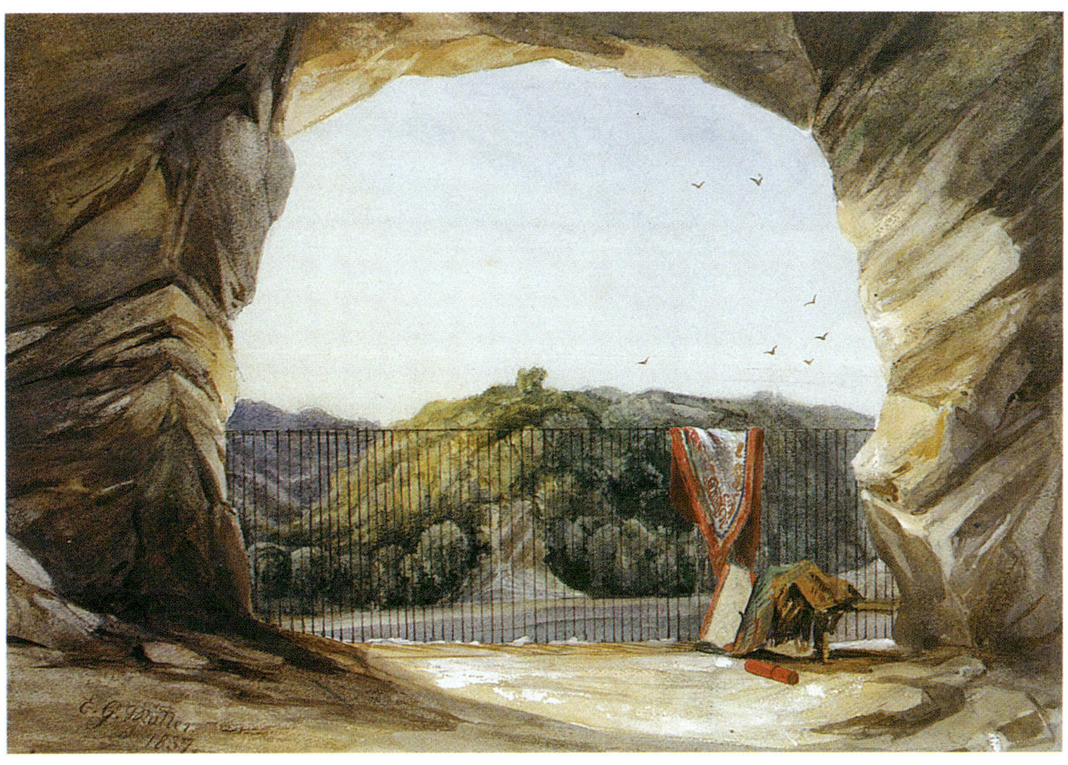

79 Rolinda Sharples 1793-1838
Rownham Ferry 1820-22
Oil approx. 870 x 1200 mm Whereabouts unknown

ROWNHAM FERRY WAS NOT ALWAYS AS BUSY. Rolinda Sharples must have been depicting it on a sunny Sunday afternoon, when so many flocked to the tea gardens of Long Ashton, then famous for strawberries and cream.

Rolinda Sharples may have deliberately placed the sailing vessel in the centre of the painting in order to obscure the rebuilding of the Hotwell House at this time, 1821-2. St Vincent's Parade is carefully depicted and above are St Vincent's Rocks and the end of Windsor Terrace.

Rownham Ferry was exhibited at the Royal Academy in 1822, where it was a considerable success. Full of incident and observation – perhaps overfull – it incorporates innumerable portraits of Rolinda Sharples' friends. She was the daughter of a professional artist, but she lived a thoroughly conventional middle-class life in Clifton with surprisingly little contact with her fellow Bristol artists. She died of cancer in 1838. Her mother, Ellen Sharples, later left a large sum of money as well as her own pictures, her husband's portraits and all Rolinda's paintings to the future Royal West of England Academy, which, in effect, her bequest founded.

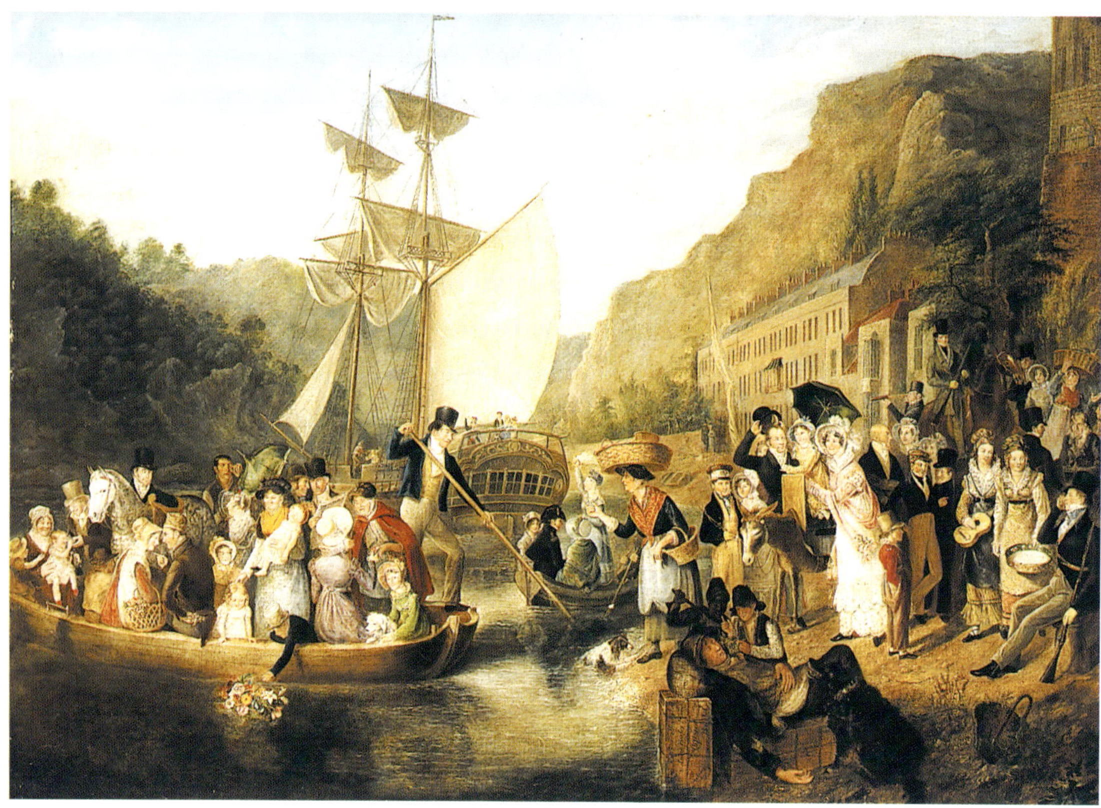

80 Rolinda Sharples 1793-1838
The Clifton Race-Course (detail) 1829-36
Oil 1105 x 1575 mm Bristol Museums and Art Gallery K1073

ROLINDA SHARPLES BEGAN THIS AMBITIOUS WORK in 1829. Her diaries record her visits to Ashton Court to paint Sir John Smyth's coach and four, which features so prominently on the left. 'Sir John was very polite…invited every day to lunch, partridges, pine apples, hot house grapes and other luxuries.'

In the summer of 1831 she mentions the completion of the ash tree, which she included for compositional reasons. The Downs were still almost treeless at this time and it was based upon the ash tree outside her window at 2 Lower Harley Place, Clifton. Progress was then delayed by the Bristol Riots in October and by her subsequent work on *The Trial of Colonel Brereton.*

The Clifton Race-Course and its multitude of figures was not completed until 1836, just two years before the races were held for the last time.

Despite the reputation of the fine turf of the Downs, serious horse racing would have been complicated by the thinness of the soil above the limestone rock. However, it was probably the growth of Clifton and Redland that engineered the end of the races. As early as 1792, the residents of Redland had complained of the 'very great evils' resulting from horse racing and boxing matches.

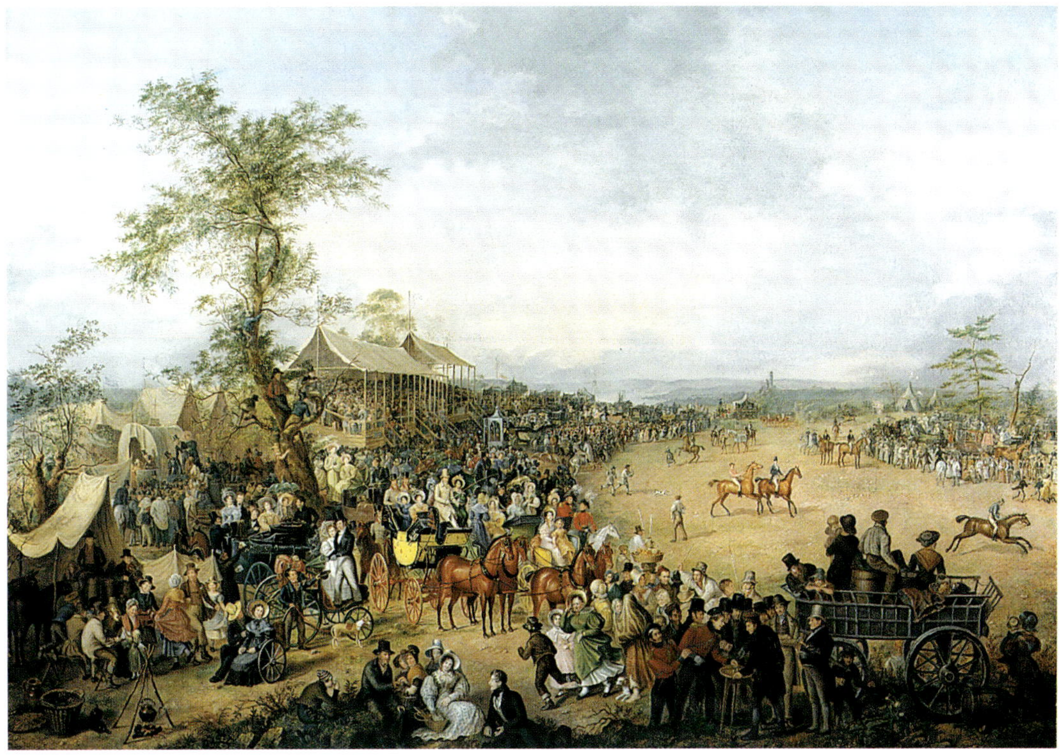

81 Samuel Jackson 1794-1869
The approved design for the Clifton Suspension Bridge   1831
Pen, ink and watercolour   636 x 1060 mm   Bristol Museums and Art Gallery K4077

THE FIRST COMPETITION FOR THE BRIDGE WAS HELD IN 1829. It was a fiasco. Thomas Telford, the distinguished but ageing engineer of the suspension bridge over the Menai Straits, rejected every submission and persuaded the committee to approve his own design for a bridge that was supported on gigantic Gothic towers rising from the muddy river banks. It was duly ridiculed. A second competition followed, which initially Brunel did not win. He finally overturned the committee's decision after what he rather defensively described as 'persevering struggles and some manoeuvres (all fair and honest however)'. He was not quite twenty-five years old.

Brunel had submitted three engineering solutions each differently clothed in so-called Saxon, Gothic or Egyptian styles of architecture. The final decision on the architecture was made after the engineering design had been selected. On 28 March 1831 Brunel wrote:

> Of all the wonderful feats I have performed…yesterday I performed the most wonderful. I produced unanimity amongst fifteen men who were actually quarrelling about the most ticklish subject – taste... The Egyptian thing I brought down was unanimously adopted.

The Bridge Committee was then quick to commission Samuel Jackson to produce this large and impressive watercolour, which was put on public display in the Commercial Rooms in Corn Street.

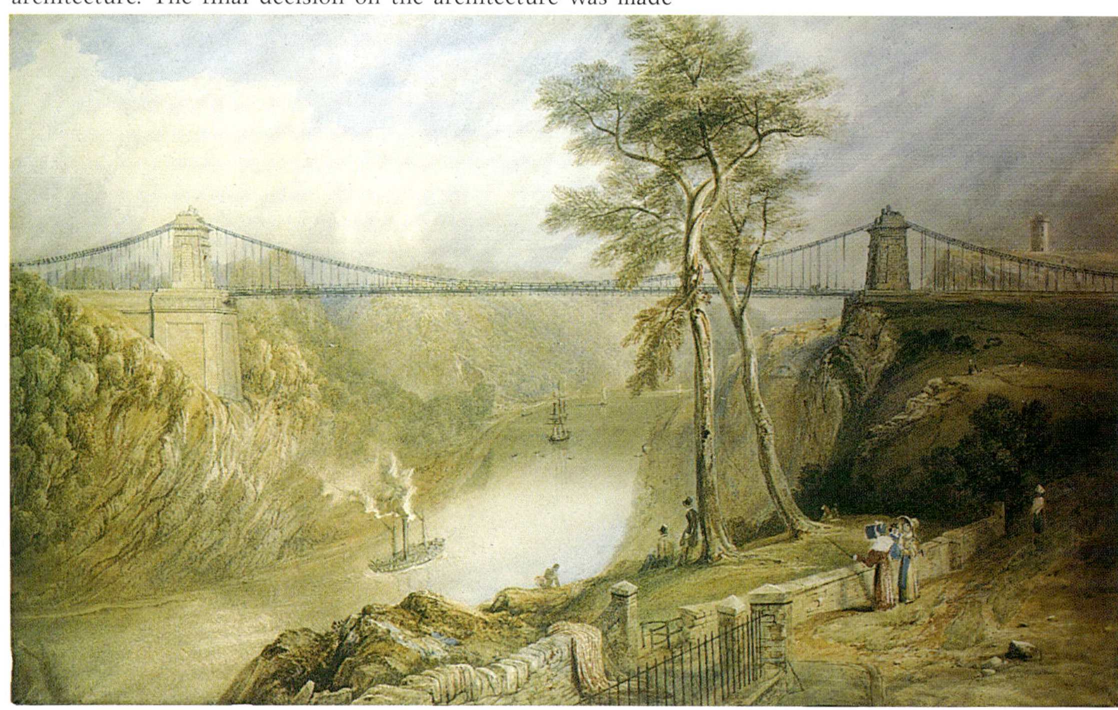

82 Samuel Jackson 1794-1869
The Leigh Woods gateway to the Clifton Suspension Bridge 1831
Pen and ink, watercolour and bodycolour approx. 300 x 500 mm Private collection

THE LARGER WATERCOLOUR, illustrated on the opposite page, shows the sphinxes facing inwards. Brunel must have realised almost immediately that it would be more appropriate to be greeted by the heads rather than the tails of these mythical beasts. So, here, the sphinxes now face us as we approach the bridge from Leigh Woods with Clifton in the distance.

The Bridge Committee described the architecture as being based on the 'beautiful designs found in the ruins of Tentyra' (Dendera in Egypt). The Egyptian style was still a relatively novel fashion in England, but it was associated with monumental and romantic grandeur and seemingly ideally suited to such a bold engineering project in such a spectacular situation.

Brunel's ornamental towers were to be encased with cast-iron plaques depicting the history and construction of the bridge. Every part of the process of the making of iron was to be described, reflecting Brunel's early acknowledgement that iron was at the very core of the industrial revolution and of almost every one of his own advances in engineering.

A Bridge Committee ledger records payment to 'Pugin' for architectural drawings in June 1831. This is very likely to be for the pen and ink architectural details in both of these watercolours and for the smaller figures in this one. Augustus Charles Pugin was to die in 1832, but it is more likely to be his work than that of his son, Augustus Welby Northmore Pugin, the great architect of the Gothic Revival.

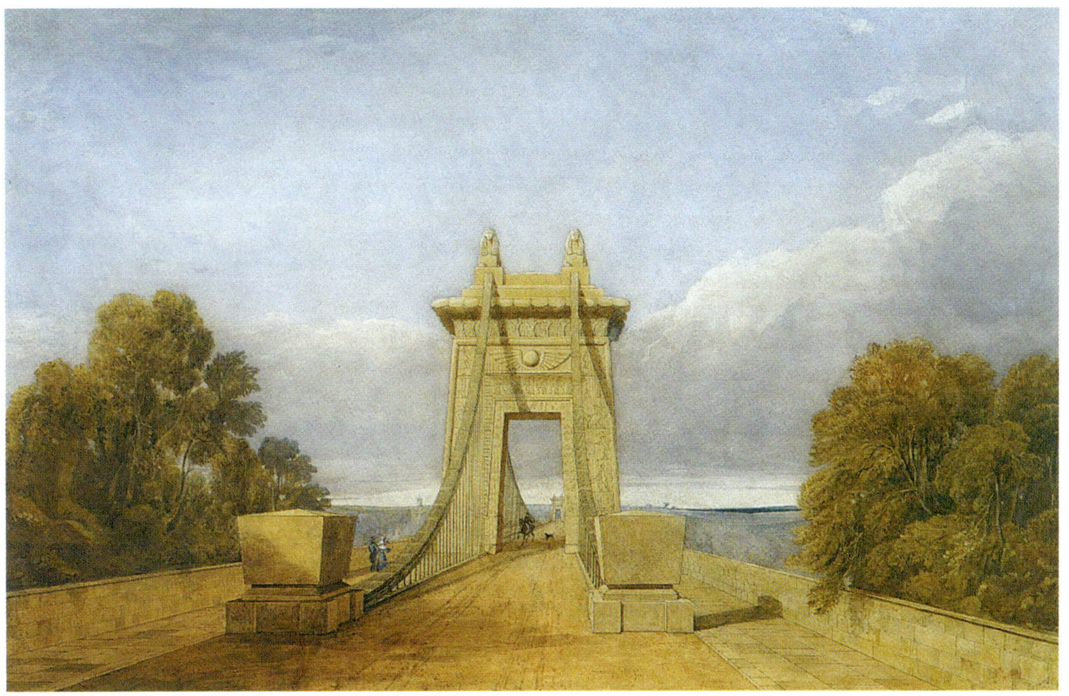

83 Samuel Colman 1780-1845
Laying the foundation stone of the Clifton Suspension Bridge   1837
Oil   869 x 1295 mm   Bristol Museums and Art Gallery K874

THERE HAD BEEN A CEREMONY IN JUNE 1831 to mark the hewing of the first stone. Sir Arthur Elton made a stirring speech, cannons were fired and the band of the 3rd Dragoon Guards played 'God save the King'. Ironically it was the same troop that cleared Queen Square four months later, bringing the Bristol Riots to an end. It was those devastating riots that brought all work on the bridge to a halt for five years.

After that first ceremony there were complaints that the public had not been given proper notice of the occasion. Samuel Colman's painting confirms that there was a vast audience five years later, when the Marquis of Northampton laid the foundation stone of the abutment on the Leigh Woods side at 7.00 am on 27 August 1836. Newspaper accounts make it very clear that the artist was not exaggerating the public's enthusiasm. The balloons, three green ones painted as globes and two larger white ones were released to great effect by the pupils of George Pocock's school.

Samuel Colman had come to Bristol from Somerset in 1816. Although he was to be influenced by the narrative paintings of Edward Bird and E. V. Rippingille and by the imaginary landscapes of Francis Danby, he seems to have had very little social contact with his fellow Bristol artists.

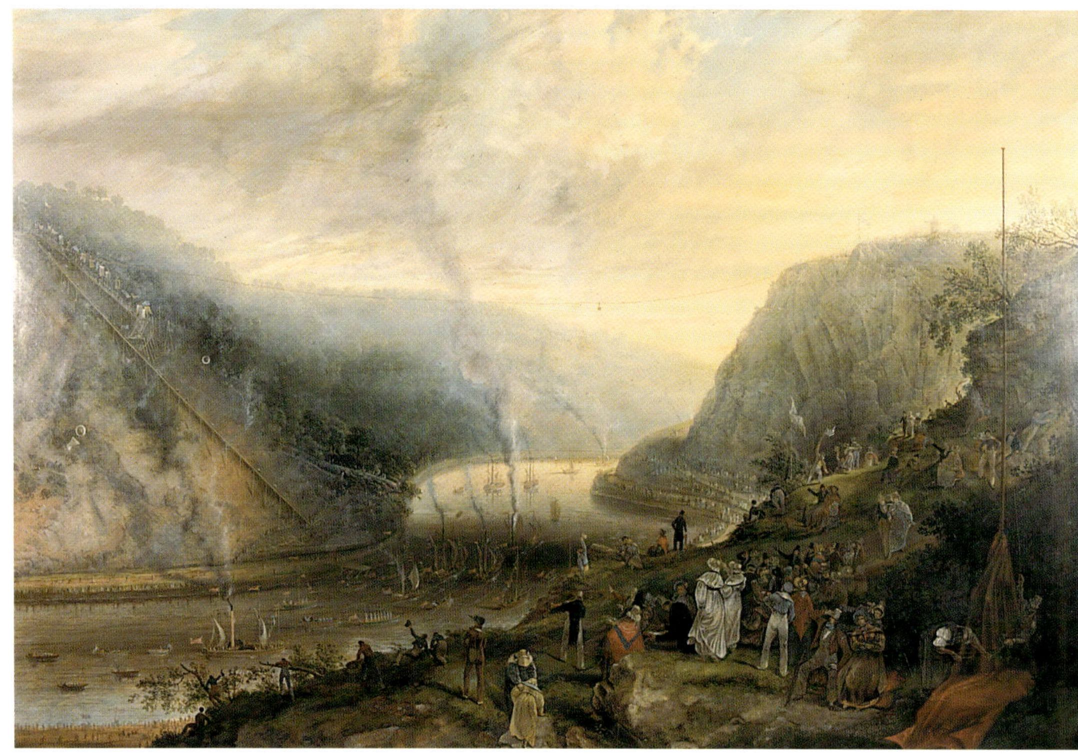

84 Samuel Jackson 1794-1869
The Avon at Hotwells c.1836
Oil 629 x 1016 mm Bristol Museums and Art Gallery K4

SAMUEL JACKSON WAS ONE OF SEVERAL ARTISTS who painted the finished Clifton Suspension Bridge long before its completion. The date of this work may be indicated by the presence of the extension on William West's Observatory, for which he obtained permission in 1834. Later on in the 1840s and 1850s, when funds were exhausted and there seemed little prospect of any further work, some artists omitted the gaunt unfinished piers, which so disfigured the gorge. It was Brunel's death in 1859 that finally inspired the completion of the bridge as a memorial to the great engineer and it opened in 1864, nearly thirty years after the probable date of Jackson's painting.

Jackson complements the modernity of the bridge with three paddle steamers. The steamer on the right is the little Chepstow steam packet *Wye* of 60 tons, which had been built in Bristol in 1826 by William Scott. This was the first steamship to be completely fitted out in Bristol, including locally made engines by John Winwood.

At the stern of the *Wye* is Rownham Ferry crowded with a coach and pair. On the right is a boatload of turtles and on the quayside a boy carries one on his head. Bristol was renowned, even notorious, for its turtles which were brought live from the West Indies. 'Too much in turtle Bristol's sons delight' wrote Lord Byron.

Samuel Jackson would have been familiar with this scene, for from 1832 to 1844 he lived at 3 and later at 8 Freeland Place, which runs up the hill just out of picture on the right.

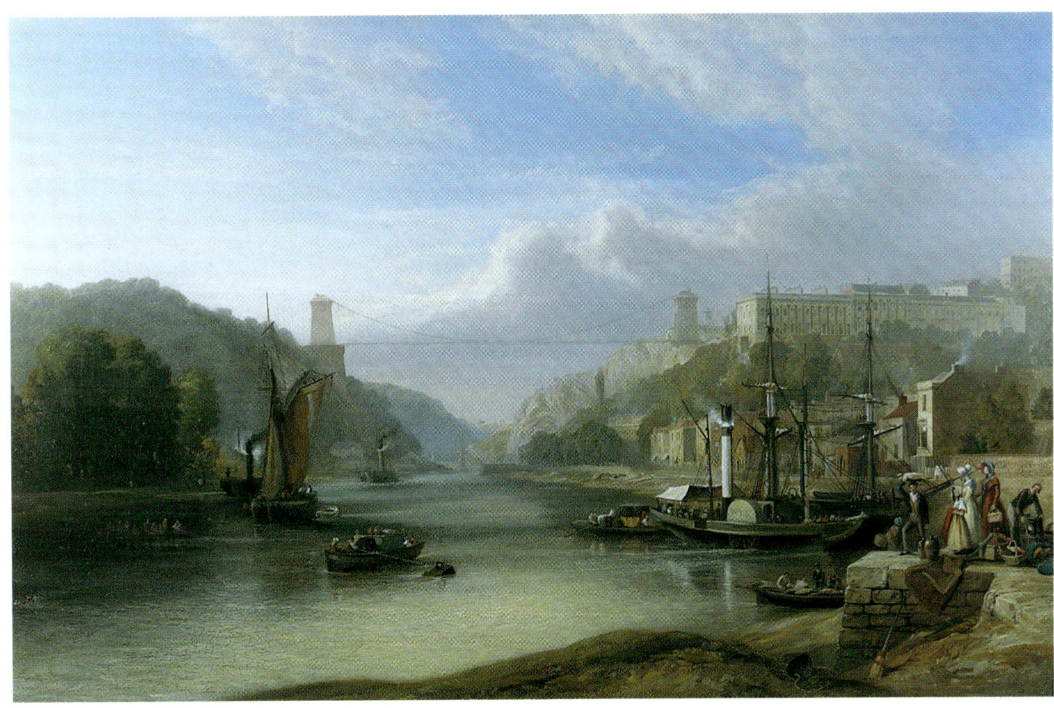

85 William James Müller 1812-1845
The Bristol Riots: the burning of the Bishop's Palace c.1831
Oil 125 x 229 mm   Bristol Museums and Art Gallery M4122

ISAMBARD KINGDOM BRUNEL himself was involved in the vain attempt to save the Bishop's Palace from the rioters on the night of Sunday 30 October, 1831. After the rioters had burnt Bristol's three prisons, they turned to the home of the bishop, who had voted against the Reform Bill earlier in the month in the House of Lords. The palace was initially defended with success, but the soldiers were called away to Queen Square where the Mansion House had been set on fire. The palace was soon ablaze and the magnificent library of three thousand books was destroyed.

Müller, who was only nineteen at the time, witnessed nearly all this destruction as it happened. His many watercolour, body-colour and oil sketches may form the most complete visual record of a national disaster before the advent of the camera. He not only illustrated the dreadful sequence of events, but also took full advantage of the pictorial possibilities of the riots. The low cloud of that wet October evening was illuminated by the fires and wherever possible Müller also used the river's reflections to enhance the dramatic effects.

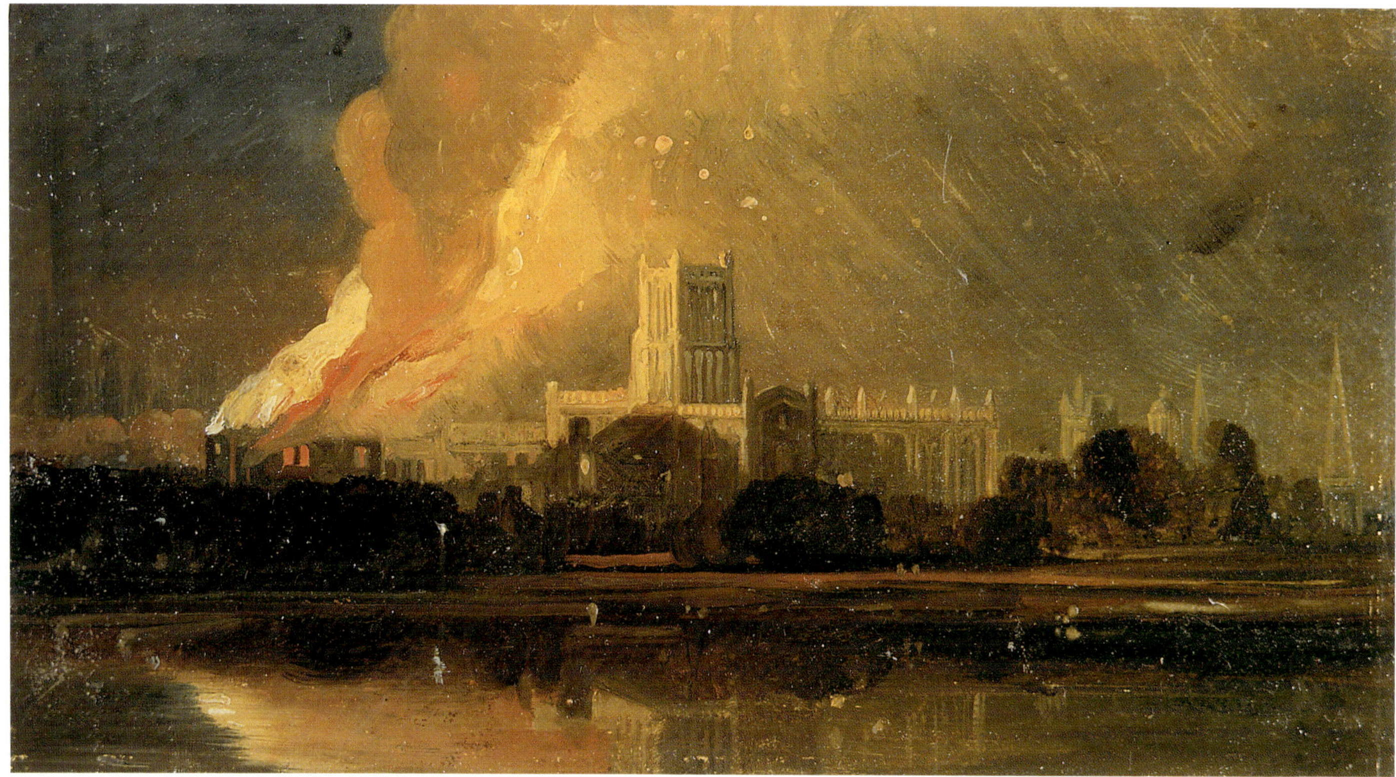

86 William James Müller   1812-1845
Bristol Cathedral from across the Floating Harbour   1835
Oil   752 x 1356 mm   Bristol Museums and Art Gallery K554

MÜLLER PAINTS HIS NATIVE CITY as if in the clear light and stillness of the Venetian Lagoon. He had returned in February 1835 from a seven-month tour in Europe with his friend George Arthur Fripp. They stayed for nearly two months in Venice.

The painting is dated 1835 and there is autumn colour in the trees matching the rich browns of the barges. Müller probably deliberately selected the modestly sized barges rather than the more likely and much larger merchantmen, in order to enhance the scale and presence of the cathedral. The viewpoint is the same as that in the very small oil painting opposite, but the river has been widened considerably. In both Müller reveals his immaculate sense of composition, cleverly reversing the simple diagonals that hold each picture together.

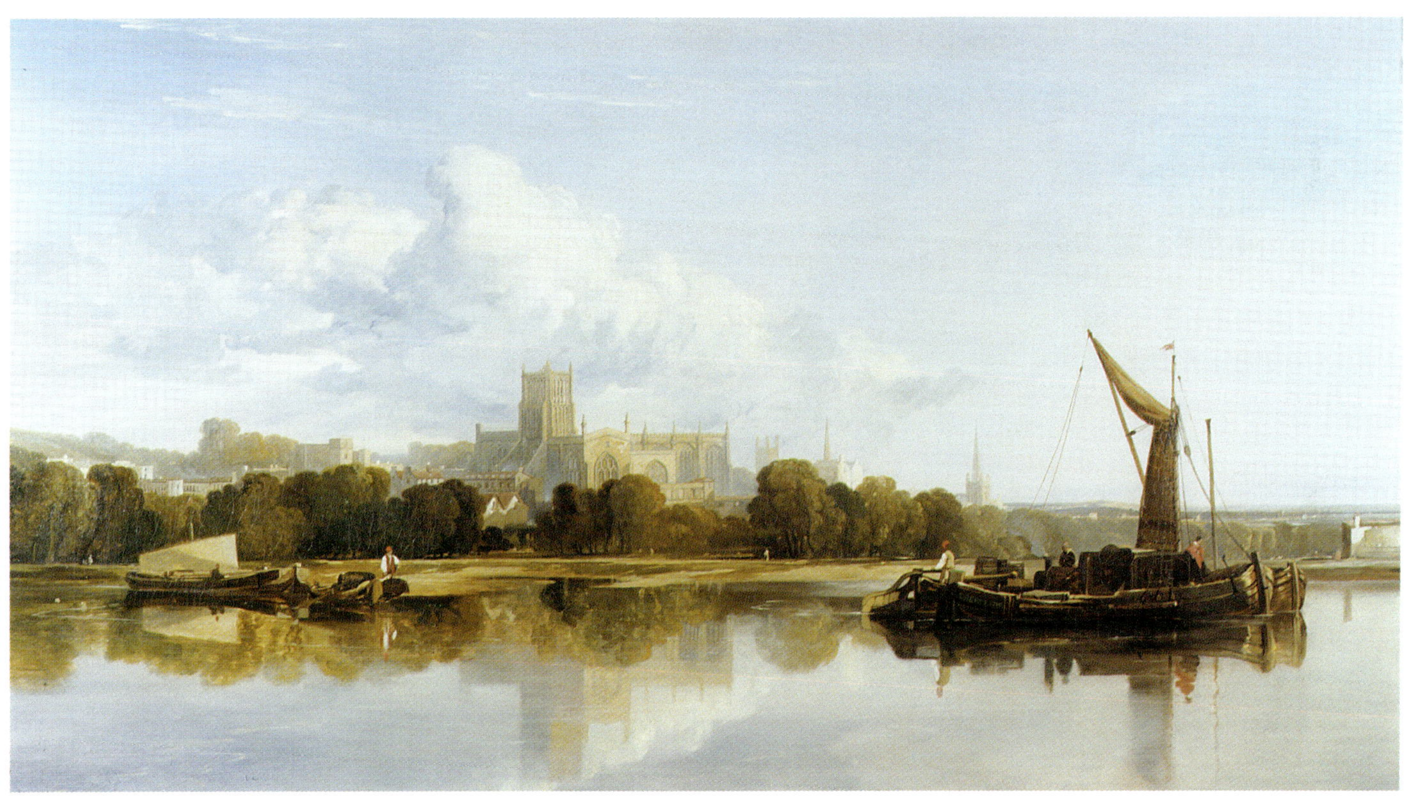

87 William James Müller 1812–1845

The Bristol Riots: the burning of the New Gaol with St Paul's Church, Bedminster c.1831
Watercolour and bodycolour 131 x 270 mm Bristol Museums and Art Gallery M4143

ACROSS THE NEW CUT, WHICH IS SEEN AT LOW TIDE, the burning gaol is reflected in the windows of the brand-new church of St Paul's, Bedminster. The Bishop of Bath and Wells, an opponent of the Reform Act, had just consecrated this church on 24 October 1831. He was mobbed and narrowly escaped injury. Cynical placards had earlier entreated the public to greet the bishop,

> with every demonstration of respect that becomes his *exalted* rank *and late vote in the House of Lords*. Refrain, therefore, from hooting, pelting, groaning, hissing, or any annoyance that may be offensive to the man who has so recently declared himself against the voice of the PEOPLE.

Six days later on Sunday evening there were said to be 15,000 people about the New Gaol. Using sledgehammers and crowbars taken from Acraman's iron works on Bathurst Basin, it took the rioters three-quarters of an hour to batter their way in, before releasing the prisoners and burning the governor's house and the treadmill.

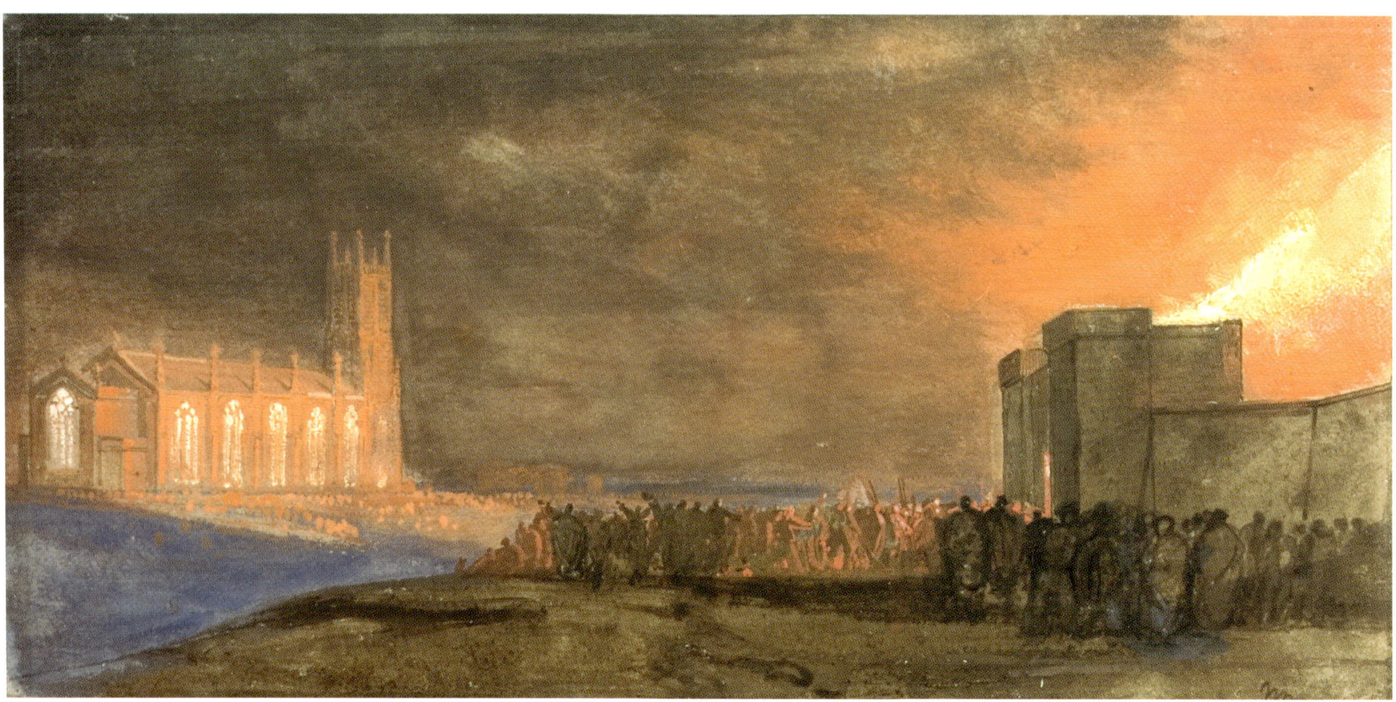

88 William James Müller   1812-1845
Bristol from Clifton Wood   1837
Oil   914 x 1727 mm   Bristol Museums and Art Gallery K1542

THIS IS THE MOST SUCCESSFUL of many large panoramic paintings of Bristol, and, for Müller, it is unusually fastidious in its topographical detail. The view stretches from the group of city churches on the far left to St Paul's, Bedminster, beyond the New Gaol on the far right. To the right of the Cathedral is the Limekiln Lane glasshouse with the domed gas holder of the Bristol and Clifton Oil Gas Company formed in 1823. Beyond is Bush House, which today houses Arnolfini. Above is St Mary Redcliffe. Even the tilt of Temple Church tower is carefully recorded.

By contrast, the lichen-covered oaks that grow from a sandy soil in the foreground owe more to the work of the Dutch seventeenth-century painter, Jacob Ruisdael, than to Clifton Wood. Although the steep eastern slopes of Clifton Wood were still largely undeveloped at this time, the foreground is a stage setting invented in the studio – a reflection of Müller's enthusiasm for art rather than for accuracy.

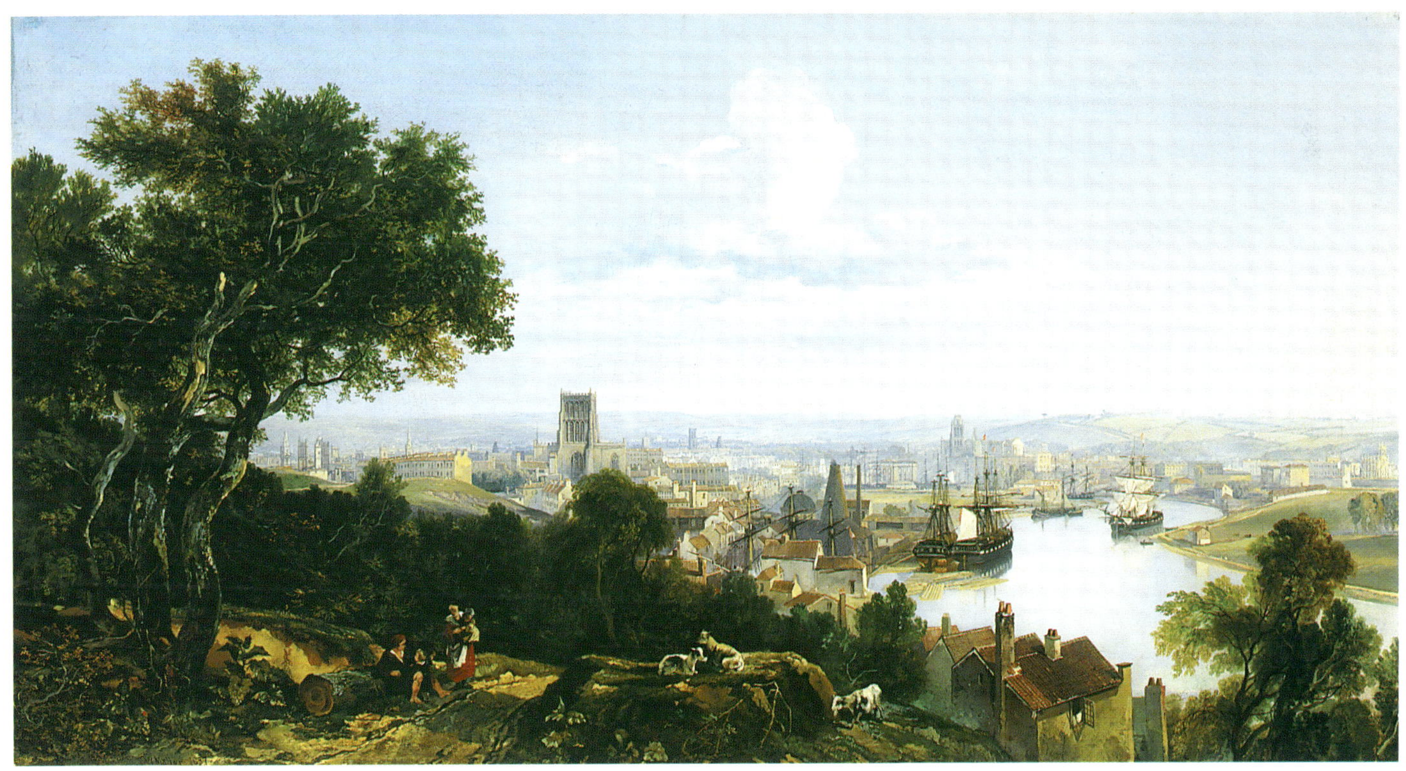

89 James Baker Pyne 1800-1870
The Avon from Durdham Down 1829
Oil 902 x 1222 mm Bristol Museums and Art Gallery K585

PYNE PAINTS ONE OF THE FINEST VIEWS IN ENGLAND, and captures the soft warm light of a gentle summer's evening. It is a painting that can add to our enjoyment of the actual view itself, and no greater compliment can be paid to a landscape artist.

To improve the composition, Pyne has invented a group of ivy-clad pines. He was unwittingly anticipating the work of the Planting and Thinning Sub-Committee of the Downs Committee, which, forty years later in the 1870s, pursued a program of beautification and embellishment of the Downs. It involved the planting of many alien shrubs and trees, including Austrian (Black) and Tyrol Pines, to the contempt of many modern ecologists as well as to the annoyance of those who want to enjoy the artists' favourite viewpoints.

Pyne was initially articled to an attorney and first exhibited in Bristol in 1824. W.J. Müller was his pupil from 1827 until 1829, when Pyne briefly shared a studio with Samuel Jackson. At this time he was painting both local views and the imaginary poetic landscapes typical of the Bristol School. He moved to London in the mid-1830s, becoming one of the most successful and distinctive of J.M.W. Turner's followers.

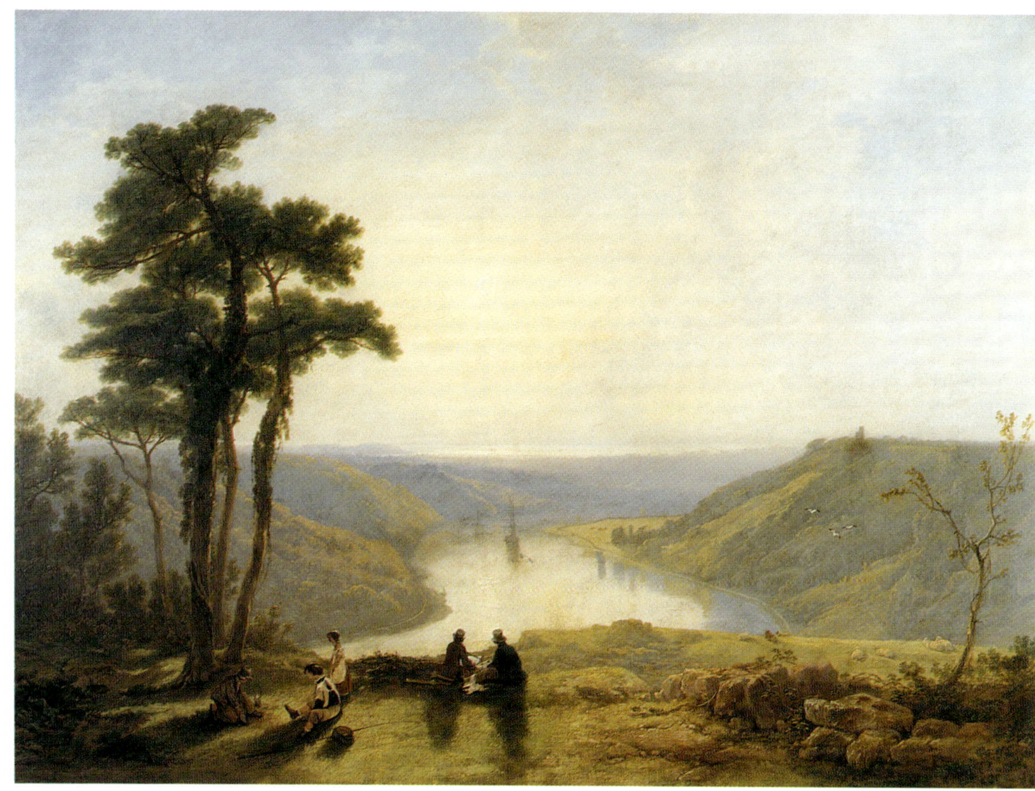

90 George Arthur Fripp   1813-1896
'View on the Avon at Clifton'   1840
Pencil and watercolour   370 x 620 mm   Private collection

THE VIEW LOOKS UP THE AVON from below Cook's Folly. The more familiar viewpoint of Sea Walls is on the left. Durdham Down and Clifton Down remain almost treeless. In the centre the camera obscura is now in place on William West's Observatory and the large extension, completed in 1838, can be clearly seen. To the left are houses on Litfield Place and below is Bridge Valley Road.

G. A. Fripp was born in Bristol, the son of a clergyman and the grandson of Bristol's outstanding marine artist, Nicholas Pocock, who had employed the same rarely used viewpoint over fifty years earlier (17). Fripp was much influenced by Samuel Jackson and he was a friend of W.J. Müller's, with whom he travelled on the Continent in 1834-5. He moved to London in 1841 and this watercolour is one of a group of seven which he exhibited at the Old Water-Colour Society in that year. It was the first time he had exhibited at the society, but he was promptly elected an associate, with full membership following in 1845. He was to be secretary of the society from 1848 to 1854.

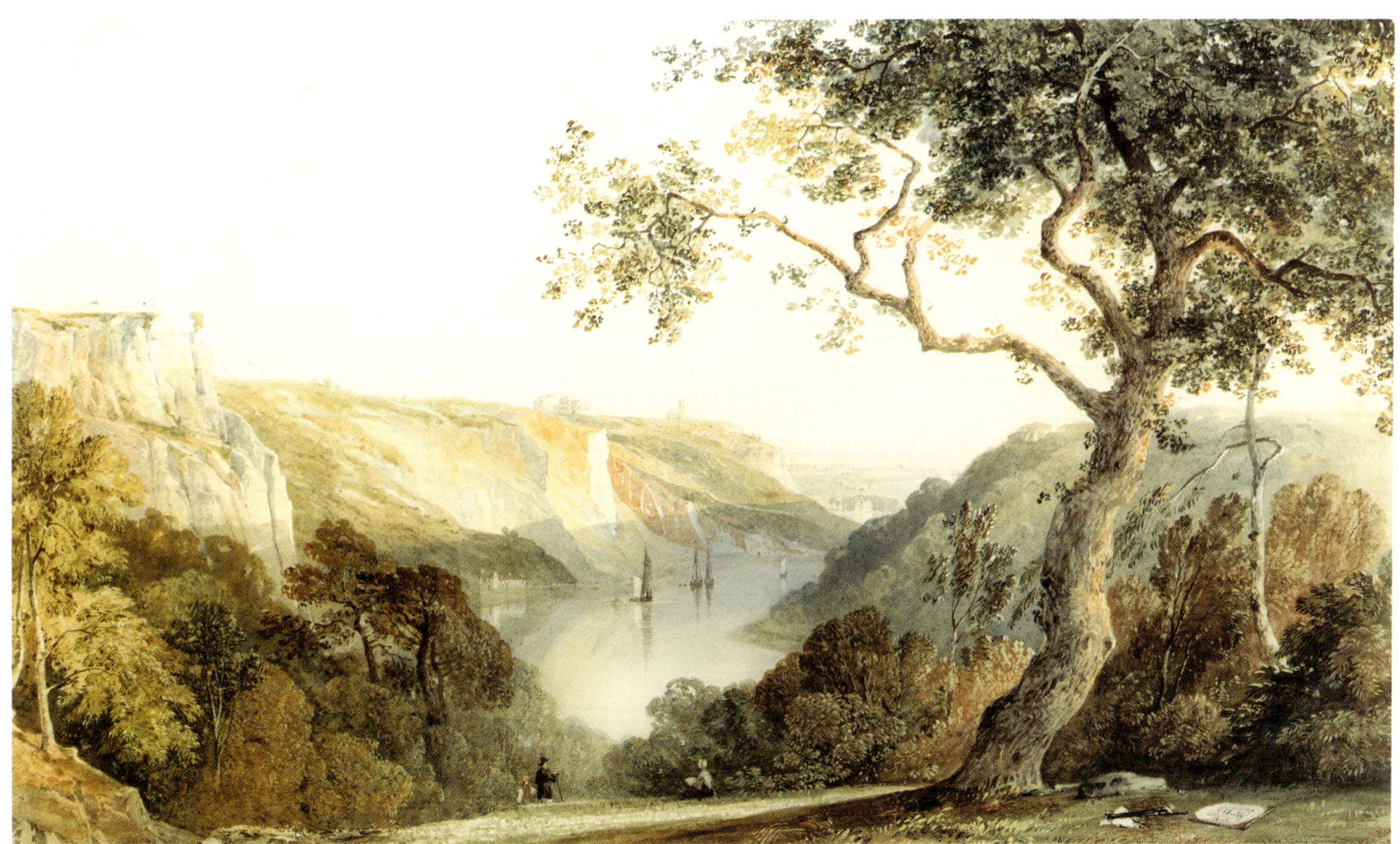

91 James Baker Pyne 1800-1870
Pill harbour c.1827
Oil 250 x 350 mm Private collection

THIS VIEW OF THE HARBOUR OR CREEK AT PILL may date from 1827
and it is perhaps the earliest of Pyne's surviving oil paintings.
The scene is one of picturesque decrepitude. It is low tide, the
Avon is behind us and the lock gates to Pill's small dock are in
the distance. There is not a single substantial building to be
seen; only the pilot boat, the vessel to the left, is well built and
properly maintained, as all these justly famous craft had to be.

In the mid-eighteenth century John Wesley came here to
preach and noted that Pill was famous for its 'stupid, brutal
abandoned wickedness'. Yet this hamlet on the Somerset bank
five miles from Bristol was vital to the city's trade.

From Pill came most of the towboat men and hobblers and
virtually all the pilots. The people of Pill were at the mercy of
the weather, press gangs, fluctuations of trade and the progress
of engineering. During the vicious winter of 1789 persistent
easterly winds and ice made the Avon unnavigable for many
weeks and the Merchant Venturers gave money for the relief of
the towboat men and the pilots. The opening of the Floating
Harbour in 1809 saw a decline in the use of Hung Road and of the
labour-intensive methods of mooring and weighing anchor there.
A still more serious threat was to come with the introduction of
steam tugs in 1836 (98).

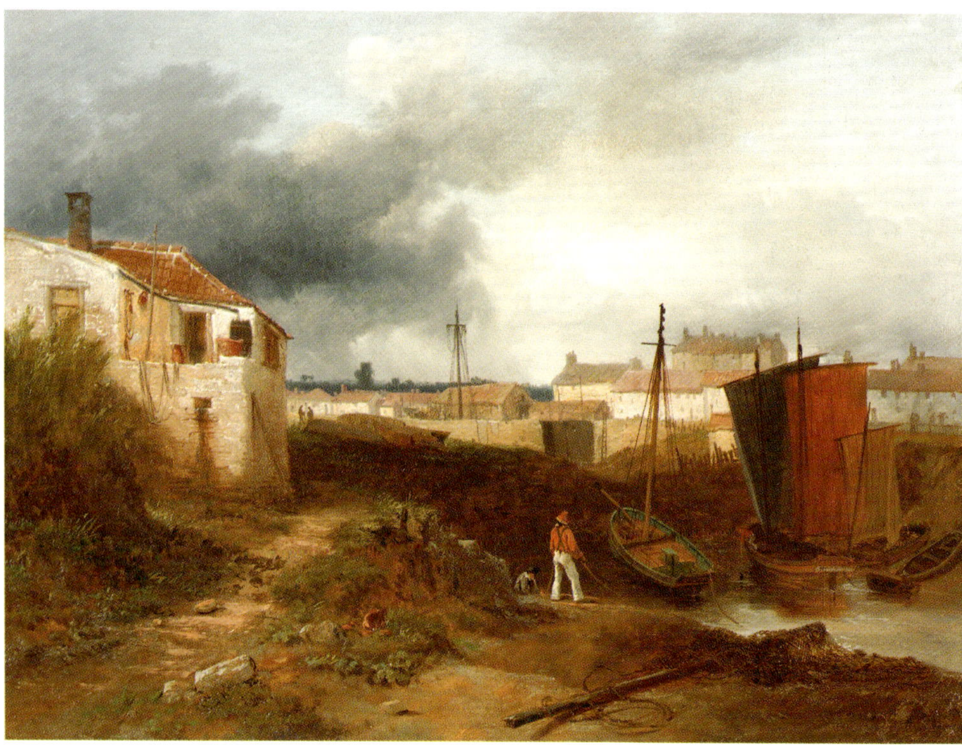

92 James Baker Pyne 1800-1870
Clifton from the Overfall Dam   1837
Oil   1143 x 1829 mm   Bristol Museums and Art Gallery K120

THE OVERFALL DAM IN THE CENTRE OF THE PAINTING marks the point at which the original course of the river had been dammed when the Floating Harbour was completed in 1809. In 1832 Brunel proposed a number of solutions to alleviate the serious silting up of the harbour that had followed and two years later a culvert was cut low into the dam. When opened, it enabled the mud, which had been dredged from the harbour and dumped in front of the dam, to be flushed into the tidal New Cut. In due course the Overfall Dam became known as the Underfall, a name preserved by the neighbouring Underfall Yard – the workshop of the Floating Harbour.

When this very large and spectacular work was shown at the Royal Academy in 1837, a critic wrote: 'It is…very poor and thin; with no colour, disagreeably white. Mr Pyne is a man of great talent, and we cannot imagine in what sick fit he painted this picture.' Pyne was to be J.M.W. Turner's most successful follower, and his admiration for that great artist was partly to blame.

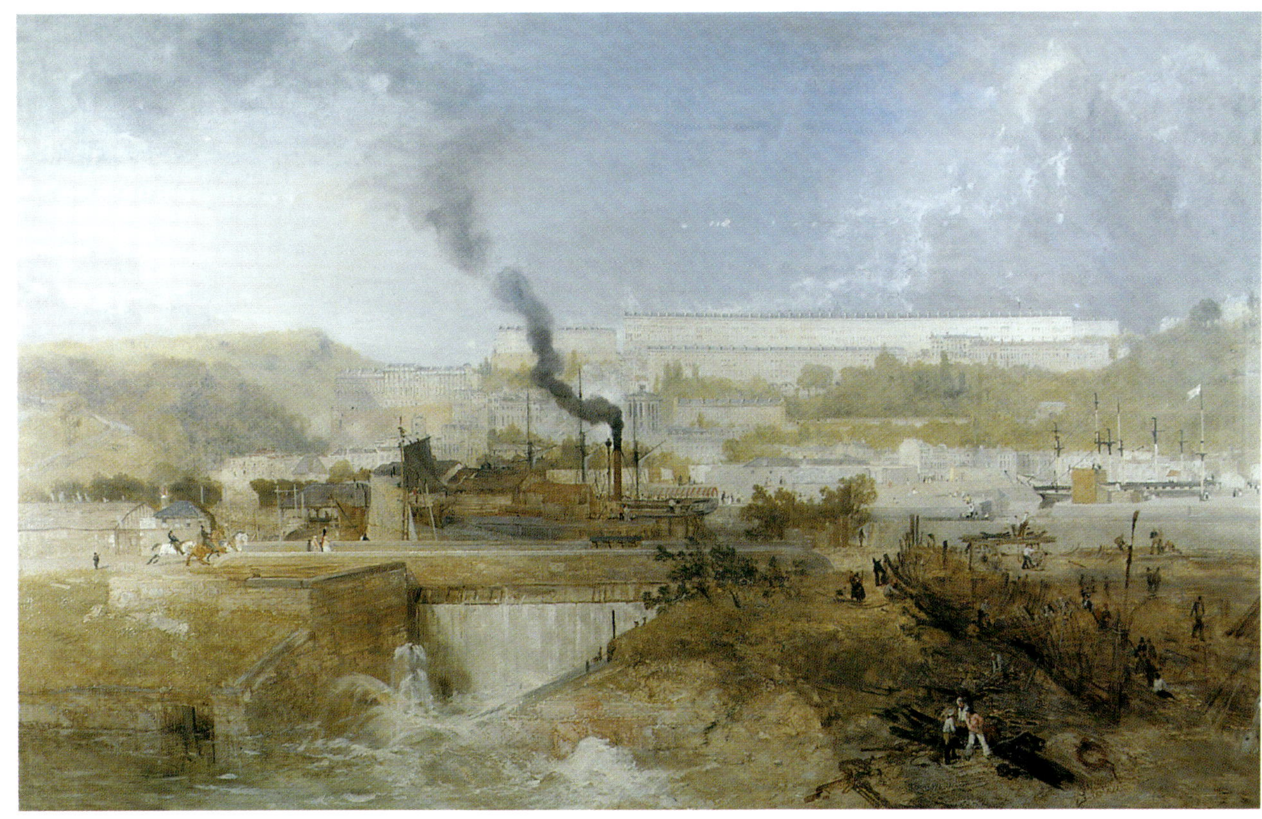

93 Joseph Walter 1783-1856
Bristol Harbour from Wapping   1836
Oil   660 x 915 mm   Bristol Museums and Art Gallery K923

FIFTY YEARS EARLIER, NICHOLAS POCOCK had painted the same view looking down St Augustine's Reach from Wapping (14).

In the foreground, old spars are tied to a mooring post and a raft of new timbers lies next to a Severn trow. Canon's Marsh below the Cathedral had been developed in the decade after Pocock's view and Walter sets a timber ship, distinguishable by the hatch near the waterline in the bow, against the timber yards. On the opposite side of St Augustine's Reach there is still only one steamer at Narrow Quay amongst the many sailing vessels. The merchantmen by Bush House, today's Arnolfini, are drying their sails, suggesting that they are recent arrivals.

Bush House had been built 1830-31 to the designs of R.S. Pope as warehouse and offices for Acraman's, the iron founders. Four years later it was doubled in size by the addition of tea warehousing for Acraman, Bush, Castle & Co, a company formed in 1834 to take advantage of the ending of the East India Company's monopoly of the tea trade just a year earlier. Both companies were to fail in the 1840s and in 1846 the bonded warehouse keepers George and James Bush acquired the building.

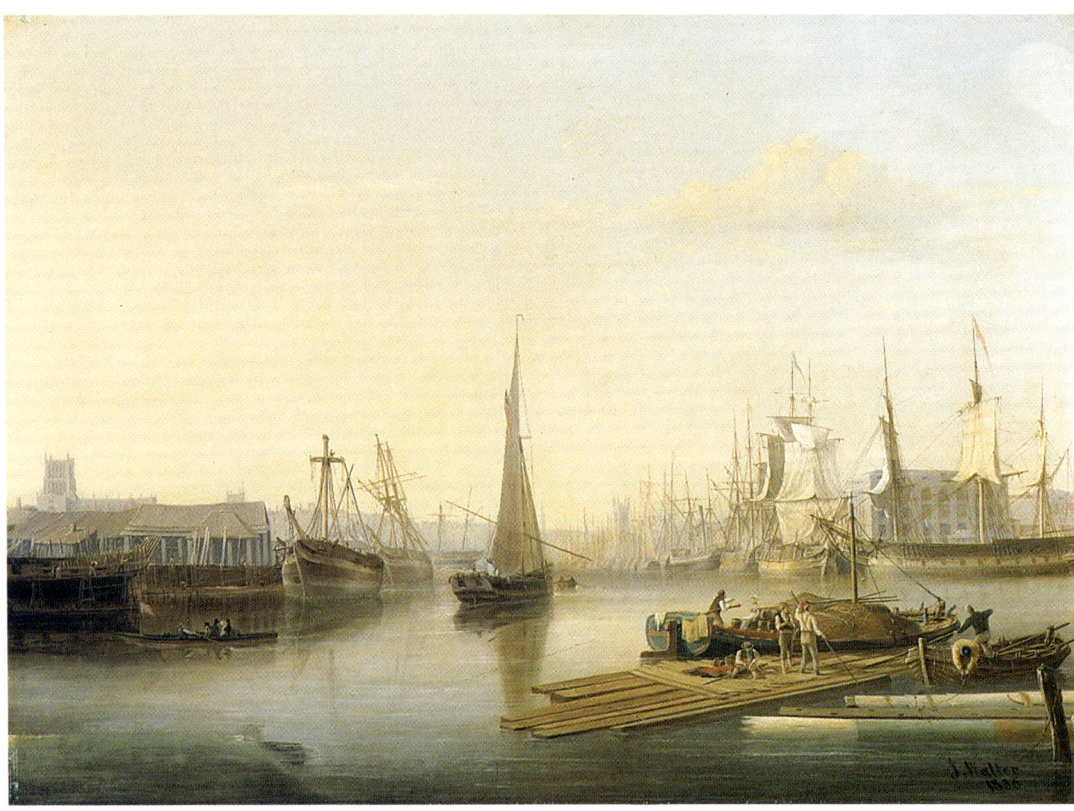

94 Joseph Walter   1783-1856
The Floating Harbour with Prince Street Bridge   1842
Oil   660 x 920 mm   Bristol Museums and Art Gallery K1178

THIS BUSTLING EARLY-MORNING SCENE with a dramatic sunrise above St Mary Redcliffe highlights the small size of the first Prince Street Bridge, completed in 1809. It was to continue as a toll bridge until it was purchased by Bristol Corporation in 1876. Three years later the present bridge was opened.

Joseph Walter was nearly sixty years old when he painted this intimate scene of the life of Bristol's harbour. He had been born in Bristol and lived much of his life in the parish of St Augustine near the Cathedral, almost certainly practising as an accountant. It was not until 1832, when he was in his fiftieth year, that he first exhibited a painting in the city. Four years later he is listed in the local directories as a marine painter. There is no reason to believe that Walter had any of Nicholas Pocock's experience of the sea as a mariner. But his great knowledge of ships and shipping and his passion for the port of Bristol were profound.

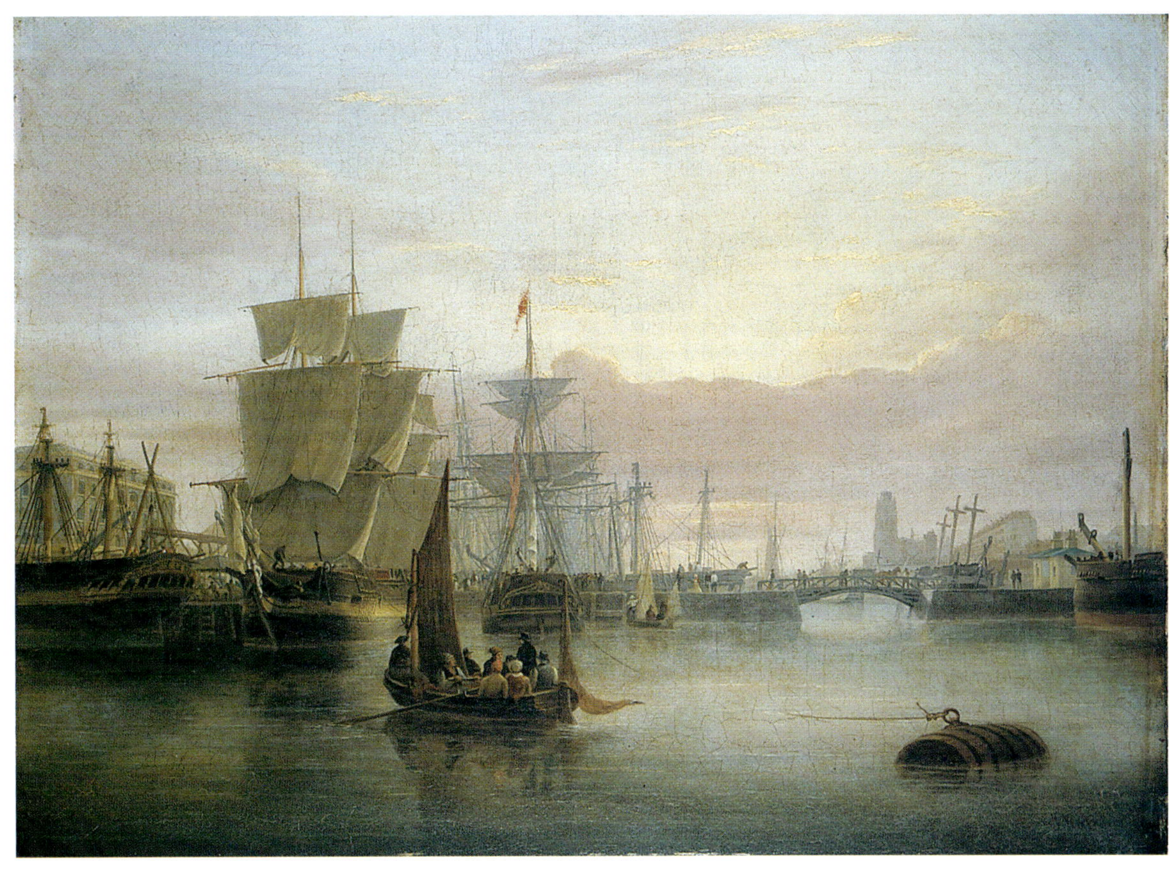

95 Joseph Walter 1783-1856
The Great Western *leaving Cumberland Basin on the 18 August 1837*
Lithograph   200 x 305 mm   Bristol Museums and Art Gallery M256

JOSEPH WALTER WAS THE CHIEF PORTRAITIST of Brunel's two great Bristol-built steamships, the *Great Western* and *Great Britain*. His many paintings and prints proudly celebrate these ships as triumphs of engineering. The two pictures illustrated here also seem to acknowledge that these steamships marked the end of an era in the history of Bristol's harbour.

The *Great Western* was built by William Patterson at Wapping on the site of today's Bristol Industrial Museum. Conceived as an extension to New York of the Great Western Railway from London to Bristol, she was the largest steamer afloat and the first to be built expressly for crossing the Atlantic. Launched on 19 July 1837 before a crowd of 50,000 people, we see her here one month later squeezing out of the entrance lock of Cumberland Basin and about to turn the perilously sharp corner into the tidal Avon. She was towed by the steam tug *Lion* and assisted by the two steam packets *Benledi* and *Herald*.

The *Great Western* proved to be exceptionally reliable, completing sixty-seven transatlantic voyages in eight years. From 1838 until 1841 she sailed from the Bristol Channel, taking on her passengers, coal and cargo at King Road or at moorings at Broad Pill on the Avon below Pill. She still had to pay Bristol's exorbitant dock dues and it was no surprise that in 1843 Liverpool became the terminus for all her future voyages. The passenger trade of the port of Bristol has been negligible ever since.

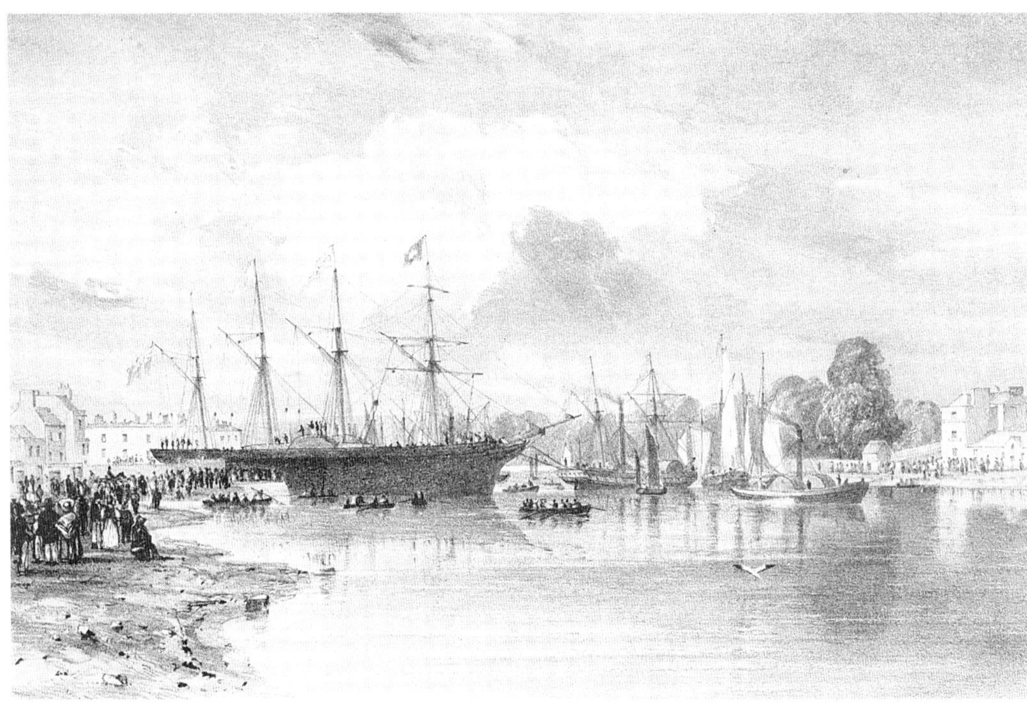

The Great Britain *being towed down the Avon Gorge on 12th December 1844 on the start of her voyage to London to complete her fitting out* Oil   420 x 660 mm   Collection of the *ss Great Britain* Trust

BRUNEL'S *GREAT BRITAIN* WAS the first iron-hulled and screw-propelled vessel in the world. She was also the largest ship of any kind. She was launched in July 1843 in the presence of the Prince Consort from the specially constructed dock to which she was to return in 1970. After the launch she remained locked in the Floating Harbour like a great beached whale for almost eighteen months while Bristol's Dock Company delayed its commitment to enlarge the Cumberland Basin locks.

Finally on 11 December 1844 on a high spring tide she was eased through the first lock only to get stuck in the second before being desperately pulled back to avoid being wedged, suspended and crushed as the tide ebbed. Throughout the day, Brunel supervised the removal of the upper courses of masonry from the sides of the locks. Then, during the night by the light of blazing tar barrels, the *Great Britain* was finally squeezed through the lock and allowed to ground on the mud as the tide went out.

Here, on the following day, high in the water and pulled and nudged by four tugs, she makes her only journey down the Avon. The riverbanks are crowded but it is not the excitement but the pathos of this cold winter morning that the artist seeks to convey. The *Great Britain* was to be based in Liverpool from the very beginning.

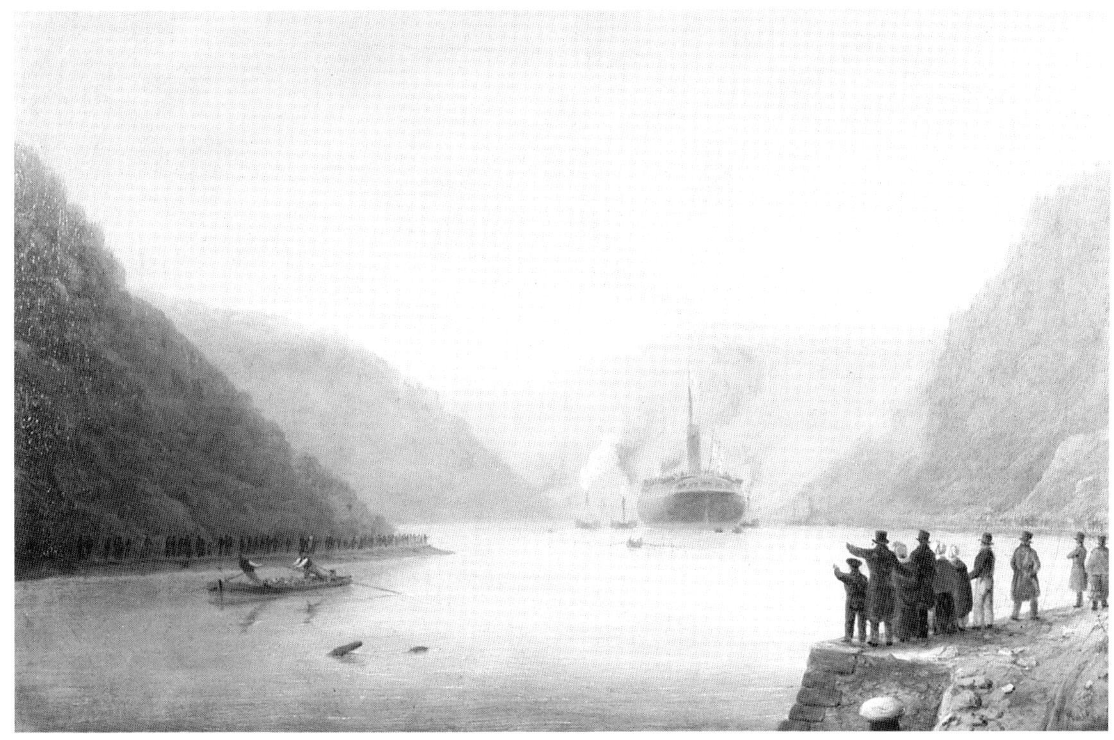

97   Joseph Walter 1783-1856
Sea Mills   1844
Oil   669 x 914 mm   Bristol Museums and Art Gallery   K2410

SEA MILLS IS HALF WAY BETWEEN BRISTOL and the mouth of the Avon. No trace of the important Roman harbour now remains but the ruins of the largely unsuccessful eighteenth-century dock can be seen to the left of the sails in the centre of this painting. Today, the quaysides to the entrance of the early floating dock of 1712 can still be traced.

A steam packet hastens upstream and a steam tug tows a merchantman down river towards King Road, her destination signalled by the sequence of flags on her main mast. Joseph Walter would have been very much aware of the novelty of vessels going in opposite directions on the river, a feature of both of the paintings on these two pages. For the first time, we can no longer make presumptions about the state of the tide, beyond suspecting, in this instance, that it might be on the turn.

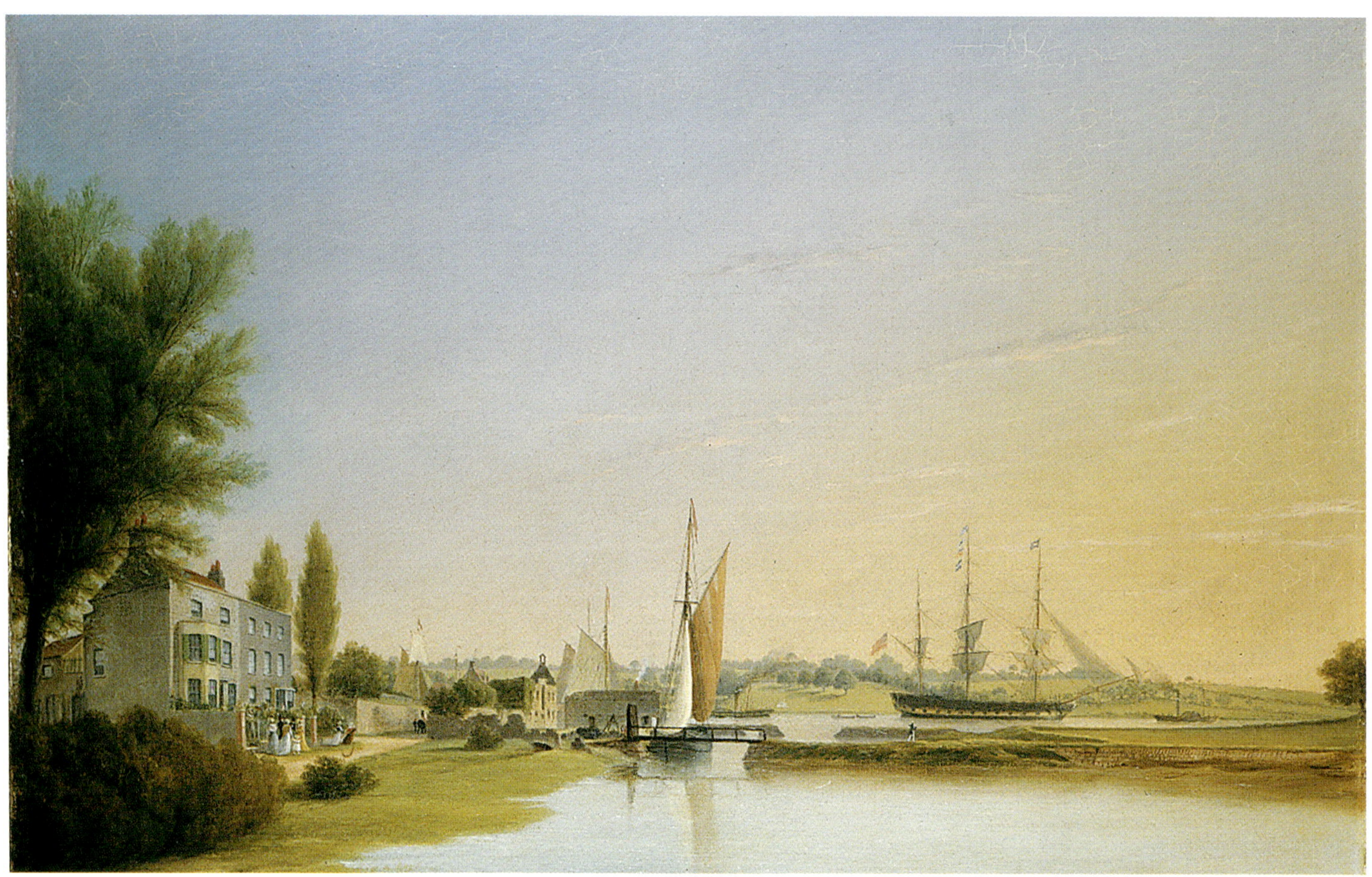

98 Joseph Walter   1783-1856
A steamer on the Avon passing Pill   c.1835
Oil   500 x 750 mm   Private collection

A STEAM PACKET ROARS PAST PILL. Its arrogant wake is about to rock the pilot cutters that would be moored in Crockern Pill, the small harbour or creek just behind the stern. The view is from the Lamplighters Inn on the Shirehampton bank. The artist may have deliberately chosen to celebrate the speed and power of the packet boat against the background of the one community on the river that was already suffering the consequences of the introduction of steam power.

The first steamer to operate a regular passenger service in the West Country was the *Charlotte*, which in 1813 and 1814 ran on the Avon between Bristol and Bath. Not until 1821 was there a regular service from Bristol into the Channel and beyond. By the following year there were scheduled services between Bristol and Cork, Dublin, Swansea, Newport and Chepstow. Other services soon followed, but by the 1860s the expanding rail network was causing a rapid decline in the steam packet fleets.

When the first resident steam tug, *Fury*, appeared in 1836, the towboat men of Pill boarded her at night in King Road and set her adrift. It was a hopeless protest and the population of Pill was to decline steadily over the next few decades.

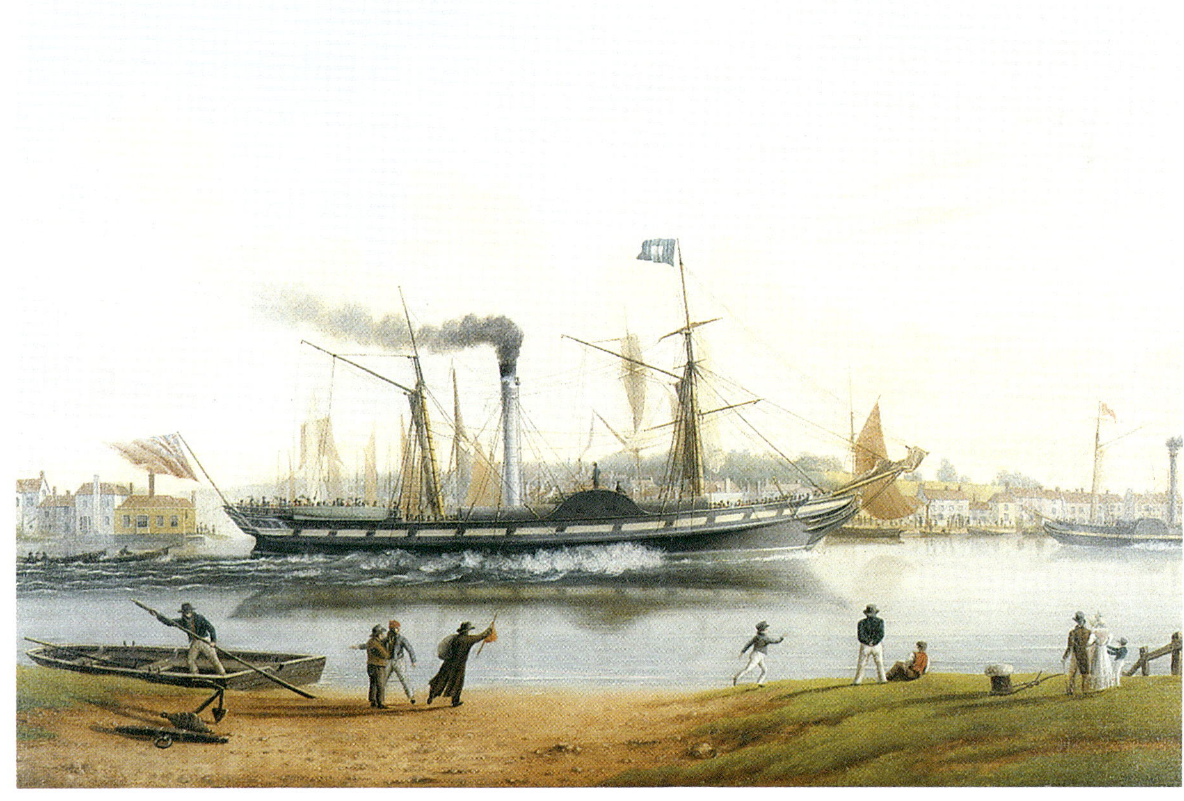

99 Joseph Walter 1783-1856
The Great Western *passing Portishead on her maiden voyage to New York on 8th April 1838* c.1839
Oil   500 x 700 mm   Private collection

IN APRIL 1838 THE FIRST VOYAGE OF THE *GREAT WESTERN* developed into a race with the much smaller steamer *Sirius* for the record of opening the first regular transatlantic service by steam. The Sirius left Cork three days earlier and arrived in New York just three-and-a-half hours before the *Great Western*. *Sirius* was empty of coal and had consumed much of its cabin furniture and deck fittings, but the *Great Western* had bunkers of coal to spare. Both ships were given a tumultuous welcome.

In the distance just behind the foremast, the Royal or Portishead Hotel can be seen. Built in 1830 by Bristol Corporation in an austere Tudor style, it is still there today. Its completion opened a decade of major development for the village both as a resort and as a place of permanent residence. Steam packets were vital to the hotel's early success. A steep stone pier or landing stage was erected nearby and a regular packet-boat service from Bristol began in 1834. The following year a regatta was arranged with four steam packets transporting the visitors from Bristol for the day.

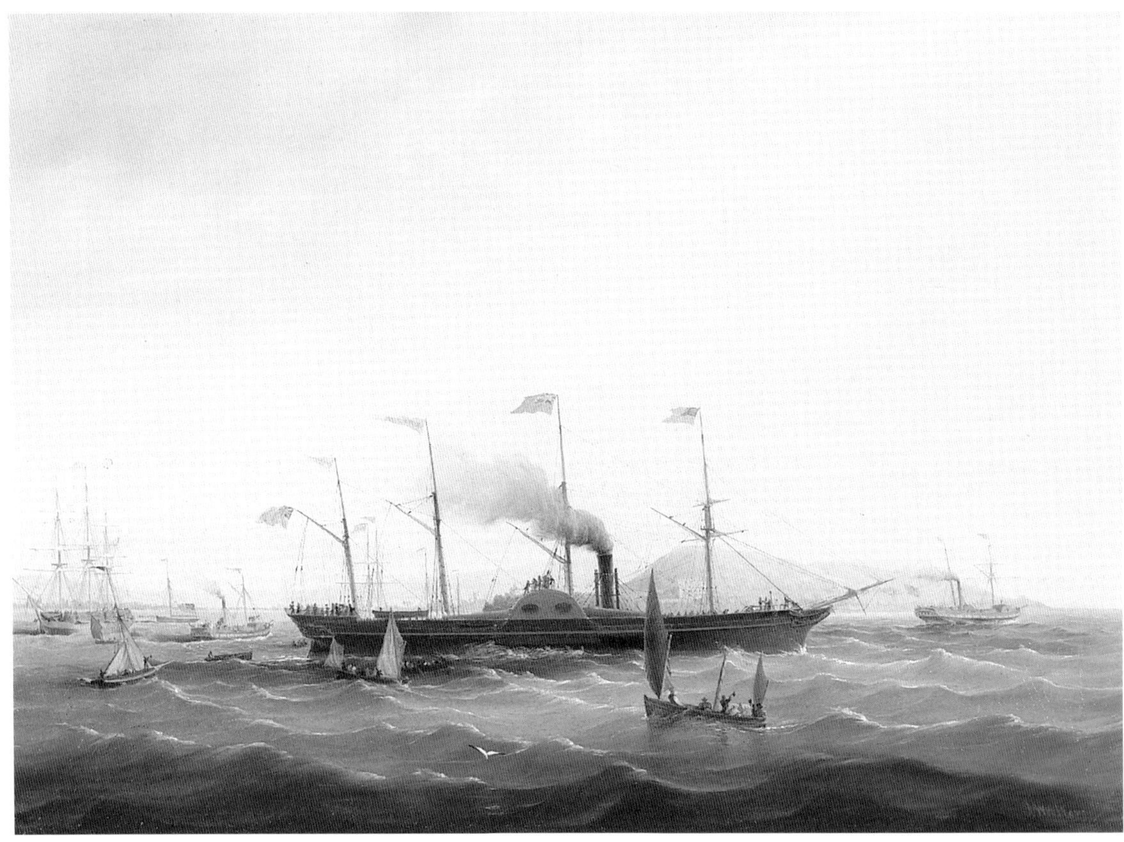

PORTBURY FLOATING PIER, LANDING PLACE, & STEAM PACKET HARBOUR c.1840
Colour lithograph   650 x 370 mm   Bristol Museums and Art Gallery J592

THE *GREAT WESTERN* WAS OBLIGED to take on her passengers in King Road, an ignominious start to a transatlantic voyage. When in December 1839, Brunel made several proposals for the improvement of the Floating Harbour, he also outlined the need for docking facilities at the mouth of the Avon to meet the needs of the larger ships. His proposal for a floating pier and harbour at Portbury near Portishead, which is illustrated here, was drawn by Joseph Walter.

Bristol Corporation had been the owner of much of Portishead since the seventeenth century, but the marshes at Portbury were in the possession of James Adam Gordon, who had both promoted and withdrawn a bill in 1841 for the building of a large dock at Pill, which he also owned. The Bristol Corporation and the Merchant Venturers opposed both the Pill Docks bill and a subsequent bill for a pier at Portbury in 1846 on the grounds that they would injure Bristol's trade. Not until 1877 was the first Avonmouth Dock to be completed. One hundred years later West Dock, later Royal Portbury Dock, was opened by H.M. The Queen on the very site depicted here.

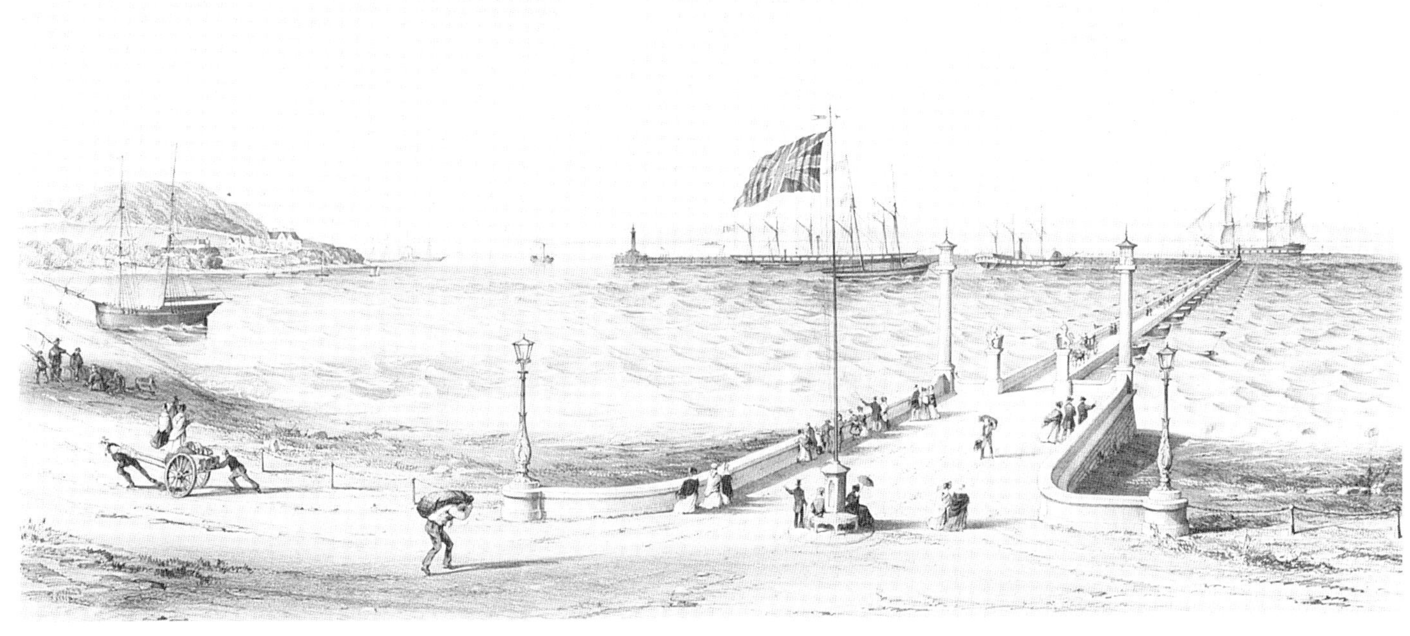

101 Joseph Walter 1783-1856
View from Portishead towards Wales c.1832
Oil 480 x 635 mm Bristol Museums and Art Gallery K4551

AN AUTUMN STORM PURSUES A STEAM PACKET, a merchantman and several coastal craft up the channel and around Portishead Point to the shelter and anchorage of King Road. On the far right is the small Customs watch-house or Preventive Station built in 1810. The tramlines of stubble, the muck spreading and the sudden rush of wind that bends the taller trees heighten the exceptional sense of actuality – of a particular moment recorded.

This painting may be Joseph Walter's earliest surviving work. He was to develop a more fluent technique and a more conventional approach to composition, but the concentrated observation and the convincing effects of light and atmosphere that we see here were not to be excelled in his later work.

When Joseph Walter first exhibited three paintings at the Bristol Society of Artists in 1832 he gave his address as Portishead. For a short period, perhaps when he retired from accountancy to become a professional artist, he evidently moved out of Bristol. Until recently, this painting had been tentatively dated to about 1832 for that reason. The house under construction on the right now confirms that year as the date of this painting. It is still there and it is called Mariners Cottage. '1832' is engraved in stone in the middle of the façade.

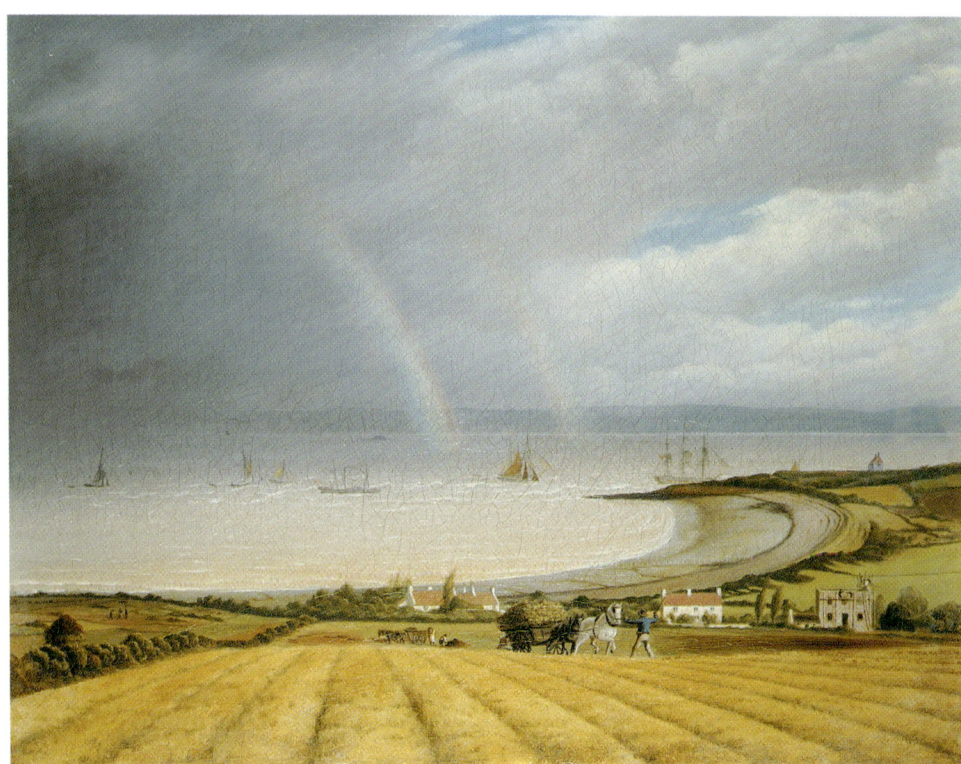

102 Joseph Walter   1783-1856
King Road and the mouth of the Avon   1837
Oil   863 x 1244 mm   Bristol Museums and Art Gallery K462

KING ROAD HAS NEVER BEEN MORE EXPRESSIVELY or knowledge-
ably depicted. No steam ships are included and there is such a
careful record of the consequences of wind and tide that Walter
may have been intending a deliberate tribute to the age of sail.

   The wind is easterly and the tide is on the ebb. The ship with
her sails ready to be unfurled has her port anchor fished. Her
outer jib and fore topsail are set and are bringing her bow round
to point down the Bristol Channel. The pilot would already be on
board to take her beyond Flat Holm and Steep Holm. To the left
another ship signals her departure and prepares to get under way.

In the centre above the shoreline is Penpole Point on King's
Weston Hill. Below are two Severn trows waiting for the flood
tide to take them up river. Beyond them and to the right a large
topsail cutter is reaching out of the river followed by other
smaller craft. To the right two larger ships are just reaching
open water and are already under courses and topsails and are
outward-bound. The two small rowing or pulling boats have
some well-dressed passengers in them who have, perhaps, just
been saying their goodbyes aboard an outward-bound ship.

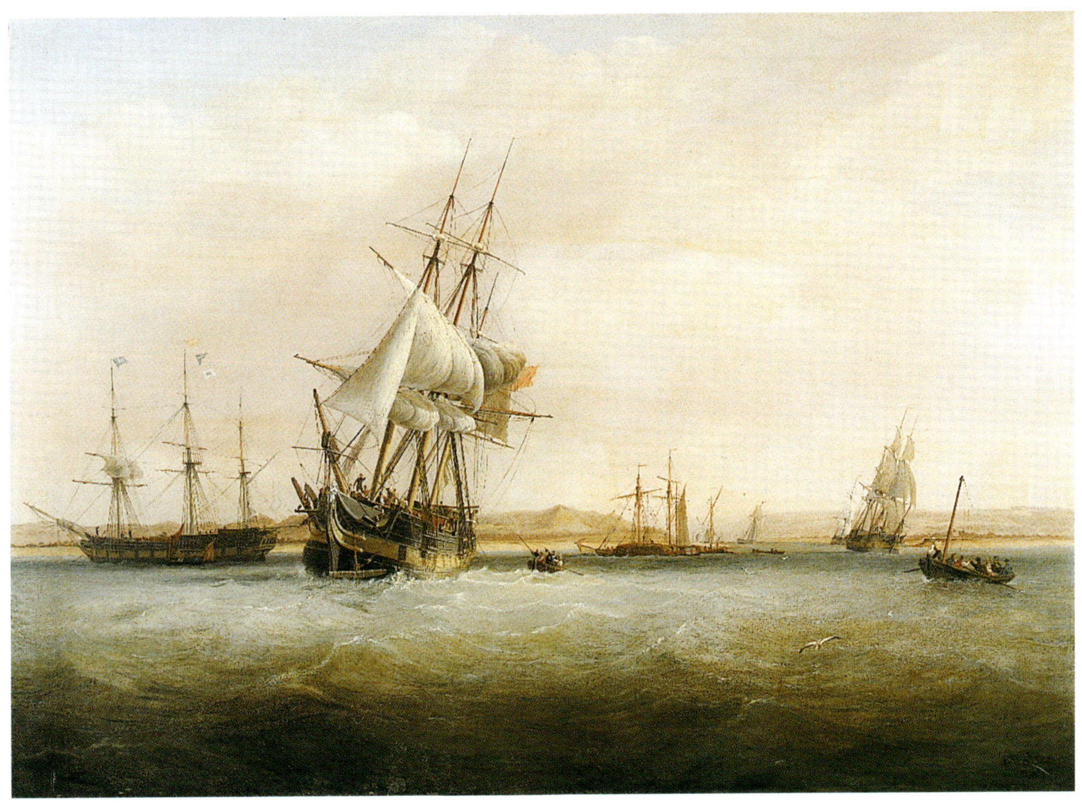

Bristol Harbour with the Demerara *and Clifton Wood*   1853
Watercolour   335 x 495 mm   Bristol Museums and Art Gallery K1110

IN THE *GREAT BRITAIN*'S DRY DOCK ON THE LEFT, is the paddle steamer, *Demerara*. It is 1853, two years after she was first launched, but the nineteen-year-old artist does not hint at the sorry story behind this peaceful evening scene of the Floating Harbour and Clifton Wood.

William Patterson, who had constructed the *Great Western* for Brunel and who had assisted with the design of the *Great Britain*, was both the designer and the builder of the *Demerara*. She was almost as big as the *Great Britain*, but more like the *Great Western* in design, being wooden-hulled and a paddle steamer. Launched in 1851, she was being towed to Glasgow to have her engines fitted when she struck the Gloucestershire bank of the Avon just a mile down river. The ebbing tide then slewed her across the river and she was severely damaged. The pilot was later disciplined for speeding by the Merchant Venturers.

The *Demerara* was hauled back to Bristol, eventually sold in 1854 and then converted to a sailing vessel of over 3,000 tons. She was to be lost in a hurricane in the West Indies in 1867, when only two of sixty ships survived. The *Demerara's* figure-head, an exotic figure in a feather headdress, was to decorate an auctioneer's in Quay Street until 1937. Today there is a replica on a building near the Hippodrome theatre on St Augustine's Reach.

The wreck of the *Demerara* had an immediate effect on ship-building in Bristol and it was nearly fifty years before a ship of similar size was launched in Bristol – the *Bristol City* built by Charles Hill and Sons Ltd in 1899.

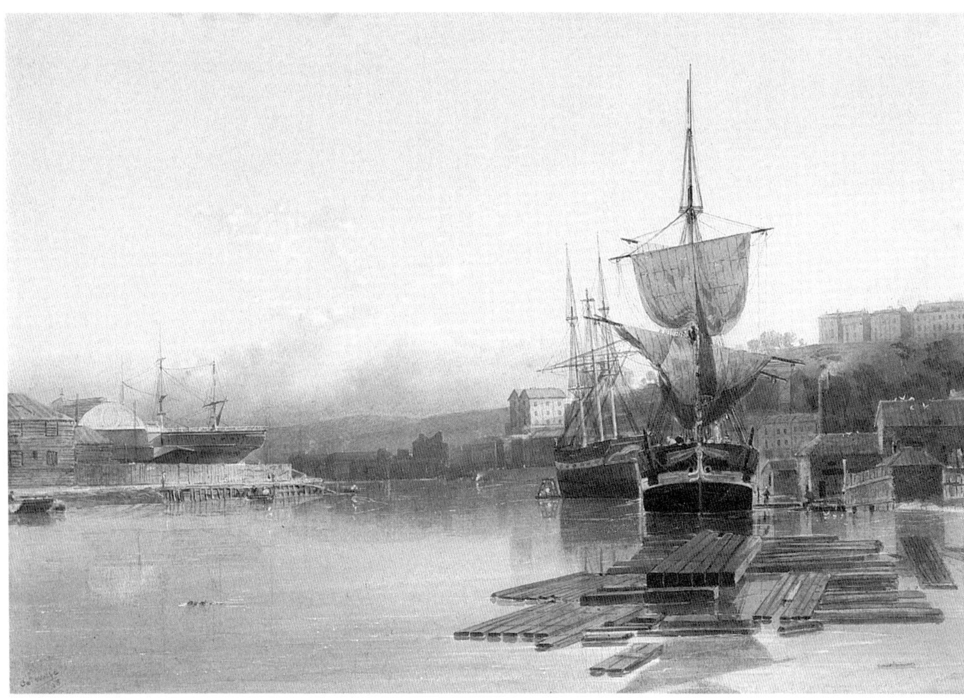

104   George Wolfe   1834-1890
The Wye *in the Bristol Channel*   1854
Watercolour   310 x 480 mm   Bristol Museums and Art Gallery J41

THIS FINE PADDLE STEAMER WAS BUILT IN BRISTOL in 1843 as a successor to the *Wye* depicted in Samuel Jackson's famous oil painting (84). Like its predecessor it ran between Bristol and Chepstow. A collision with another steam packet in thick fog in the Avon in December 1850 led to alterations that further improved her performance. Thereafter the journey was scheduled to take only one hour and thirty-five minutes.

George Wolfe is said to have been born in Hotwells and to have spent much of his life in Bristol, but we know surprisingly little about him. He started painting at the age of seventeen and may have shared a studio briefly with Samuel Jackson. He was to exhibit much in London and his mature works are often of coastal scenes with fine sunset effects. They are also painted with a more meticulous and denser technique than these two very early works.

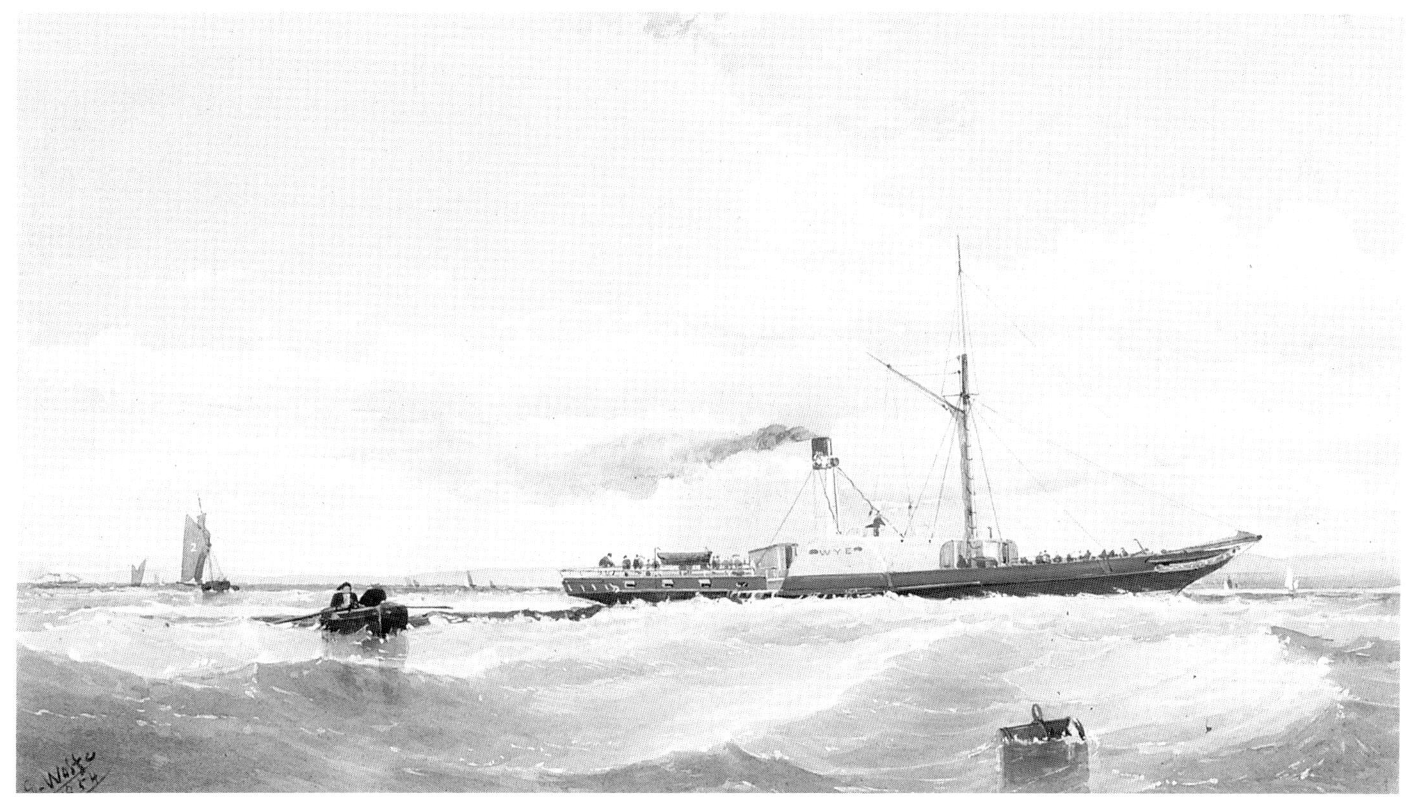

105 after John Lavars c.1810-1889
    'BALLOON VIEW OF AVONMOUTH BRISTOL' 1877
    Colour lithograph 292 x 368 mm Private collection

THE OPENING OF BRISTOL'S FIRST DEEP-WATER HARBOUR at Avonmouth in 1877 was the most important development in the history of the port of Bristol since the creation of the Floating Harbour nearly seventy years earlier.

The railways on either side of the Avon had preceded the docks, both here at Avonmouth and at Portishead, where the new dock was completed in 1879. The Bristol Port Railway and Pier line that curves around Avonmouth dock basin was opened in 1865. It took passengers from a station a few yards down river from the Clifton Suspension Bridge to Severn Beach and the shortest crossing to Wales before the opening of the Severn railway tunnel in 1886. The Bristol and Portishead Pier and Railway Company's line in the foreground opened in 1867. A section of it has very recently been revived to carry imported coal from Royal Portbury Dock.

The muddy lump of land to the far left is the treacherous Dumball Island on which a gibbet had once stood (8). It was later to be incorporated into the Royal Edward Dock, whose entrance lock sliced straight through it. At the far-left corner of the basin is the Corporation of Trinity House lighthouse built in 1840.

Despite the title of this colour lithograph and the actual presence of a balloon in the sky, there is, as yet, no other evidence that Lavars made use of a balloon.

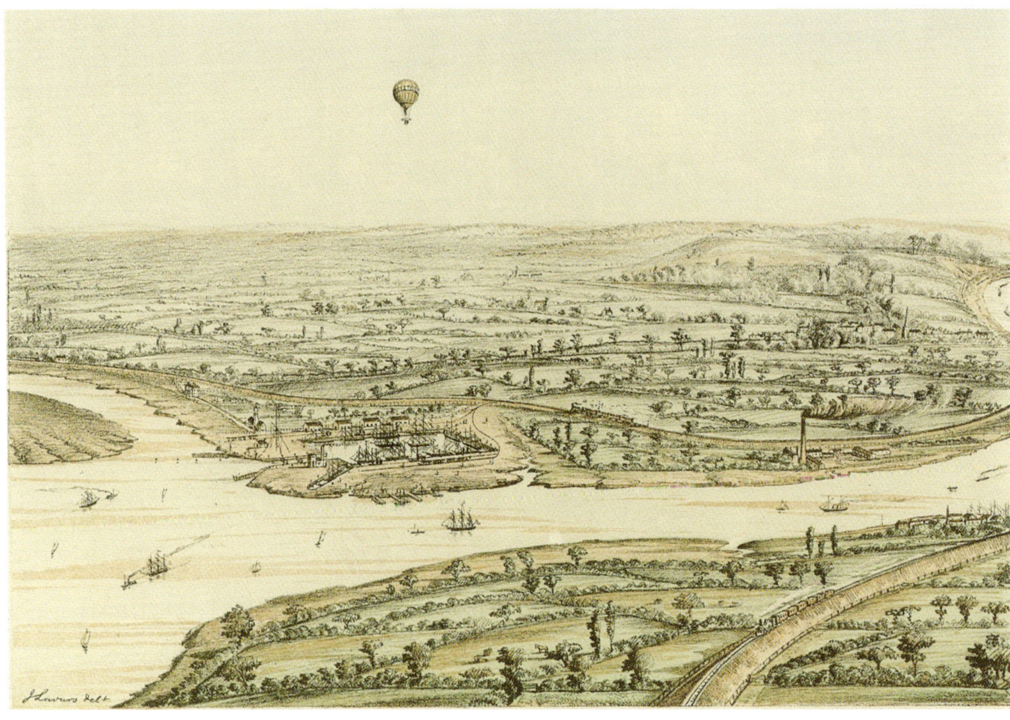

106 after Edward C Lavars
Bird's eye view of Bristol 1887
Colour lithograph 335 x 850 mm Bristol Museums and Art Gallery M3336

BREATHTAKING IN ITS DETAIL and in its accuracy, this work is equal to many of the finest of eighteenth- and nineteenth-century panoramas of the world's great cities. It was conceived as a celebration of Queen Victoria's golden jubilee and few more impressive tributes were paid to her.

Once again the view is as if seen from a balloon, but the landscape is now enlivened by light and shade and the shadows of clouds. A rainstorm passes over the Severn in the far distance and there are dark clouds over Bedminster and its colliery in the foreground.

John Lavars had founded Lavars & Co. in 1838 and it became the most successful lithographic printers in Bristol. It specialised in maps and plans and later in fashion plates and other commercial work. When the founder died in 1889, his son Edward took over and there is inconclusive evidence that it was Edward who was responsible for this remarkable panorama. It is Edward who signs both of the lithographs illustrated on the next two pages, but the view of Avonmouth, illustrated opposite, bears the printed signature of John Lavars.

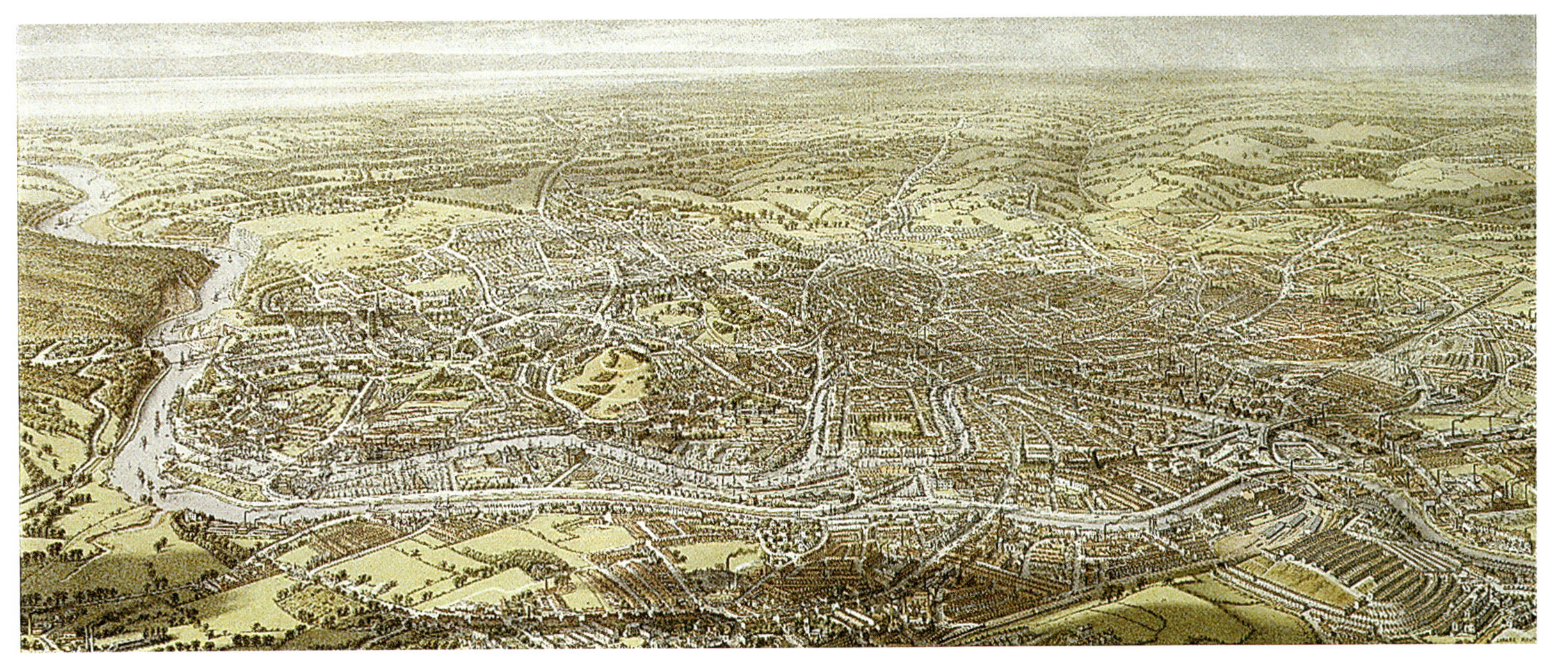

107 after Edward C. Lavars
'THE AVON AT HORSE SHOE POINT One of the Proposed Points of Dockization' (detail) c.1865
Colour lithograph   105 x 190 mm   Bristol Museums and Art Gallery M287

ON THE LEFT IS THE LOWER PORTION OF HORSESHOE BEND and above is the creek, known as Chapel Pill. In the distance is the Georgian mansion, Ham Green (31), with Hung Road to the right. Just above the merchantman being towed upriver by two paddle steam tugs is the Powder House. Here, the heavily armed privateers and merchantmen of the eighteenth century were obliged to leave their gunpowder in order to lessen the risks of violent explosions at Bristol's crowded quaysides. The floorboards of one of the storehouses were fastened with copper nails to reduce the risk of sparks. The quay, but not the storehouses, survives.

The title of this small lithograph well illustrates the endless proposals and counter-proposals for the improvement of Bristol's harbour facilities between 1839, when Brunel proposed a floating pier at Portbury (100) and 1877, when a private company opened the first dock at Avonmouth (105). There were repeated proposals for straightening the river either by cutting off Horseshoe Point or putting a canal through it. There were also 'dockisers', who were in favour of 'dockization' and they had a choice of several plans for 'dockising' the river. One of their preferred sites for damming the river was this one – just below Horseshoe Point. Thankfully, both the river and the English language have survived.

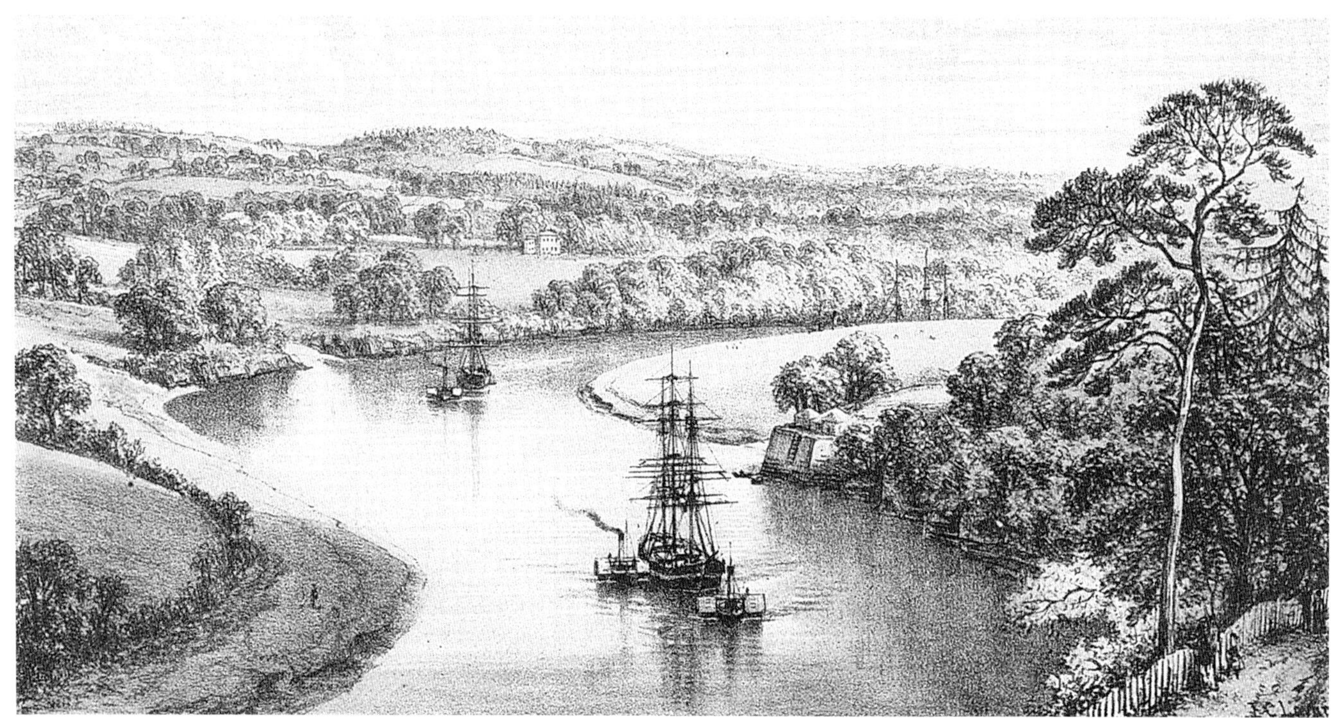

108 after Edward C. Lavars
'SUSPENSION BRIDGE FROM SION HILL CLIFTON St Vincent Rocks Hotel & Baths' c.1875
Colour lithograph   215 x 430 mm   Bristol Museums and Art Gallery Mb2799

THE CLIFTON SUSPENSION BRIDGE had finally been completed in 1864 and the railway running beneath it opened three years later. During the bridge's first three years, innumerable prints were published and photographs were taken of the Avon Gorge, spanned by the new bridge and with the Hotwell House below. They give little indication of the spa's decline. In 1867 the Merchant Venturers were happy to sell the Hotwell House to Bristol Corporation who immediately demolished it and blew up the point on which it stood to improve navigation. As this colour lithograph demonstrates, the spa had, in effect, long since moved up the hill.

In 1793 a lawyer and developer of Sion Hill had drilled some 250 feet down through the limestone rock below his house and successfully tapped into the warm Hotwell waters. Ten years later Sion Spring was marked on a Clifton map as the 'New Hot Well.' The water was soon being pumped to houses throughout much of Clifton. The supply was vital to the development and fashionable appeal of the area. In this lithograph of about 1875, Sion Spring or New Hot Well has become the St Vincent Rocks Hotel and Baths. The hotel continued until 1999.

Very few artists notice the differences between the two Suspension Bridge towers. Edward Lavars records the disparities with a fastidiousness that is yet another reason for attributing that remarkable panorama (106) to his hand.

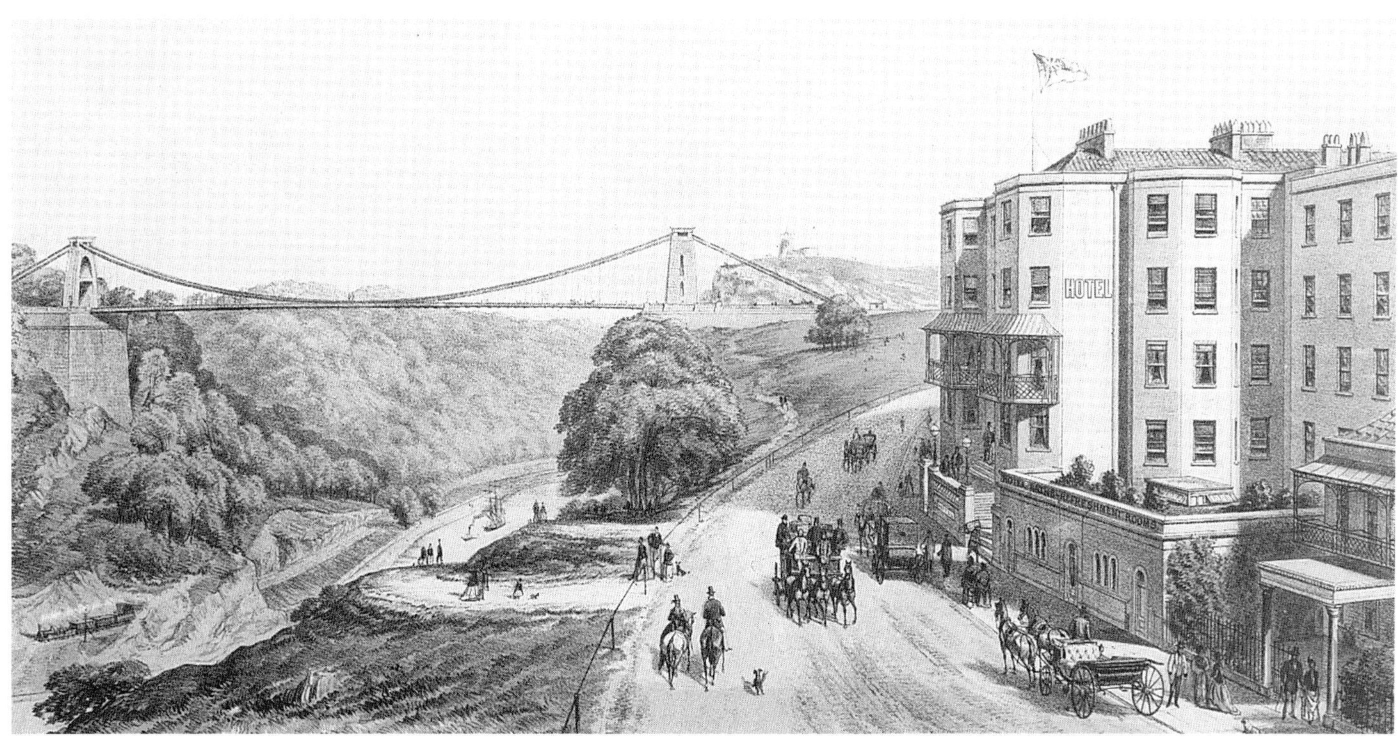

109 Albert Goodwin   1845-1932
Bristol docks by moonlight with the Sierra Cadena   c.1895
Pen, ink and watercolour   272 x 365 mm   Bristol Museums and Art Gallery K4260

THE *SIERRA CADENA* WAS A THREE-MASTED IRON SHIP of almost 2,000 tons that had been built in Liverpool in 1884. Here, she is berthed at Bush's Corner alongside Bush House, today's Arnolfini. Her stern would have projected far into St Augustine's Reach and her masts rose to nearly twice the height of the warehouse. Below her prow is a view down Prince Street to the tower of St Stephen's Church.

Another version of this view, dated 1893, depicts the same scene with the same figures by daylight. Although it is probable that this moonlight scene was drawn later in the studio, this watercolour has an impressive sense of actuality and an enthusiasm for the life of a busy port. Goodwin was fascinated by a wide variety of atmospheric light effects, including those enhanced by the industrial pollution that is so evident in the sky of the scene on the opposite page.

Goodwin was born in Maidstone and was first taught by two important Pre-Raphaelite artists, Arthur Hughes and Ford Madox Brown. In 1872 he travelled to Italy with John Ruskin. Goodwin passed his later years at Bexhill-on-Sea, but from 1877 to 1905 he had lived at Ilfracombe in Devon.

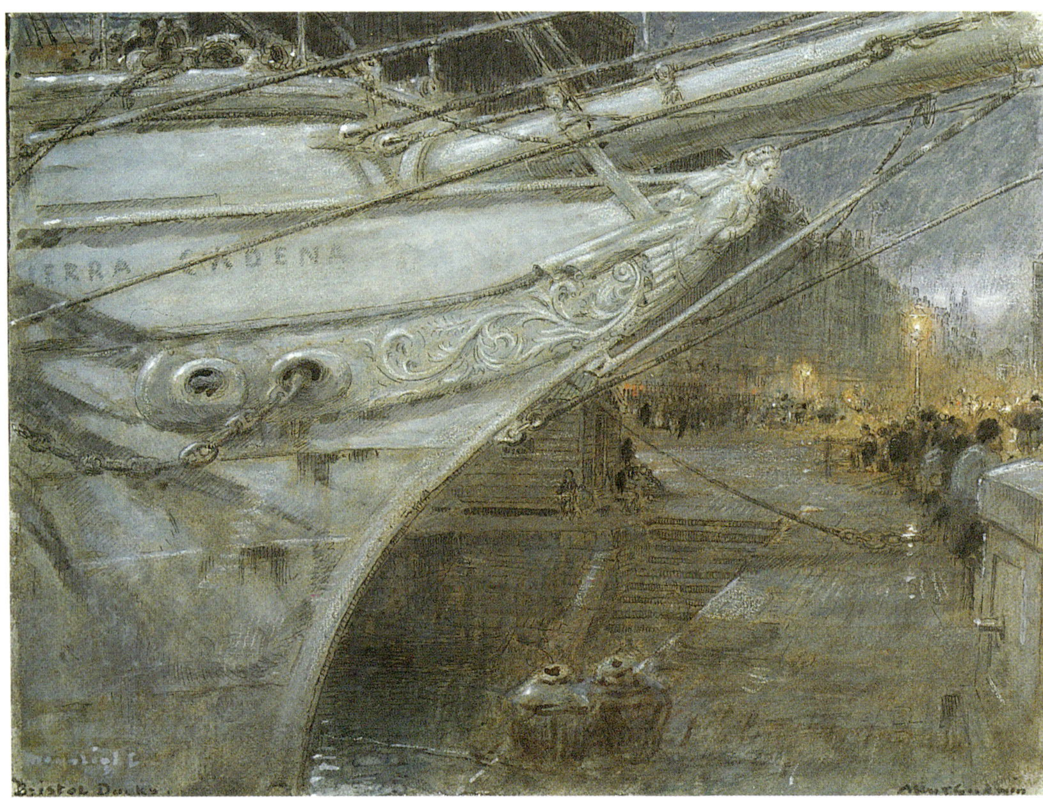

110 Albert Goodwin   1845-1932
'Bristol Dock'   c.1895
Pencil, crayon and oil   275 x 375 mm   Private collection

A BARQUE IS BEING TOWED THROUGH PRINCE STREET BRIDGE. The waiting crowd, in which there are red-coated soldiers and horse-drawn carts, enjoys the spectacle. Beyond the ship is Bush House with its recent addition of a turret on the roof for the reception of grain. The tower of the hydraulic engine shed, from which the bridge was once powered is to the right. A tug is moored in the foreground with the distinctive red, white and black livery of the stevedores and tug-owners C. J. King & Sons.

The last square-rigged sailing ship to be built in Bristol was the *Favell*, a three-masted barque of the type depicted here. She was built in the Albion Dockyard in 1895 by Charles Hill & Sons, who sold her two years later to a Finnish company, when the Bristol company resolved only to run and own steamships. The *Favell* was to take part in many of the famous grain races to and from Australia and she continued as a training ship until 1937, when she was finally broken up.

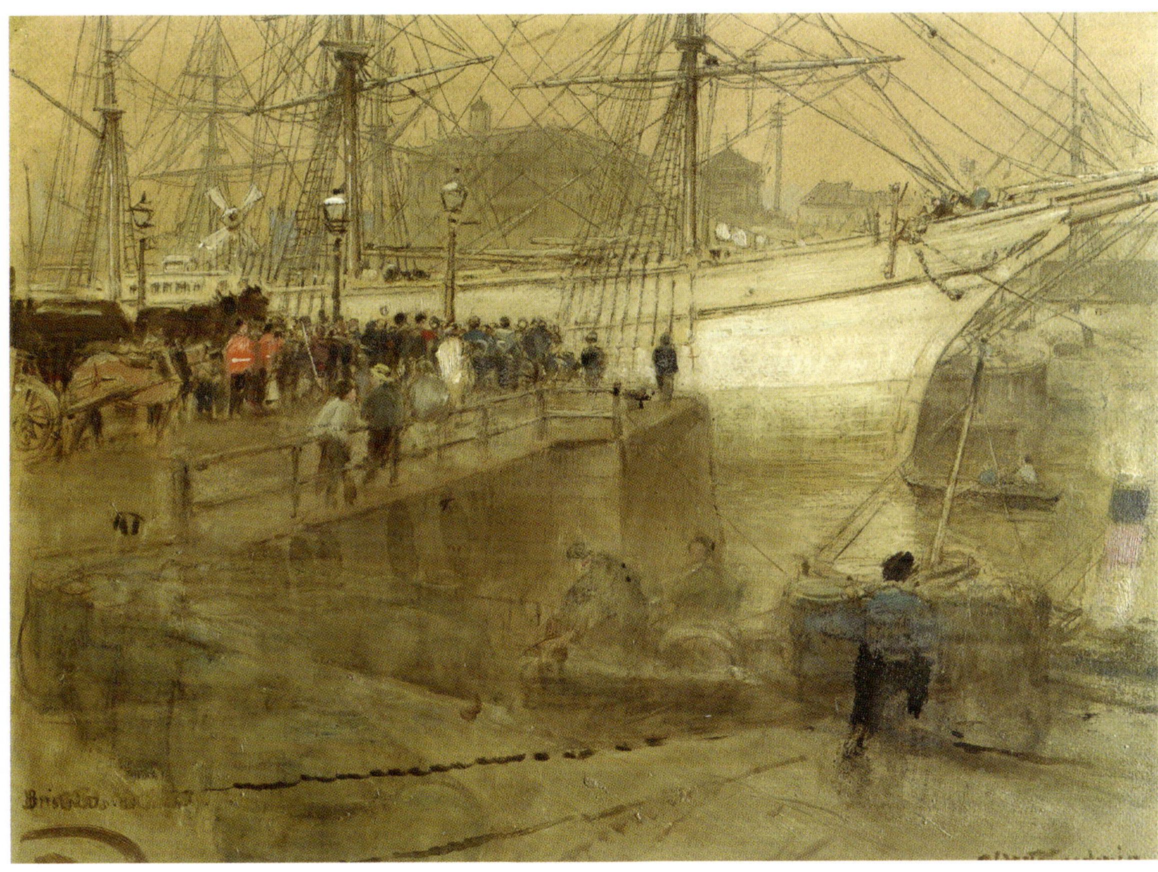

111 Charles Parsons Knight   1829-1897

'On the Floating Harbour, Bristol, before the destruction of St Werburgh's Church…'   1879
Oil   730 x 1070 mm   Bristol Museums and Art Gallery K34

THE BRISTOL ARTIST, C.P. KNIGHT, has taken purposeful advantage of much of the detail in the photograph, illustrated opposite, which was taken ten years earlier. He adds evening light and a sense of mood – of quiet at the close of day. This light also enables him to differentiate and articulate the architecture more clearly and to create a much greater sense of depth.

We also see more than the fixed viewpoint of the camera permitted. Despite the fact that Knight has subtly lowered the viewpoint, he adds in the towers, spires and cupolas of churches that could actually only be seen from much higher up. On the skyline to the left is St Michael-on-the-Hill. In the distance in the centre is St James's and just before the dominating tower of St Stephen's is the spire of St John-on-the-Wall. Finally, on the right, are St Werburgh's, Christ Church and All Saints'. In fact St Werburgh's gothic tower in Corn Street had already been taken down and re-erected in 1878 in Mina Road amidst great controversy.

The title is taken from the artist's inscription on the back of the canvas. This inscription confirms that despite the painting's distortion of the facts and its atmosphere of calm, the artist was actually making a deliberate statement of record and regret.

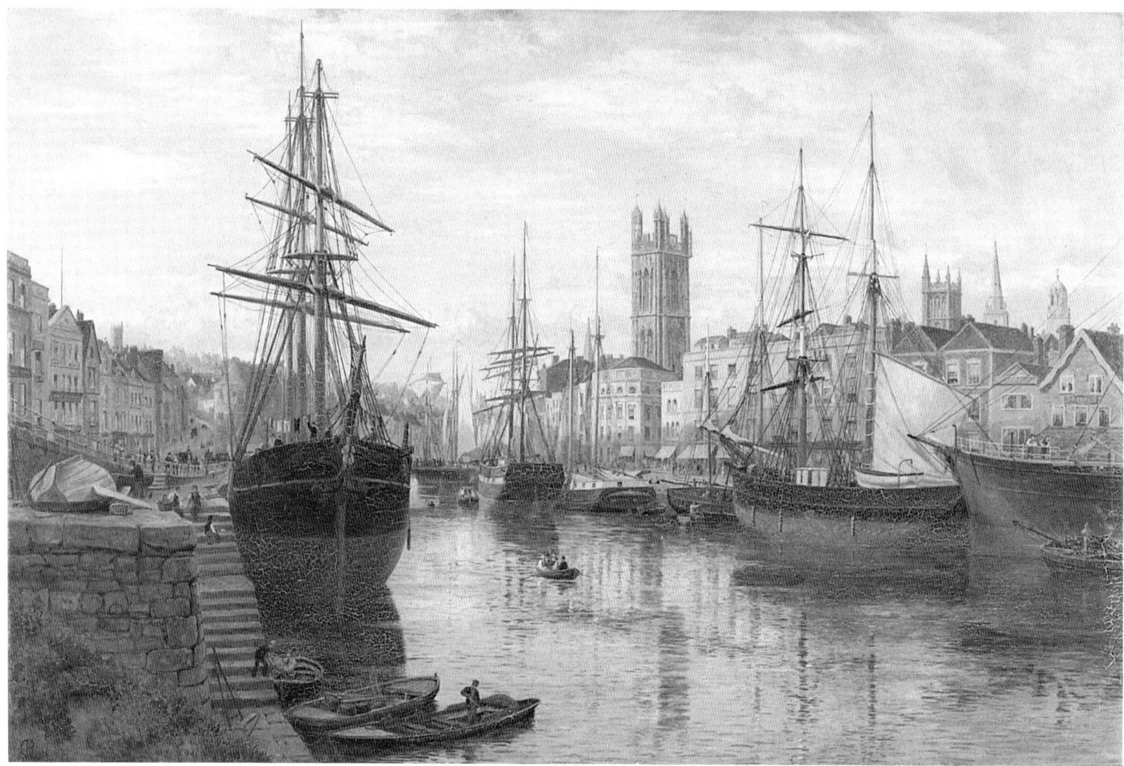

St Augustine's Reach   1868
Photograph   280 x 380 mm   Bristol Museums and Art Gallery J4787

THIS PHOTOGRAPH WAS TAKEN FROM A POINT VERY CLOSE to that at which the covering over of the Frome now begins. Today, from the same spot and in the same direction, the heart of Bristol's great medieval harbour is now represented by a parade of piddling waterspouts.

In 1868, the date of this photograph, the future of this area was already a matter of controversy. The drawbridge, which is largely obscured at the very centre of this view, was replaced during that year. Proposals to fill in the basin beyond it up to the Stone Bridge at the head of the quay had already been made and this was to be finally carried out in 1892-3.

Surprisingly perhaps, an impressive number of the surrounding buildings do remain amongst many twentieth-century office blocks. The modest size of the earlier buildings still dictates that the scale of this large space is at odds with the name that is now so commonly and misleadingly given to it. 'The Centre' is merely a contraction of Tramways Centre.

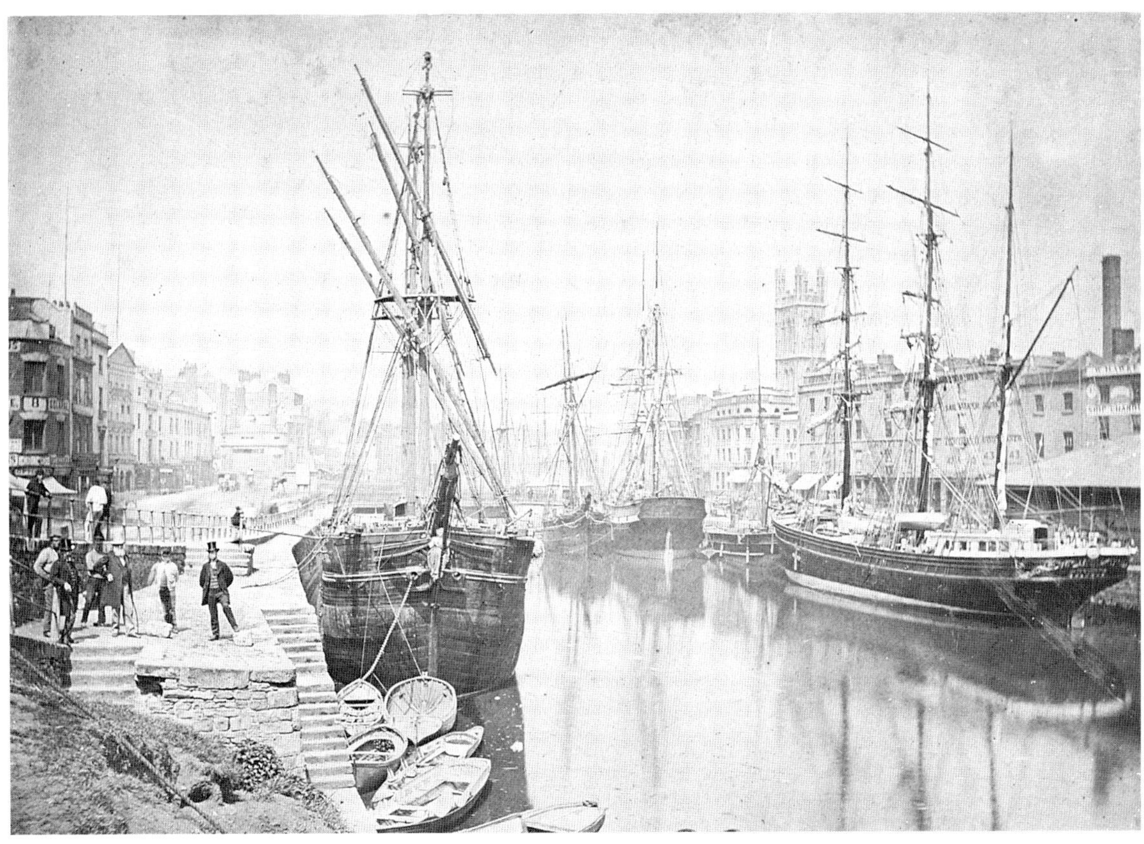

Winter in the Floating Harbour with the Corporation Granary and Prince Street Bridge   c.1895
Oil   400 x 600 mm   Private collection

WE STILL UNDERESTIMATE MANY OF OUR VICTORIAN landscape painters. With some courage, they depicted both rural and urban landscapes under the more unfriendly extremes of British weather. The black-brown snow-laden clouds depicted here are rare; so too is the portrayal of such a determinedly contemporary scene.

On the right is the vast Corporation Granary, seven stories high and built of the local Cattybrook brick. Erected in the mid-1880s, it was largely used for American grain. It was destroyed in the bombing of 1941 and later replaced by today's transit sheds, one of which now houses the Industrial Museum. Beyond is Prince Street Bridge renewed in 1879 and in between in the far distance is a glimpse of St Mary Redcliffe's spire, rebuilt in 1872.

On the left is a 20-ton crane more recently erected in 1893. It was to be dismantled in 1961 but the tall circular tower, on which it sat, survives at the apex of the forecourt to the Lloyds Bank Headquarters. To the left of the crane the temporary grain elevator on top of Bush warehouse can just be seen.

Branwhite was from the third generation of an impressive dynasty of Bristol artists that included Nathan Cooper Branwhite, Nathan and Charles Branwhite and Rosa Müller, née Branwhite.

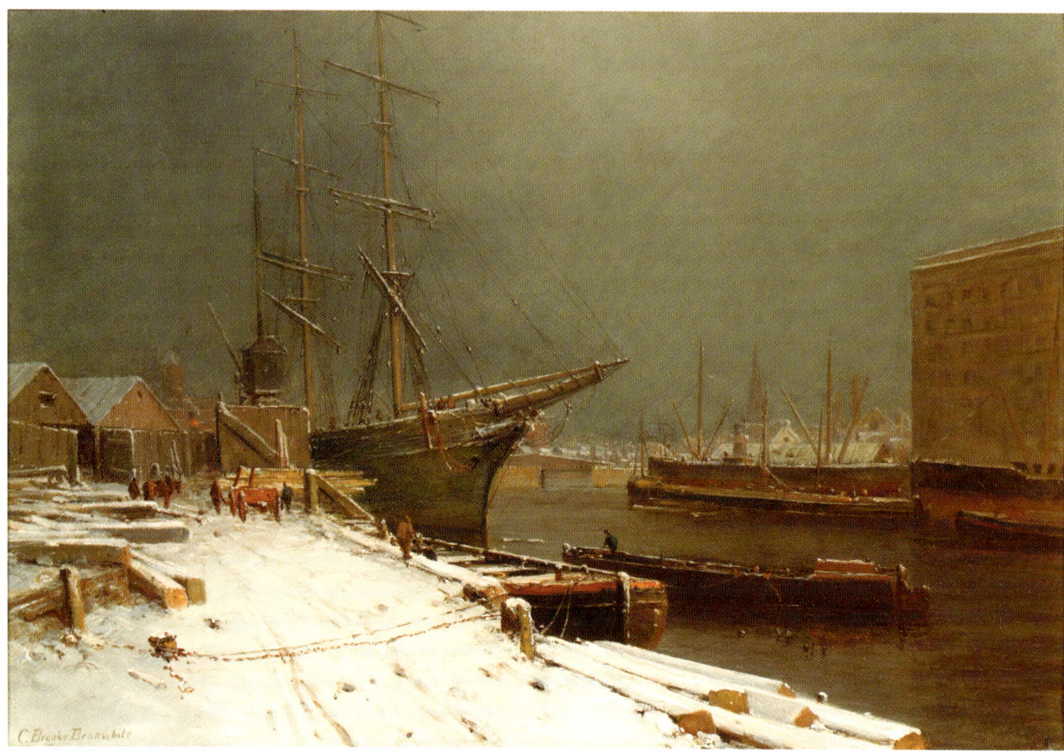

114   Arthur Wilde Parsons 1853-1931
Bristol Harbour   1912
Watercolour   360 x 540 mm   Private collection

Arthur Wilde Parsons belongs with Nicholas Pocock and Joseph Walter as one of Bristol's outstanding marine painters. And yet, here, he makes no attempt to record the prominent features of Bristol's harbour; indeed, were it not for the great block of the Corporation Granary in the distance, there would be no means of identifying the port depicted. The viewpoint is from the water itself, just off the Albion dockyard by the *Great Britain*.

The artist's principal concern was to catch the sense of space and sparkling light on a largely overcast day. Water, smoke, steam and the broken clouds hold the light. The clippers, steamers, tugs and smaller local craft, many of them active, surround the middle ground, emphasising both the light and the space. It is an apparently ordinary day in the life of a port, but one transformed by the artist's observation.

Wilde Parsons knew the port of Bristol intimately. He had been born in Fishponds, where his father ran a lunatic asylum, but he was largely brought up in Hotwells at 13 Dowry Square, the Clifton Dispensary. He later lived at Hampton Park. A founder member of the Bristol Savages, he was their president in 1908. His brother was to be vicar of Crantock near Newquay and Wilde Parsons is perhaps best known for his stormy Cornish coastal scenes and landscapes.

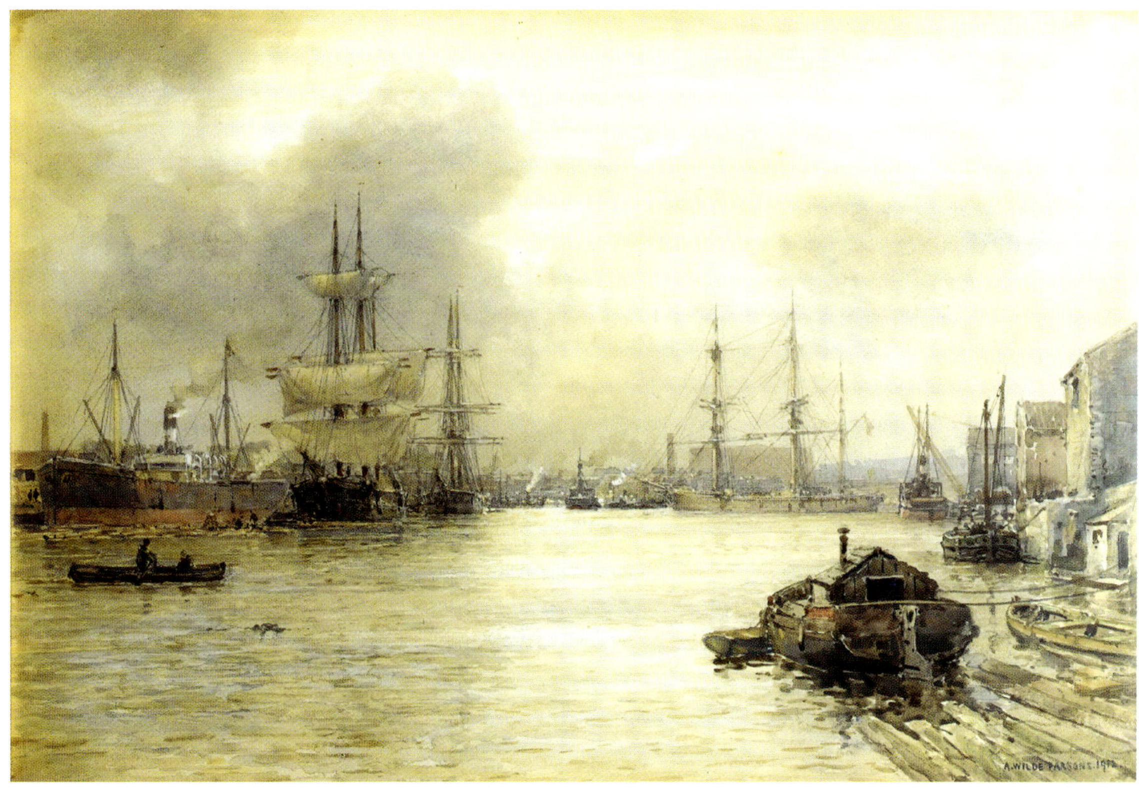

115   Arthur Wilde Parsons   1853-1931
The last days of H.M.S. Formidable   1904
Watercolour   720 x 1110 mm   Bristol Museums and Art Gallery K52

WITHOUT UNDUE SENTIMENTALITY, WILDE PARSONS suggests the fragile dignity of a warrior's old age. Built at Chatham Naval Dockyard in 1825, this 84-gun ship is seen anchored in King Road, off Portishead, nearly eighty years later. She was employed as a training centre for wayward and homeless boys from 1869 to 1906 when she was finally towed away to be broken up. She was succeeded by Portishead's National Nautical School on the hillside in the distance, the building of which began in 1902.

Photographs of the ship reveal that the artist flattered his subject. H.M.S. *Formidable* was in such a poor state in her last two years that tugs were almost permanently standing by in case she began to sink. Wilde Parsons heightened her masts and restored her rigging – a discreet facelift that was especially understandable in the year before the first centenary of the Battle of Trafalgar.

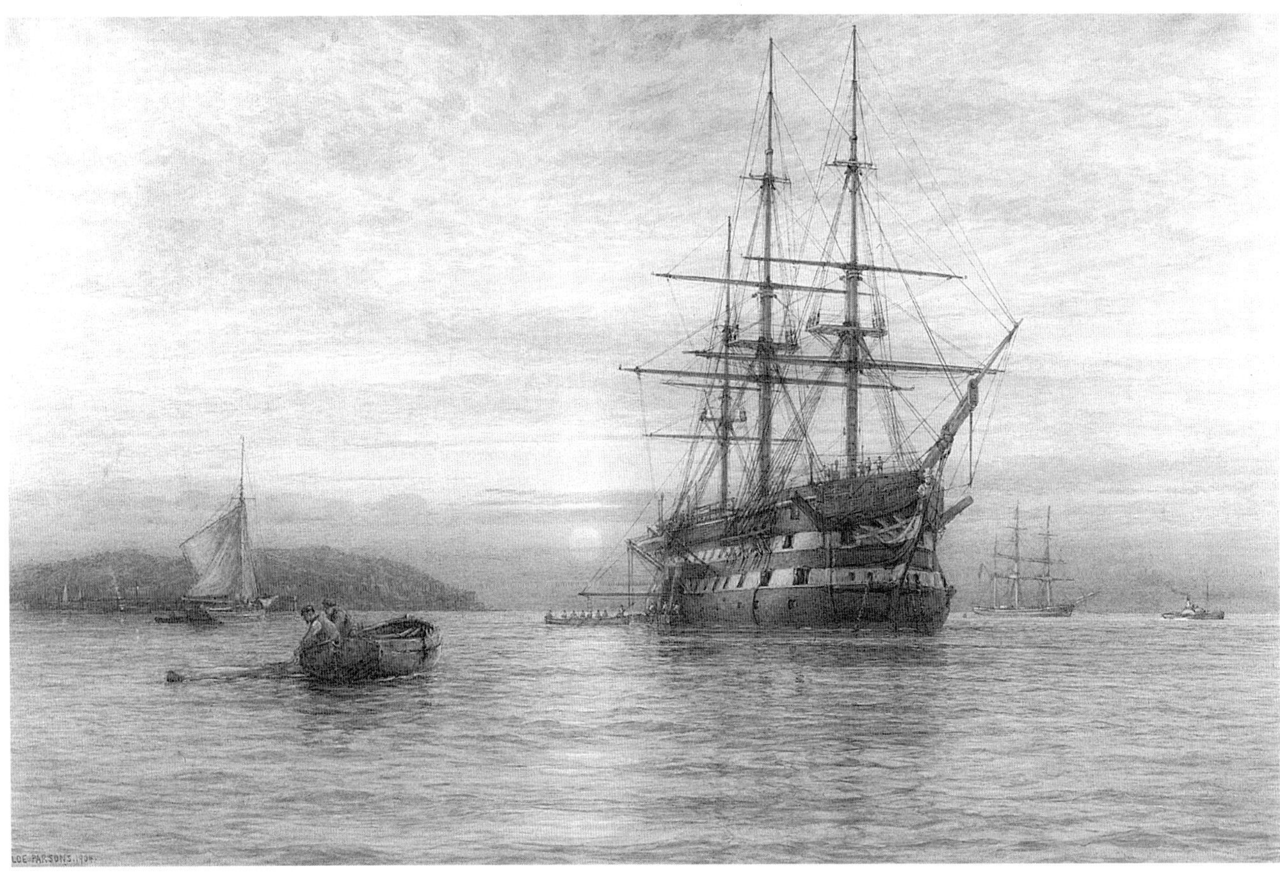

116 Arthur Wilde Parsons 1853-1931 *'Opening of the Royal Edward Dock, Avonmouth, July 9 1908, by his Majesty King Edward VII,*
accompanied by her Majesty Queen Alexandra and H.R.H. Princess Victoria, on board the Royal Yacht...' 1909
Oil   1270 x 2120 mm   Bristol Museums and Art Gallery K164

BY THE 1880S IT WAS ALREADY CLEAR THAT STEAMSHIPS were being built that were too big for Avonmouth's entrance lock, completed in 1877. In 1901 an Act of Parliament was passed authorising the building of a vast new dock at Avonmouth that would, at last, be ahead of demand for many decades to come.

On the day that the Royal Yacht *Albert and Victoria* was guided into the Royal Edward Dock by the tugs of C. & J. King & Sons, *Sea Prince* and *King*, the royal party had first been entertained to lunch in Bristol Art Gallery, opened just three years earlier. Perhaps it was there, before the main event, that a group of Bristolians resolved to commission a painting to record the great occasion. But that July day became wet, blustery and grim. A year later, when the painting was duly presented to the

Art Gallery, the local newspaper reported that the original subject 'was about as bald and uninspiring as any artist could be confronted with.'

The writer generously acknowledged, however, that Wilde Parsons had skilfully balanced the need to record the new sheds, the powerhouse and the great size of the dock itself with the stately royal yacht. The yacht was also surprisingly sombre in appearance and the artist contrasted it with the newly and brightly painted tugs and the colourful flags and bunting. The movement of the water was admired and 'there is life, too, in the grey rain clouds racing over the dock.' It was a bold commission and the subscribers were justly rewarded. Today, the painting hangs in the dining room of the Mansion House.

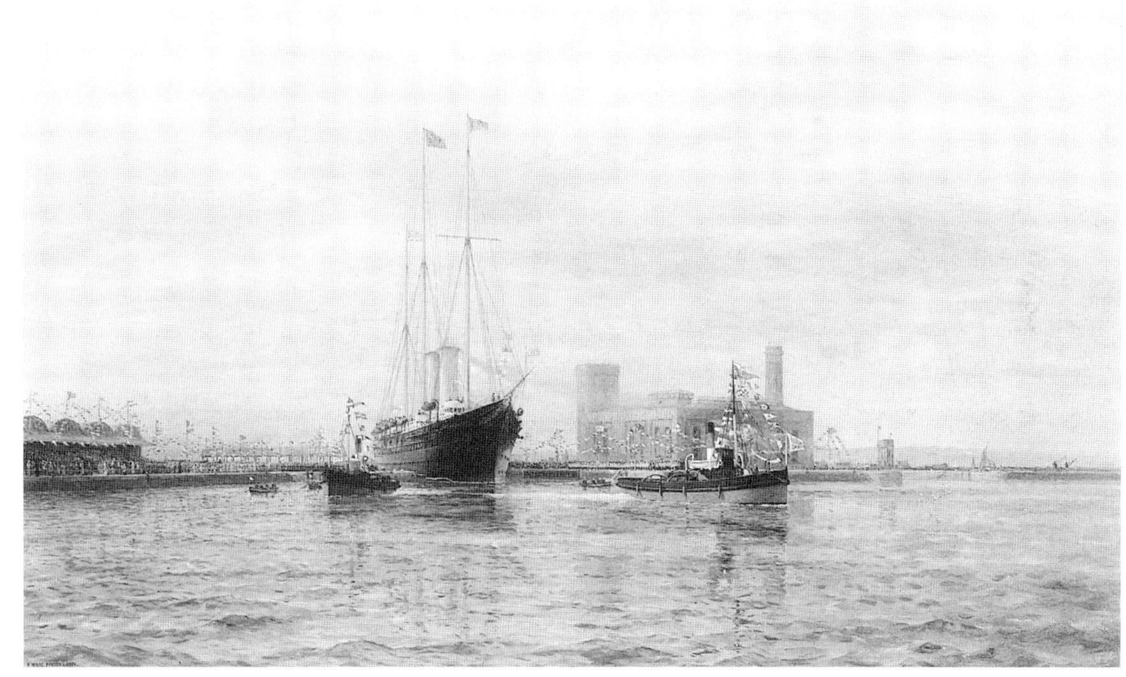

The Lock, Feeder Road c.1926
Etching and drypoint 124 x 174 mm   Bristol Museums and Art Gallery M4644

BY THE EARLY TWENTIETH CENTURY ETCHING had achieved an almost equal status with watercolour or oil as an original medium of artistic expression rather than simply as a method of illustration or reproduction. The outstanding Principal of the Bristol Municipal School of Art, Reginald Bush, ensured that Bristol had an unusually high number of good etchers, especially in the 1920s. For many years E. Willis Paige was Bush's Assistant Principal.

The Lock, Feeder Road is perhaps Paige's finest work. It is intense, crowded and atmospheric and its lines and shapes seem to interlock both on the surface and in depth. It depicts the only scene above Bristol Bridge to be included in this book and well deserves to be the one exception to the rule.

Many smaller vessels could travel up the New Cut on the tide and enter into either the Floating Harbour or the Feeder Canal through this lock behind Temple Meads Station. The bridge carried the new Feeder Road, sanctioned by an Act of 1806. The tollhouse is just to the left of the bridge and appears to be still bearing its old tariff boards. The lock was deliberately filled in during the Second World War to avoid the risk of the Floating Harbour being drained should the lock be damaged.

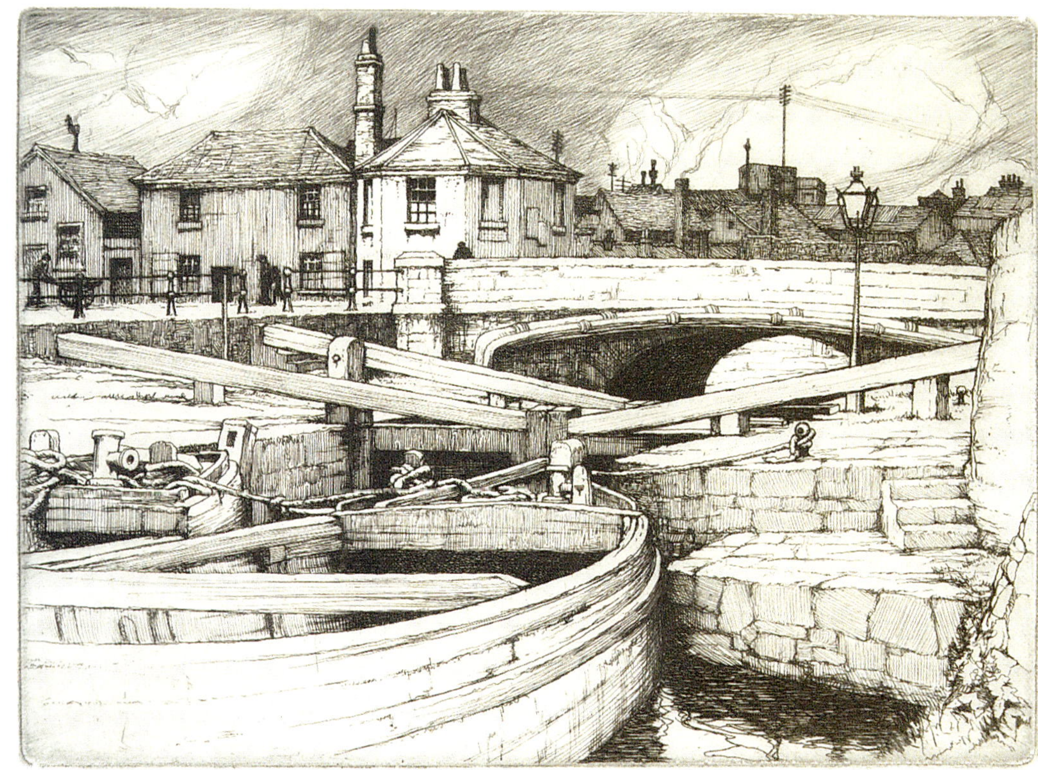

118 Harry Banks 1869-1947
Broad Quay c.1922
Etching 154 x 145 mm Bristol Museums and Art Gallery M4306

TOBACCO CASKS – HOGSHEADS – ARE BEING UNLOADED
at No 1, Dublin Shed, built in 1861 and the earliest of
all the transit sheds. Almost all tobacco imports were
soon to be landed at the new No 29 Bond, the subject
of the etching on the next page.

In the distance below Colston Hall is the new
fixed bridge completed in 1893. At the same time the
Frome was culverted from there to the Stone Bridge.
The long process of filling in a large part of the
medieval harbour had begun.

Harry Banks lived in Dorset and his connection
with Bristol is unusual. For five or six years from
1917 he and his family lived in Clifton during term-
time while his daughter attended school.

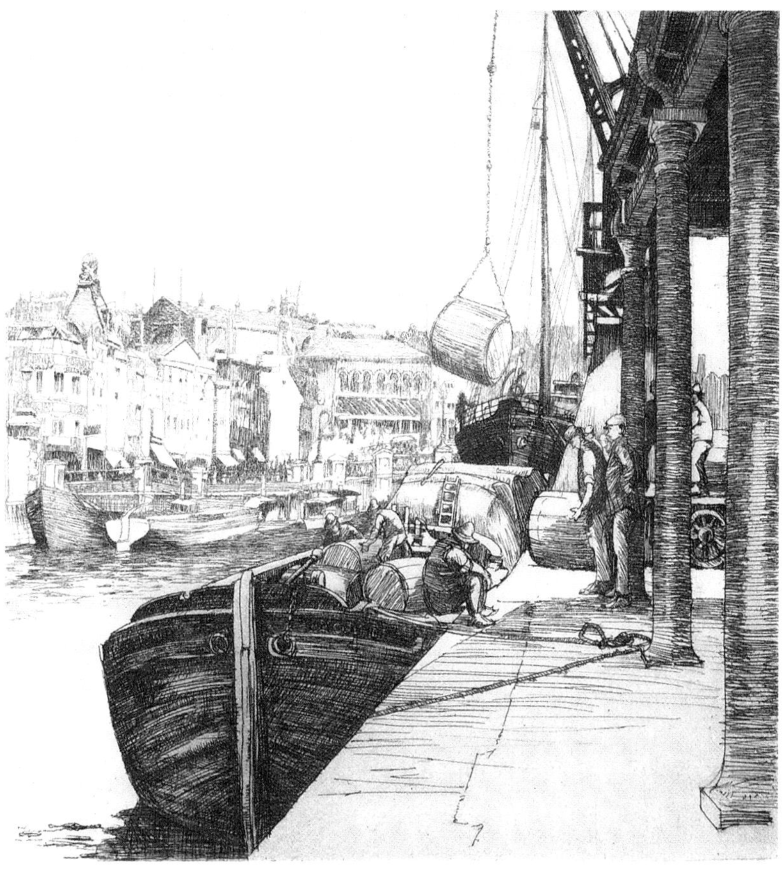

119 Edward Sharland   c.1888-1967
Tobacco Bonds, Canon's Marsh   c.1922
Etching   380 x 550 mm   Bristol Museums and Art Gallery J3757

THIS GIGANTIC WAREHOUSE, NO 29 BOND, was completed in 1922 for Canon's Marsh Tobacco Bonds Ltd, in which Imperial Tobacco was the major shareholder. By the 1930s still more space was needed for the storage of the casks of tobacco leaf, an indication of the enormous scale of this business.

To the right of the warehouse is Bristol Cathedral. In the centre is the 20-ton crane erected in 1893 (113). The crane's tower remains at the apex of the forecourt of the Lloyds Bank Headquarters, the building that succeeded the Tobacco Bonds after their demolition in 1988.

Edward Sharland was the son of a Bristol cabinetmaker and was largely self-taught as a printmaker. In this large work and in a series of etchings of the construction of the University Tower, there is a vigour to the drawing and an excitement in the sheer scale of the subject that is often lacking in his many topographical prints.

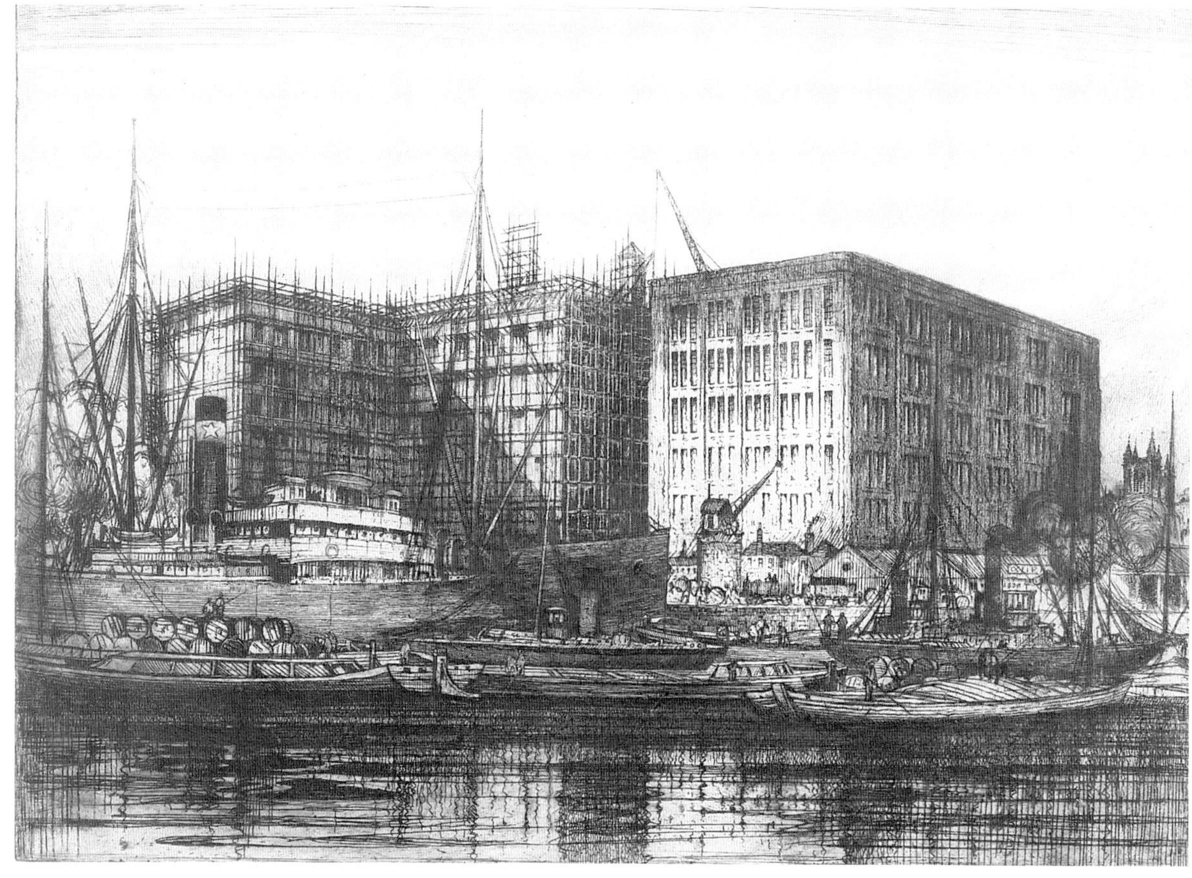

120 Dorothy Woollard RWA RE 1886-1986
'The Mill on the Harbour' 1913
Etching 257 x 112 mm Bristol Museums and Art Gallery M4998

DOROTHY WOOLLARD WAS FIRST TAUGHT at Bristol Municipal School of Art by Reginald Bush, of whom she was to be a life-long friend, and then at the Royal College in London by the master printmaker, Sir Frank Short. It is no surprise that she should have been a fine technician, or that, at her best, her work can recall James Abbott McNeill Whistler's etchings of scenes on the Thames executed half a century earlier.

But for the swirling smoke, the distant chimneys of Fry's chocolate factory in the Pithay and the closer chimney of the granary, this scene has survived remarkably intact. The towers of All Saints', Christ Church, St Nicholas' and St Mary-le-Port are all still just visible from this spot. The quay-less cliff face of the mills on Redcliffe Wharf opposite Welsh Back has been justly cherished by the City's planners. To the right of the masts is the early reinforced concrete building of 1893, the Western Counties Association warehouse, now converted to housing. Buchanan's warehouse, which is on either side of the single chimney, has also been converted into flats. It was the granary and mill built 1883-4 for Proctor Baker, chairman of the Docks Committee.

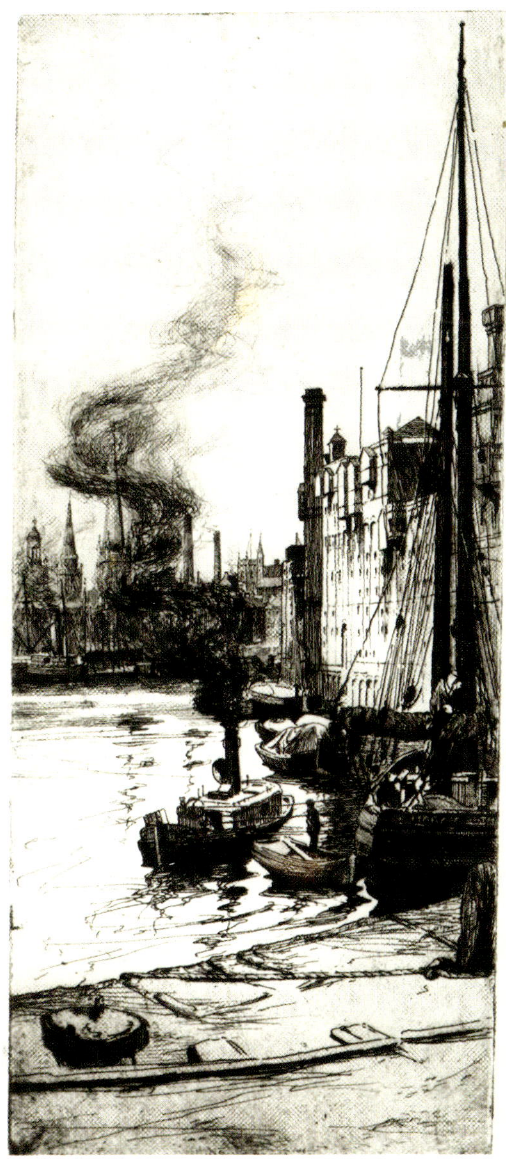

TIMBER IS BEING UNLOADED AT BALTIC WHARF to be added to the open corrugated-iron sheds to the left. Two of P. & A. Campbell's White Funnel fleet of paddle steamers are moored at Underfall Yard. Beyond them is the chimney of the New Hydraulic Engine House completed in 1887. Its hydraulic power could once operate all the Floating Harbour's lock gates, sluices and swing bridges as well as B-Bond's tobacco presses. B-Bond, the massive redbrick tobacco-bond warehouse, was completed in 1908 for Bristol Corporation. Today it houses the city's Record Office and the Create Centre.

Preparatory drawings confirm that John Nash took great care over the composition. Stacks of timber, steamers, warehouses, chimneys, masts – all are carefully placed and poised with the balance of an abstract sculpture by Anthony Caro. There has been some selection and simplification and some incidental details may have been ignored, but the forms, shapes and textures, even the cobbled quayside, are all very accurately realised.

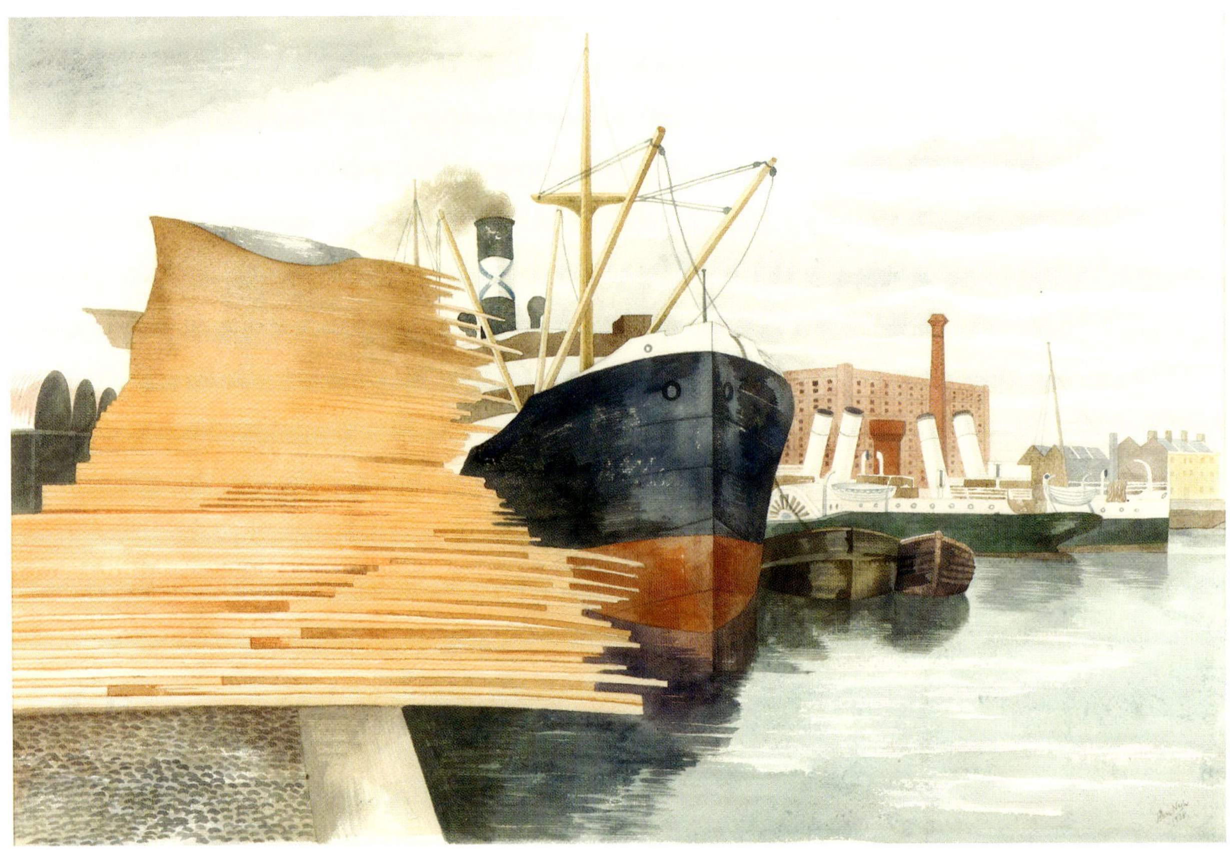

122 John Nash CBE RA 1893-1977
'Nocturne' 1938
Pencil and watercolour   400 x 580 mm   Bristol Museums and Art Gallery K1456

THE ELEGANT PADDLE STEAMERS of the White Funnel fleet are in their winter quarters moored by the railway lines along the Hotwell Road with the Cathedral and the gas works in the background. The vessel is almost certainly the *Britannia* (Fig. X) which Nash's friend, Eric Ravilious, also painted on the same visit from a different angle.

John Nash has inscribed the title *Nocturne* below his signature. It is a title that recalls James Abbott McNeill Whistler's paintings of the Thames at night to which Whistler gave the same title. For both Whistler and Nash the musical connotations were deliberate. Here, they are reflected in the subtle transitions of the limited range of colours and, more obviously, in the succession of rhythmical, echoing curves.

John Nash was the younger brother of Paul Nash. It was Paul who persuaded his brother not to undergo any formal art education so that his own genius might find free expression, unfettered by the influence of other artists. It was a theory that worked well for John Nash, but which has plagued art schools ever since.

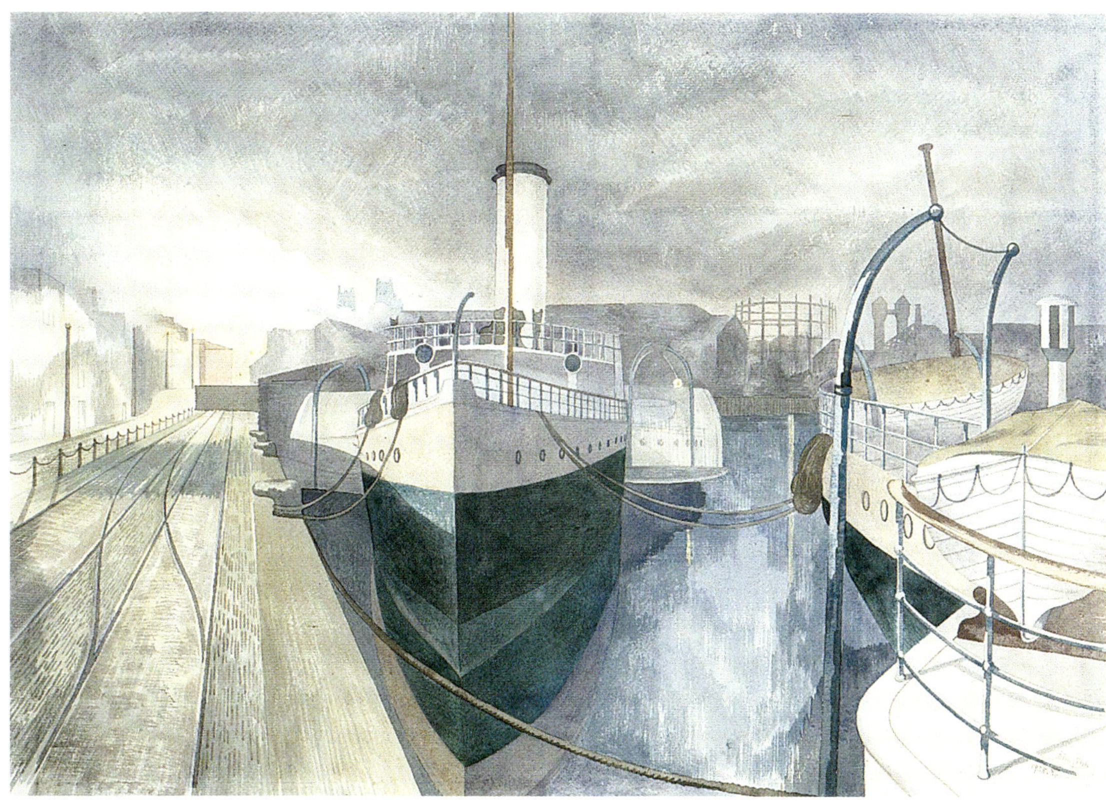

CABOT TOWER AND THE UNIVERSITY'S WILLS TOWER rise above No 29 Bond, the bonded tobacco warehouses on Canon's Marsh. In the foreground are the crowded marshalling yards of the Bristol Harbour Railway, the line that ran under St Mary Redcliffe's churchyard.

No 29 Bond survived the war but was demolished at seven o'clock on the still and clear morning of 29 May 1988. It had been built of concrete. Some minutes after the dramatic detonation, the dust settled and the air cleared. A thick white film, unmoving and seemingly solid, now covered the Floating Harbour. For a few minutes it was as if the City Council's arrogant demand for the powers to fill in the harbour, mercifully rejected in committee by the House of Lords in 1969, had finally been realised.

John Piper had been a mature student at the Royal College of Art in the late 1920s. In the 1930s he produced abstract paintings and reliefs and he was closely associated with such artists as Ben Nicholson and Henry Moore. Abstracts did not sell well and Piper took to writing articles. In 1938 his *Shell Guide to Oxfordshire* was published. Thereafter, topography and the textures, colours and poetry of landscape dominated his work. As an Official War Artist, Piper was given various subjects to paint, including transport, and he is known to have visited Cardiff and Avonmouth, and presumably also Bristol, in July 1944. He was to paint three of Bristol's blitzed churches.

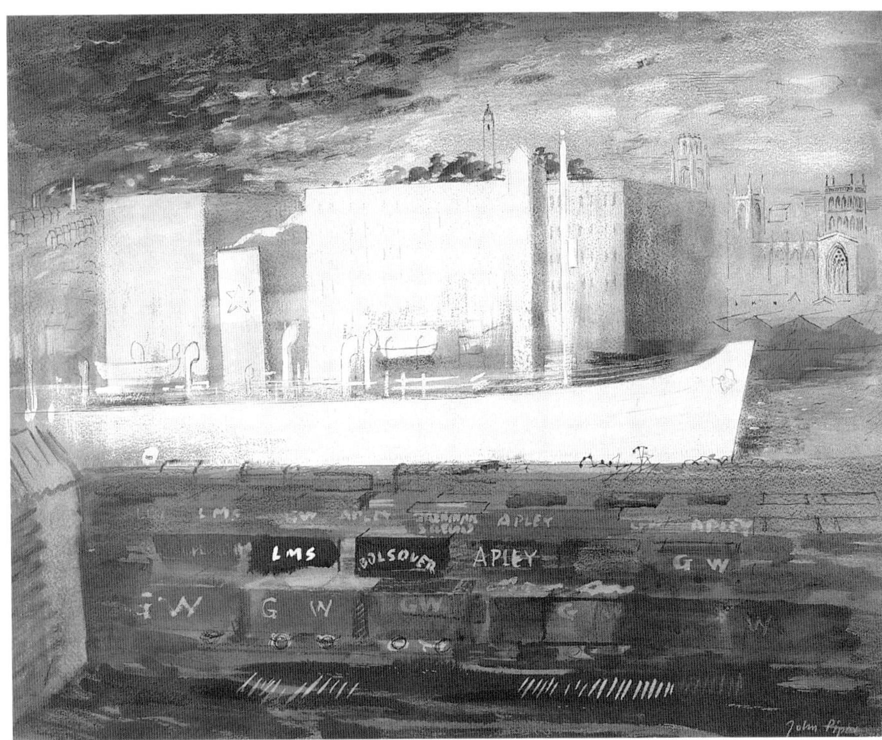

124 Paul Nash 1889-1946
The Avon Gorge 1939
Pencil, chalk and watercolour   283 x 388   Bristol Museums and Art Gallery K5797

PAUL NASH WAS ONE OF THE MOST IMPORTANT BRITISH PAINTERS of the first half of the last century. In March 1939 he stayed briefly in Bristol drawing in the Avon Gorge and carrying out research on the Clifton Suspension Bridge for an article in the *Architectural Review*, published the following September. The title of the article, 'The Giant's Stride', was a reference to local legend, but also to Nash's own fascination for the way in which man has moulded the landscape over many centuries.

From his vantage point at Sea Walls, Nash worked quickly in pencil and crayon, possibly adding the colour later. He took advantage of the sweeping curves of the new road, the Portway, opened in 1926 and of the riverbanks, creating an hourglass design of the gorge capped by the bridge. A steam train emerges from the tunnel on the south side and there is a dense grey March sky above. Strong reflections in the river animate the vast open space before the viewer. The bridge binds the two sides of the gorge and the road, railway, bridge and observatory seem an integral part of this ancient landscape.

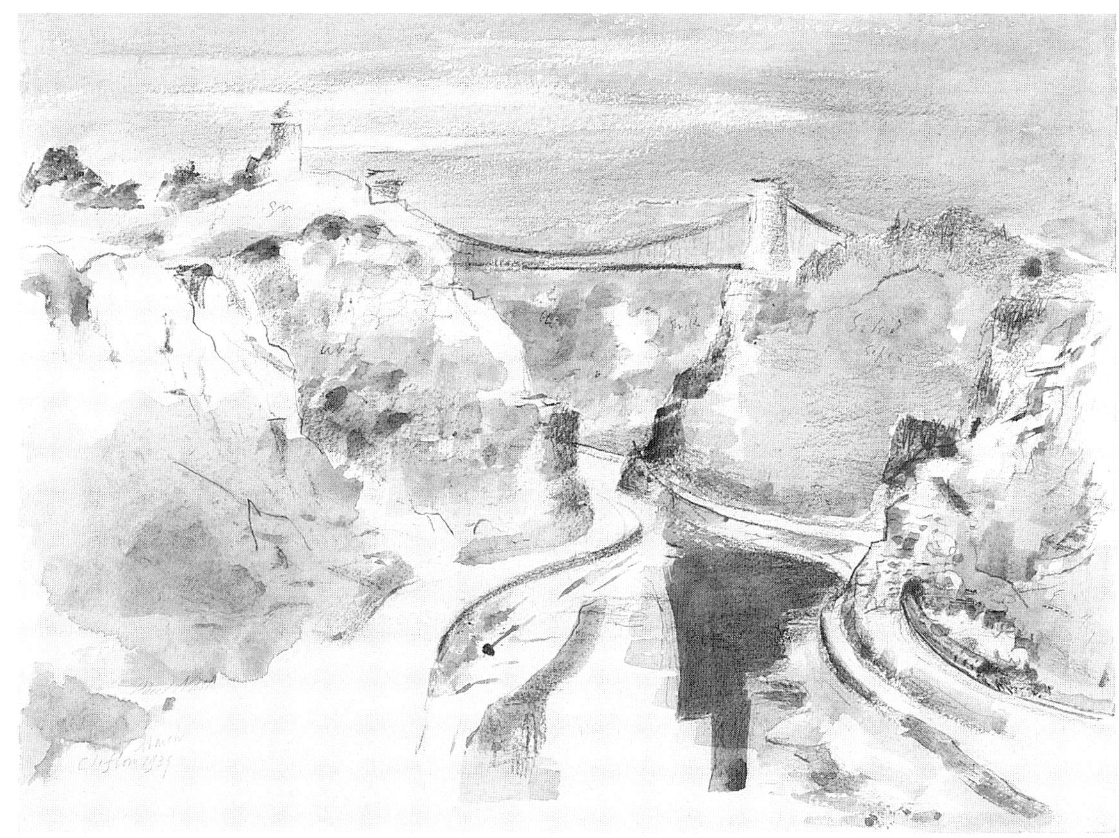

125 Gordon Nicholl 1888–1959
Clifton Suspension Bridge c.1935
Colour lithograph 1010 x 620mm Private collection

GORDON NICHOLL'S DESIGN IS THE MOST STRIKING of several British Railways posters promoting rail travel and tourism to Bristol. The bridge and the Avon Gorge are the main subjects but the steam train on the Bristol to Portishead line draws attention to the scenic wonders of rail travel as well as subtly exaggerating the height of the bridge.

The sleek P. & A. Campbell steamer gliding below the bridge was also a major tourist attraction. Not only Bristolians, but many others from further afield travelled to Bristol annually to enjoy a crowded but stylish, almost luxurious cruise down the Avon Gorge to Portishead, Clevedon, Flat Holm and Steep Holm, Ilfracombe or the Welsh coast.

Since the 1880s most paddle steamers were being built expressly for pleasure cruises. The elegant vessels of the White Funnel Line fostered a habit of trips into the Bristol Channel amongst successive generations of West Country families. Several of these paddle steamers were to see active service at Dunkirk and as minesweepers during both world wars. In 1946 the *Bristol Queen* was built in Bristol, but demand was falling and she proved to be the last of her line.

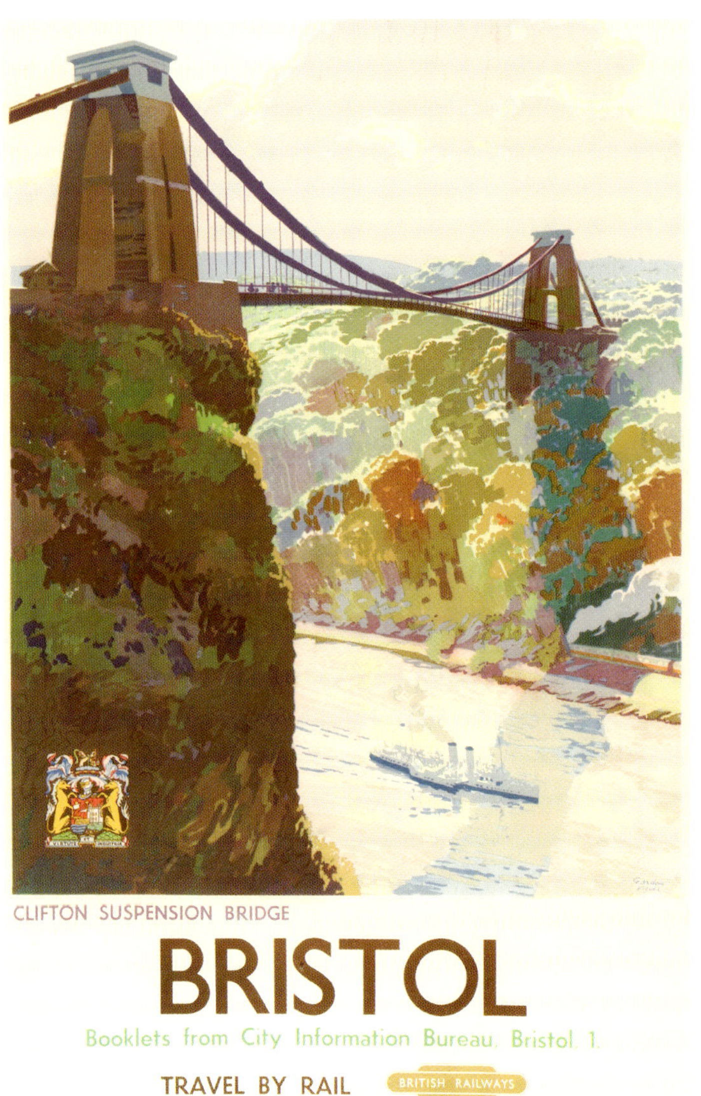

'TOWN CENTRE'; St Augustines Parade   c.1946
Colour lithograph   495 x 760 mm   Bristol Museums and Art Gallery K5475

BRISTOL'S GIANT ROUNDABOUT had been created just before the Second World War began, when a second portion of the medieval harbour had been filled in. It was plans for an inner circuit road that had prompted this massive in-fill of the harbour. Redcliffe Bridge, opened in 1939, and a new road that sliced diagonally across Queen Square were part of the same scheme.

In the distance the trees opposite the colonnaded façade of St Mary-on-the-Quay mark the part of the harbour that had been covered over in the 1890s. It was this area that then became the Tramways Centre, although by the time of the war the double-decker bus had evidently already superseded the tram.

Phyllis Ginger's skill as a topographical artist had led to her involvement in 'Recording Britain'. Begun in 1939, this scheme was the brainchild of Sir Kenneth Clark, who saw it as an exten-

sion of the Official War Artist programme. Driven from London by the relentless bombing, Phyllis Ginger came to Keynsham to stay with friends and did many drawings in Bath, Bristol and Cheltenham for 'Recording Britain'. This lithograph was commissioned immediately after the war and was based on both new and earlier studies. It was simply titled 'Town Centre' and was one of the series of School Prints produced in 1946 and 1947. This bold project was the initiative of Brenda Rawnsley, who had written to such artists as Henry Moore, John Nash and Julian Trevelyan explaining that it was 'a means of giving school children an understanding of contemporary art.' Twenty-four prints, each by a different artist, were produced. This admirable scheme ultimately foundered on the unforeseen costs and difficulties of distribution to over 4,000 schools.

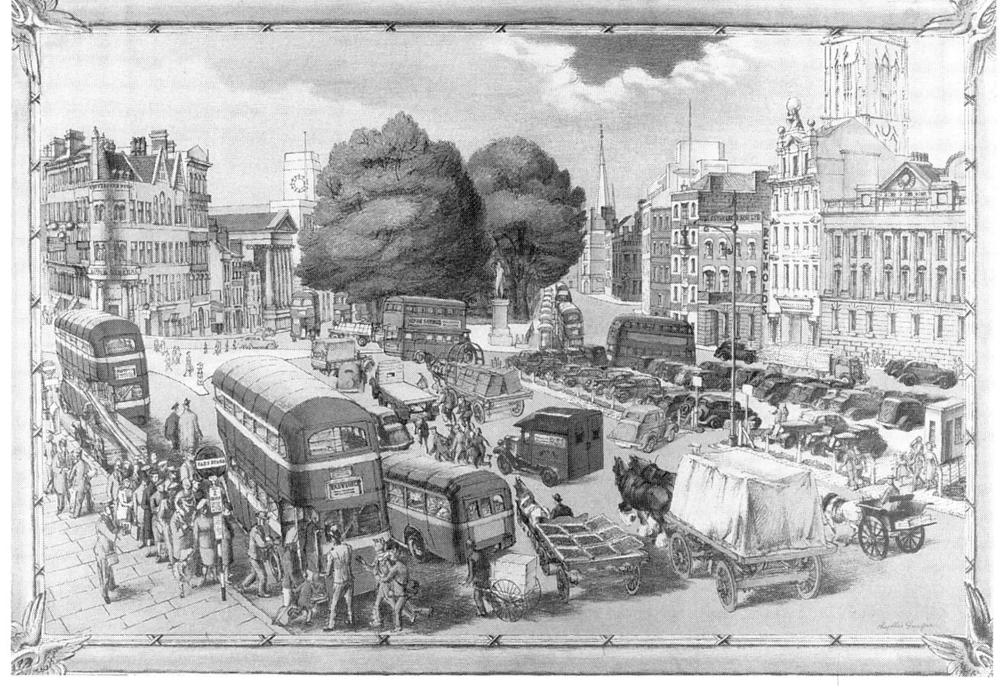

127 Tristram Hillier RA 1905-1983
'The Inner Pool, Bristol' 1960
Oil   601 x 812 mm   Bristol Museums and Art Gallery K2919

THE ARTIST'S TITLE IS BOTH MISLEADING AND REVEALING. The nearby Bathurst Basin might well be described as an inner pool, but the river in this view is part of the Floating Harbour, the once-tidal Avon. The topographical and architectural detail is no more accurate than the title. St Mary Redcliffe and Redcliffe Parade are easily recognisable, but that is all. Instead the title may more purposefully refer to the stillness of the water and the pervasive spiritual calm of the painting.

In the 1930s Hillier had been a determined supporter of surrealism and a surreal quality was to persist in his work. There is a clarity to the light and a sharpness of outlines that is unreal. Immaculate technique and a precision to his perfectly balanced compositions heighten the feeling that his paintings are principally inventions of the studio and landscapes of the mind.

Hillier travelled extensively, but after the war he lived near Shepton Mallet in Somerset. He had been a pupil at Downside School and in 1946 he re-entered the Catholic Church. Here he transforms one of the most familiar views in Bristol into a confident statement of his faith. He does not exaggerate the height of the soaring tower and spire as so many artists have done. Instead, although the church may lock the composition together as a whole, it is the conjunction of the church and the still waters – the inner pool – that gives this work its spiritual assurance.

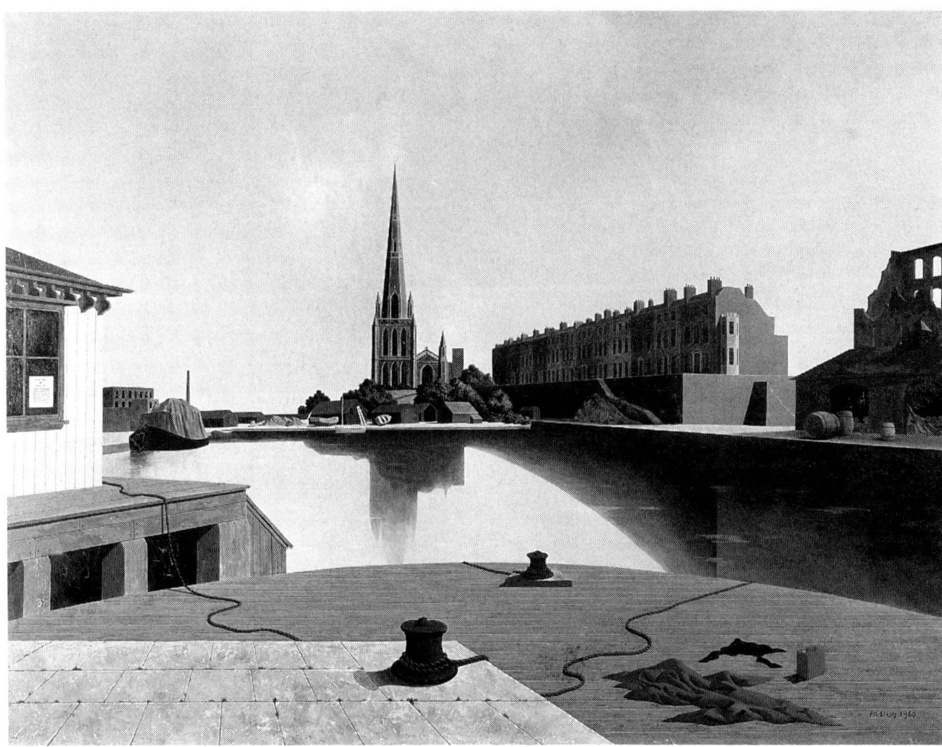

128 Clifford Hanney ARWA 1890-1990
Cumberland Basin from the Paragon c.1961
Oil   Collection of the Bristol Savages

THIS WELCOME REVERSAL OF THE USUAL VIEWS that look up towards the Clifton terraces was painted from 14 The Paragon. Clifford Hanney lived here for many years before moving to No. 3. It is possible that the artist was deliberately recording a view that he knew was about to change. The Plimsoll Bridge with its bewildering maze of approach roads was to be completed in 1964.

The reflected light from the snow makes this detailed night-scene possible. The snow also exaggerates the strong blue of the solitary gas lamp by the Cumberland Basin, where the s.s. *Kyleglen* of Liverpool has just entered the lock. The end of Windsor Terrace in the foreground is echoed by the bonded warehouse in the distance. Below the solitary figure, the gardens between Windsor Terrace and the back of Freeland Place have yet to be filled by a block of flats. On the far right is the modest railway station of Ashton Gate, which was first opened in 1906, just for football followers. A regular service began in 1926, but the station was last staffed in 1962 and has now all but disappeared.

Hanney was born at Publow near Pensford a few miles south of Bristol. He was a pupil of Reginald Bush at the Bristol Municipal School of Art and was later to be Principal of Crewe Art School.

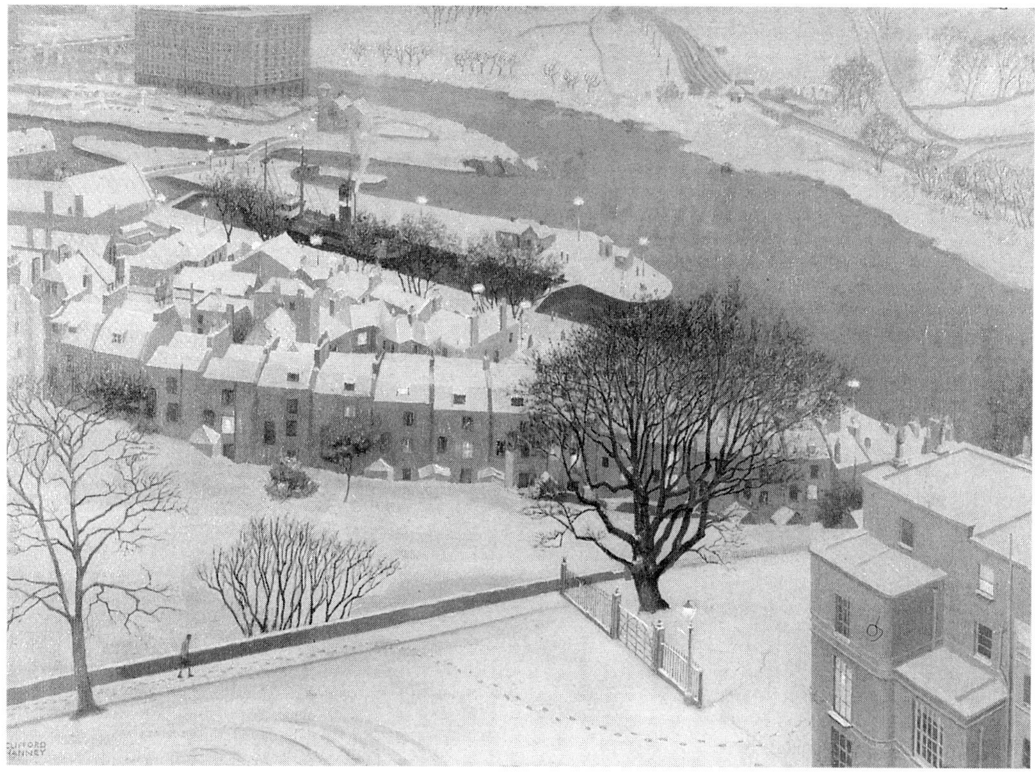

129 Peter Reddick RWA born 1924
Balloon Ascent 1993 Colour lino-cut and woodcut   380 x 505 mm
Bristol Museums and Art Gallery K5610

BALLOON ASCENT CELEBRATES THE MASS ASCENT at Bristol's annual Balloon Fiesta in early morning sunlight, as seen from the Clifton Observatory. Over a hundred hot-air balloons may rise above Leigh Woods on their ascent from Ashton Court.

Peter Reddick is best known for his small wood engravings. Few other artists have brought such emotional intensity and atmosphere to such small black and white landscapes. This very much larger lino-cut and woodcut was made to raise funds for Artspace Bristol, a charity first formed in 1976 to provide studio space for artists. Peter was the founder of the Bristol Printmakers' Workshop within Artspace, now so successfully established at Spike Island on the New Cut.

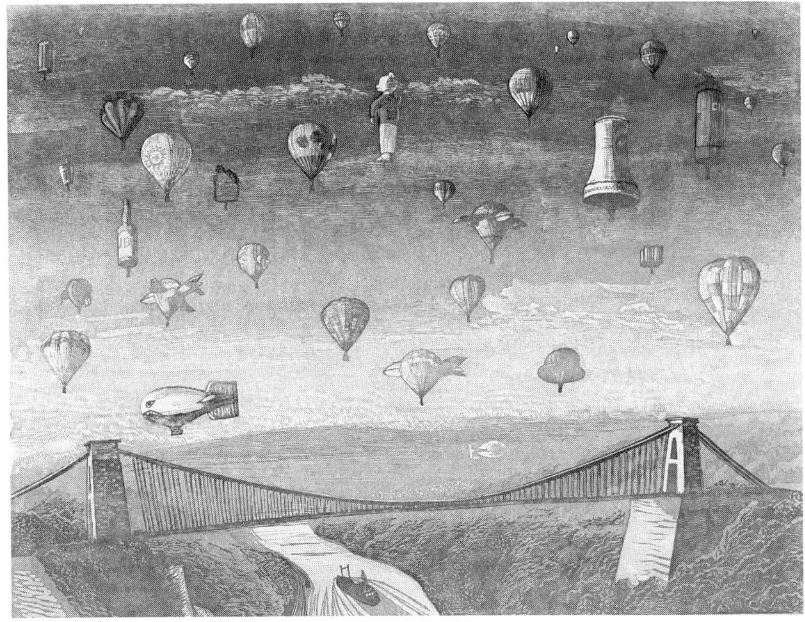

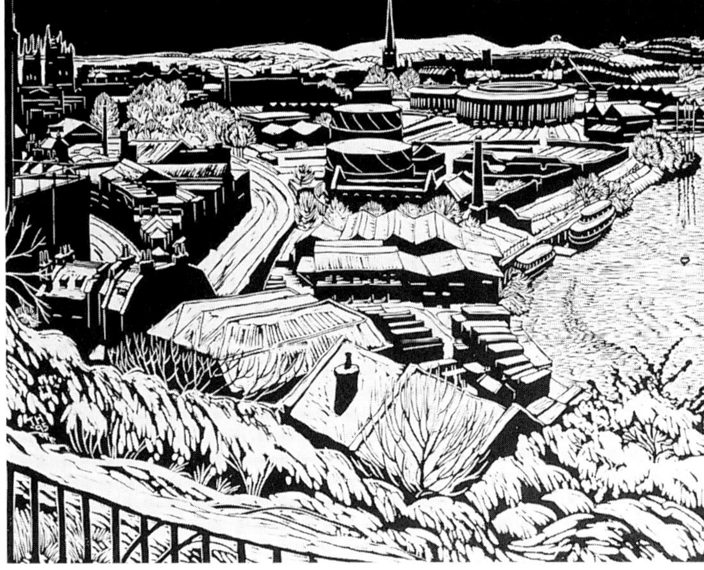

130 Trevor Haddrell born 1945
Bristol Docks from Clifton Wood in the snow 1995
Linocut 328 x 1395 mm Bristol Museums and Art Gallery K5908

THE VIEWPOINT OF THIS WINTER PANORAMA is from the steep hill-side of Clifton Wood, just a few yards above the artist's cottage, which is concealed behind the foliage on the left. As with Clifford Hanney's painting (128), it anticipates change. The artist's own view across the river to the *Great Britain* was about to be blighted by Capricorn Quay begun in 1998. These apartment blocks, arguably among the best of so many recent developments around the harbour, succeeded the warehouses and timber stacks on either side of the site of the old Limekiln Dock.

This 1995 work records the many changes since the artist had come to live in Clifton Wood twenty-six years earlier. The gasometers to the left have since gone, but the Lloyds Bank rotunda had just been completed. Trevor Haddrell witnessed the return of the *Great Britain* in 1970, and in 1976 the launch of the *Miranda Guinness*, the last substantial vessel to be built in Bristol and launched from the dock in the centre of the view. The marina to the right followed soon afterwards, and the Baltic Wharf development, still further along, was completed in 1985. The popularity of Baltic Wharf's broad tree-lined walkway is a compliment to the City planners' concept of a continuous walkway around almost the entire Floating Harbour.

Trevor Haddrell trained at Bath College of Art and after thirty-three years as a schoolteacher is now a full-time professional artist. His views and panoramas of Bristol document the changing appearance of the city with no less knowledge, skill and affection than that of Bristol's artists in the 1820s.

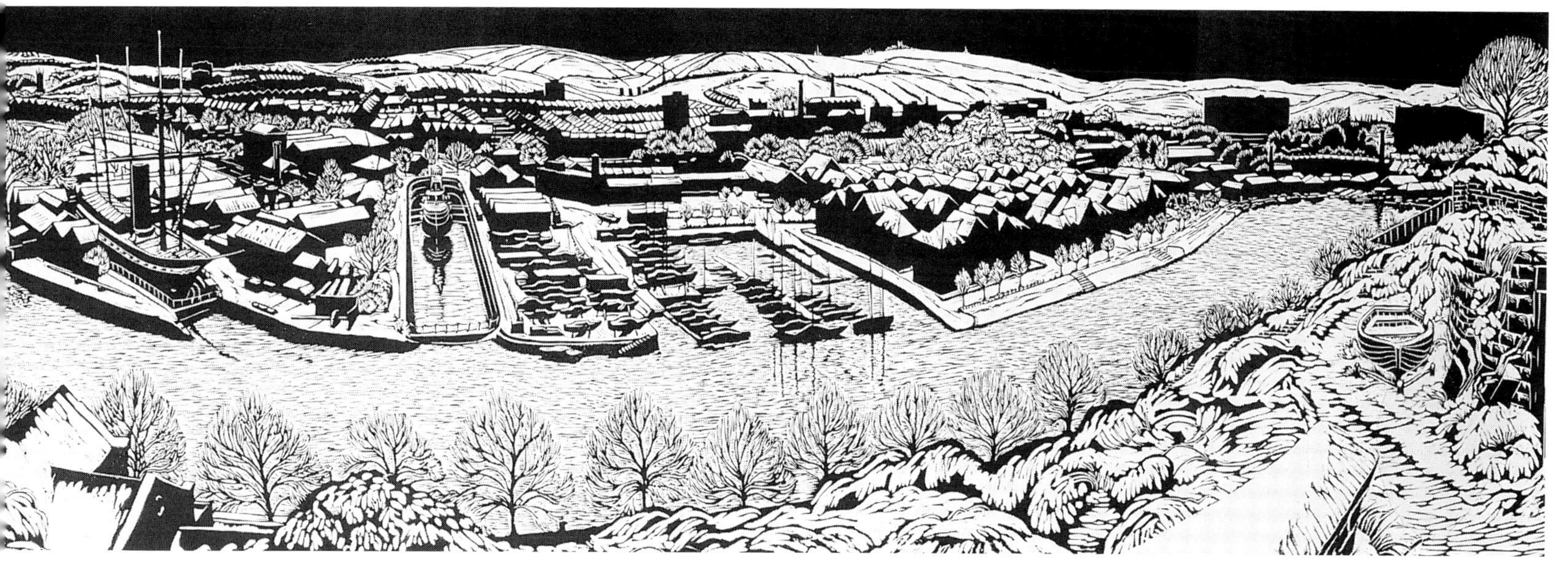

131 Robert Hurdle   born 1918
Welsh Back   1950
Oil   560 x 660 mm   Bristol Museums and Art Gallery K5636

AFTER MILITARY SERVICE ROBERT HURDLE went to Camberwell School of Art and Crafts, where he was taught by William Coldstream, a leading figure of the Euston Road School. The artists of this movement were very much aware of the growing alienation of art from the general public and they saw realism, the objective and measured appraisal of the subject before them, as the only valid way forward.

Welsh Back was painted over several months in the year of Robert Hurdle's move to Bristol in 1950, where he still lives. It has the concentrated and sustained observation of the Euston Road School. But it also has a balance to the composition, a subtlety to the sequence of colours and the more reflective approach that comes from much additional work on the canvas in the studio.

The artist's later works are signed with a seal, which was made for the artist in Hong Kong. This seal reflects Robert Hurdle's passion for oriental ceramics and for the meditative character of much oriental art. Richard Long, his most distinguished student at Bristol's West of England College of Art, shares his sympathy for Buddhist philosophy and has often used a similar seal.

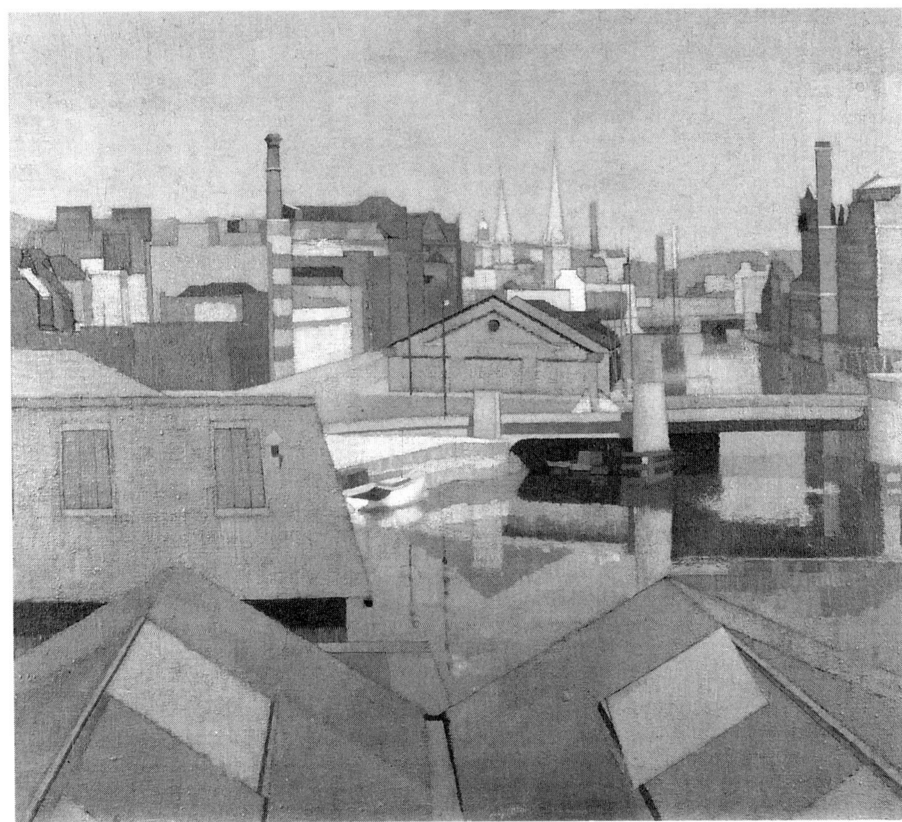

132 Richard Long born 1945
  'River Avon Mud Circle' 1991
   The Hayward Gallery, London from *Richard Long, Walking the line* (2002) p.194, with the artist's permission

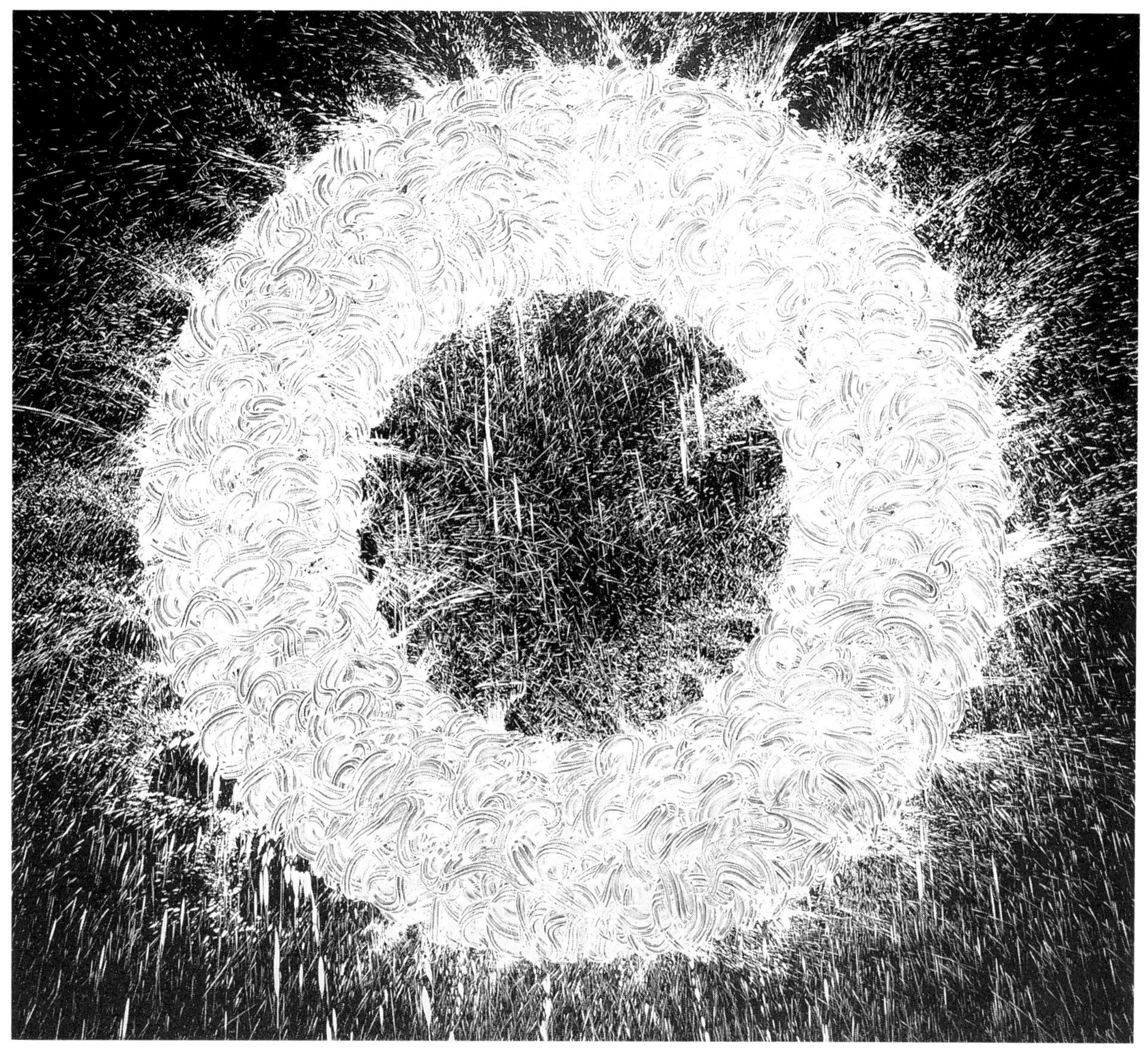

Richard Long and Bristol

BRISTOL HAS AN ARTIST OF WORLD RENOWN, an artist whose influence more than matches the extraordinary extent of his travels in almost every continent. His work might so easily have been of no relevance to this anthology. Instead the rise and fall of the River Avon is of profound importance to him.

Richard Long was born in Bristol and he still lives a few miles from the Clifton Suspension Bridge. Every year his father, a primary school teacher, would take his inner-city pupils and his son on a walk along the towpath to Pill. There they would cross by the ferry and take the train back to Bristol. Each year also, his father would take him to Pill to see it flood in the spring tides. And the only object he remembers making as a child was a plaster model of a riverbed in a baking tin. There were mud banks, creeks and inlets, which he slowly filled and emptied of water to make the tide come in and out.

After Bedminster Down School, Long went to the West of England College of Art at Bower Ashton, where Robert Hurdle (131) was a lone voice in his support. In 1966 after a gap of eighteen months, he went to study at St Martin's School of Art, then a centre of experiment and innovation in sculpture.

Just two years later, Long had his first one-man exhibition at Konrad Fischer's gallery in Düsseldorf. For the invitation Long used an overprinted postcard of the Avon Gorge and the Clifton Suspension Bridge (133). Recognition in this country was slow, and slower still in Bristol. It was fifteen years before Arnolfini gave him a one-man-show. At this time he wrote:

> The source of my work is nature. I use it with respect
> and freedom. I use materials, ideas, movement and time
> to express a whole view of my art in the world. I hope
> to make images and ideas which resonate in the imagi-
> nation, which mark the earth and the mind.

Long's mud works are a combination of careful preparation and precise preliminary drawing and then of great energy, virtuosity and spontaneity. He is familiar with Zen Buddhism, as he once was with Einstein's Theory of Relativity. When asked about the meaning of his circles, Long replied that 'they are universal and timeless, like the image of a human hand. For me that is part of their emotional power, although there is nothing symbolic or mystical in my work. They are also easy to make.'

The simplicity and practicality is deceptive. With economy, there can be clarity, beauty, and even grandeur in both the image and the idea. 'I see it as abstract art laid down in the real spaces of the world.'

Whether walking through the landscape and mapping, measuring and recording his journeys, making ephemeral marks on the landscape using the landscape's own materials, or bringing those materials into the gallery, Richard Long interacts with nature. He may justly deny that his work is romantic, but he shares with the Romantic poets and artists a concern for the relationship between man and nature. In 1988 he responded with enthusiasm, when invited to open the large Francis Danby exhibition in Bristol, and said:

> Whether he is a Wordsworth or an Andy Warhol, every
> artist is first a local artist in the sense of using a partic-
> ular culture or locality. Francis Danby is in that tradi-
> tion – if the art is good enough – of making his local
> places potentially universal places.

We are familiar with the connection between the local and the universal. We associate Dedham Vale with John Constable, Shoreham Valley with Samuel Palmer and the Avon Gorge with Francis Danby. The eternal constancy and variety of the River Avon's great tides may belong to Richard Long, but, although Bristol is still his home, he is literally an artist of the world. 'I felt art had barely recognised the natural landscapes which cover this planet, or had used the experiences those places could offer. Starting on my own doorstep and later spreading, part of my work since has been to try and engage this potential.'

133 Clifton Suspension Bridge
   The invitation card for Richard Long's first one-man exhibition at Konrad Fischer, Düsseldorf, 1968
   Overprinted postcard   90 x 140 mm   Collection of the artist

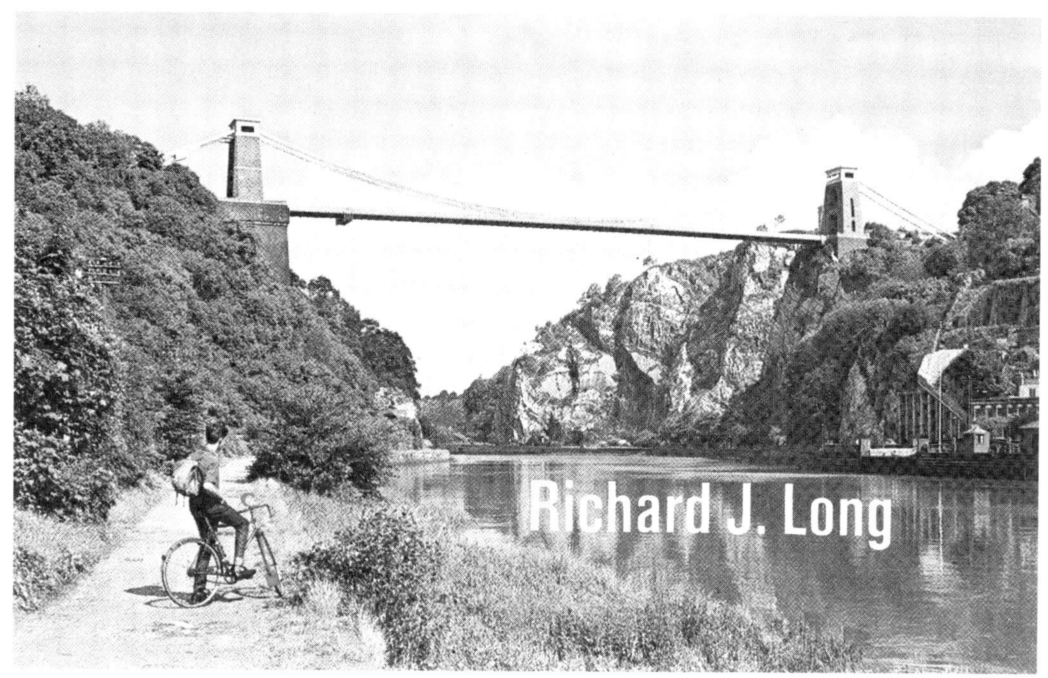

Selected bibliography

E. Adams, *Francis Danby: varieties of poetic landscape* (1973)

[E. Adams], *Bristol scenery 1714-1858, 33 drawings and watercolours from the City Art Gallery, Bristol* (1962)

J. Adams and P. Elkin, *Isambard Kingdom Brunel* (1988)

N. Allsopp, *Images of the Kennet and Avon* (1987)

A guide to watering places and sea-bathing places (c. 1806)

M. Archer, *Delftware, the tin-glazed earthenware of the British Isles* (1997)

Sir R. Atkyns, *The ancient and present state of Gloucestershire...* (1712, repr. 1984)

G. W. Barnes and T. Stevens, *History of the Clifton Suspension Bridge,* 3rd edn. (c.1965)

J. Bettey, *Bristol observed: visitors' impressions of the city from Domesday to the Blitz* (1986)

G. Body, *Clifton Suspension Bridge, an illustrated history* (1976)

B. J. H. Brown, *Weston-super-Mare and the origins of coastal leisure in the Bristol region* (1978)

Rotha M. Clay, *Samuel Hieronymous Grimm* (1941)

C. Crick, *Victorian buildings in Bristol* (1975)

R. Croft, 'Canon's Marsh Gas Works, Bristol...', *B. I. A. S. Journal,* 33 (200) 36-48

J. Dolman, *Contemplations amongst Vincent's rocks* (1755)

K. Downes, 'The King's Weston Book of Drawings', *Architectural History, Journal of the Society of Architectural Historians of Great Britain,* 10 (1967) 7-88

M. Dresser and S. Giles, eds., Bristol and transatlantic slavery (2000)

P. Elkin, *Images of maritime Bristol* (1985)

J. Evans, *Beauties of Clifton; or the Clifton and Hotwell guide,* 2nd edn. (c. 1820)

D. J. Eveleigh, *Bristol 1850-1919* (1996)

D. J. Eveleigh *Bristol 1920-1969* (1998)

G. Farr, *Shipbuilding in the port of Bristol* (1977)

G. Farr, *The* s.s. *Great Western,* 3rd edn. (1988)

G. Farr, *West Country passenger steamers* (1956, 2nd edn. 1967)

T. Fisher and J. Powell, 'The hydraulic system in Bristol Docks', *B. I. A. S. Journal,* 12 (1979) 6-11

A. Foyle, *Bristol (Pevsner Architectural Guides)* (2004)

A. E. Frey, ed., 'The Avon Gorge; Bristol Naturalists' Society Special Issue No 1' reprinted from the *Proceedings of the Bristol Naturalists' Society,* vol. 47 1987 (1989)

J. Gill, *The Bristol scene, views of Bristol by Bristol artists from... the City Art Gallery* (1975)

A. Gomme, M. Jenner, B. Little, *Bristol: an architectural history* (1979)

F. Greenacre, *The Bristol School of Artists; Francis Danby and painting in Bristol 1810-1840* (1973)

F. Greenacre, *Francis Danby 1793-1861* (1988)

F. Greenacre, *Marine artists of Bristol, Nicholas Pocock and Joseph Walter* (1982)

F. Greenacre and S. Stoddard, *The Bristol Landscape; the watercolours of Samuel Jackson* (1986)

F. Greenacre and S. Stoddard, *W. J. Müller 1812-1845* (1991)

L. M. Griffiths, *The reputation of the Hotwells (Bristol) as a health- resort* (1902)

S. Harding and D. Lambert, *Parks and gardens of Avon* (1994)

J. Hill, *Shipshape and Bristol fashion* (1951, republ. 1983)

[J. C.] Ibbetson, [J.] Laporte and J. Hassell, *A picturesque guide to Bath, Bristol Hot-Wells...illustrated...* (1793)

W. Ison, *The Georgian buildings of Bristol* (1952)

D. Jones, *The history of Clifton* (1992)

P. Jones, *Canon's Marsh, the rise and fall of the Tobacco Bonds* (1989)

A. King, *The Port of Bristol* (2003)

J. Latimer, *Annals of Bristol,* 3 vols. (1906)

J. Latimer, *The history of the Society of Merchant Venturers* (1903)

B. Little, *The City and County of Bristol* (1954)

R. Long, D. Hooker, P. Moorhouse and A. Seymour, *Richard Long, Walking the Line* (2002)

R. Long and A. Seymour, *Richard Long, Old World New World* (1988)

R. Long, 'Speech at the opening of Francis Danby exhibition' (1988) typescript, Bristol Museum and Art Gallery, Fine Art Dept.

J. Lord and J. Southam, *The Floating Harbour; a landscape history of Bristol City Docks* (1983)

P. McGrath, *The Merchant Venturers of Bristol* (1975)

P. McGrath, ed., *Bristol in the eighteenth century* (1972)

C. M. MacInnes. *Bristol: a gateway of empire* (1939, republ. 1968)

G. W. Manby, *The history and beauties of Clifton, Hot-wells and vicinity, near Bristol* (1806)

M. Manson, *Bristol beyond the bridge* (1988)

P. T. Marcy, *Eighteenth century views of Bristol and Bristolians* (1966)

Alyson Marsden, 'The second Bristol Broad Quay painting', *Journal of the Pewter Society,* 6, (2001)

J. Mathews, pub., *Mathews' Bristol guide,* 4th edn. (1815)

W. Mathews, *The new history, survey, and description of the city and suburbs of Bristol* (1794, reprinted in facsimile 1898)

T. Mowl, *To build the second city, architects and craftsmen of Bristol* (1991)

P. Newman, *Channel passage, the area around Portishead...* (1976)

J. F. Nicholls and J. Taylor, *Bristol past and present,* 3 vols. (1881-2)

E. Owen, *Observations on the earths, rocks, stones and minerals for some miles about Bristol and on the nature of the Hot-Well...* (1754)

R. Parsons, *The story of Kings, C. J. King & Sons 1850 to the present day* (1988)

W. H. Pyne, *Microcosm...for the embellishment of landscape...,* 2 vols. (1806)

Helen Reid and Sue Stops, *On the waterfront, the Hotwells story* (2002)

W. N. Reid and W. E. Hicks, *Leading events in the history of the port of Bristol* (1877)

[E. Ralph], *The Downs 1861-1961* (c. 1974)

E. Ralph, *The government of Bristol 1373-1973* (1973)

K. Ramsay, *The Bristol coal industry* (2003)

J. Rich, *The Bristol pilots* (1996)

L. T. C. Rolt, *Isambard Kingdom Brunel* (1957, republ. 1961)

R. J. G. Savage, 'Natural History of the Goldney garden grotto Clifton, Bristol', reprinted (no date) from *The Journal of the Garden History Society,* 17 no. 1

Ellen Sharples and Rolinda Sharples, 'The Sharples diaries, 1803-1836', manuscript, Bristol Reference Library

J. W. Sherborne, *The Port of Bristol in the Middle Ages,* 3rd edn. (1988)

E Shiercliff, *The Bristol and Hotwell guide* (1793)

P. Skinner, 'Pumping Bristol's water', *B. I. A. S. Journal,* 11 (1978) 14-19

G. Smith, *Smuggling in the Bristol Channel 1700-1850* (1989, republ. 1984)

Sneyd Park Residents' Association, *Sneyd Park, a local study and guided walk* (2001)

R. Southey, *Letters from England* (1807, repr. 1984)

R. Stiles, 'Bristol and the optical telegraph...', *B. I. A. S. Journal,* 29 (1996) 43

S. Stoddard, *City impressions, Bristol etchers 1910-1935* (1990)

S. Stoddard, *Bristol before the camera, the city in 1820-30* (2001)

J. Taylor, *Guide to Clifton and its neighbourhood* (1868)

Thirty letters on the trade of Bristol... by a burgess (1834)

Ethel Thomas, *Down the 'mouth, a history of Avonmouth* (1977, 2nd edn. 1992)

Ethel Thomas, *The Shirehampton story* (1983)

Jean Vanes, *The Port of Bristol in the nineteenth century* (1977)

V. Waite, *The Bristol Hotwell* (1960)

R. Wall, *Bristol Channel pleasure steamers* (1973)

M. Watts, 'John Padmore's cranes...', *B. I. A. S. Journal,* 8 (1975) 17-19

C. Wells, *A short history of the Port of Bristol* (1909)

A. F. Williams, 'Bristol Port plans...of the eighteenth century' *Transactions of the Bristol and Gloucestershire Archaeological Society,* 81 (1962), 138-188

Mary Williams, *Civic Treasures of Bristol* (1984)

A. Wilton, *Turner in his time* (1989)

C. Witt, C. Weedon and A. P. Schwind, *Bristol Glass* (1984)